THE

EVERYTHING®

HOT CAREERS BOOK

Get the in-depth insider info
on some really cool careers!

Ronald A. Reis

Adams Media Corporation
Holbrook, Massachusetts

An Everything® Series Book.
The Everything® Series is a registered trademark of Adams Media Corporation.

Published by Adams Media Corporation
260 Center Street, Holbrook, MA 02343
www.adamsmedia.com

ISBN: 1-58062-486-3
Printed in the United States of America.

J I H G F E D C B A

Library of Congress Cataloging-in-Publication Data
Reis, Ronald A.
Everything hot careers book / Ronald A. Reis.
p.   cm.
ISBN 1-58062-486-3
1. Vocational guidance. 2. Occupations–United States.
3. Professions–United States. I. Title.
HF5382.75.U6 R44   2001
331.7'02–dc21   00-050218

Many of the designations used by manufacturers and sellers to distinguish their products are claimed as trademarks. Where those designations appear in this book and Adams Media was aware of a trademark claim, the designations have been printed in initial capital letters.

This publication is designed to provide accurate and authoritative information with regard to the subject matter covered. It is sold with the understanding that the publisher is not engaged in rendering legal, accounting, or other professional advice. If legal advice or other expert assistance is required, the services of a competent professional person should be sought.
—From a *Declaration of Principles* jointly adopted by a Committee of the American Bar Association and a Committee of Publishers and Associations

Illustrations by Barry Littmann

This book is available at quantity discounts for bulk purchases.
For information, call 1-800-872-5627.

Visit the entire Everything® series at everything.com

Contents

INTRODUCTION

Colm Duggan, an animator, can't stop looking at himself in the mirror; it's part of his job.

Jami Shoemaker, a zookeeper, sneaks baby mountain lions into her apartment—all the better to bond with them.

Donna Valdez, an emergency dispatcher, spends her days fielding calls from distraught victims of rape and robbery, as well as from kids with broken toys.

And, if camera operator Mike St. Hilaire hadn't known to go "handheld," a costly and dangerous stunt on the set of *Lethal Weapon 4* might never have made it to the screen.

Such are a few insights from the more unusual careers featured in *The Everything® Hot Careers Book.* Antique appraiser, auctioneer, forensic artist, martial arts instructor, private sports coach, sign language interpreter, toy designer, voice actor are all careers you knew existed, but your high school guidance counselor may have been afraid to mention.

But that's only the beginning!

Robert Burke is an experienced, dedicated lobbyist with one of Los Angeles' most prestigious firms. He does research, prepares fact sheets, talks to legislators, and makes his client's case.

Sam Waltz is CEO and board chairman of PRSA, a public relations firm. Such a PR person must be able to work broadly across an array of disciplines: advertising, special events, management, and seminar presentations.

As a technical writer, Raymond Urgo knows he is more than a mere scribe. He deals with the broader concept of information technology.

And world-renowned chef Brad Toles is keenly aware that cooking is only a part of his job. He spends 60 percent of his time dealing with human relations problems.

These more traditional but still hot careers are explored along with other hot choices, such as residential real estate agent, graphic designer, literary agent, paramedic, professional fund raiser, stockbroker, travel agent, and copyeditor.

Then, of course, we have the world of information technology.

Stevie Case is one of today's most accomplished computer game players. She has parlayed this ability, and her fame, into a career as a computer game designer.

John Merritt is a special effects expert with a traditional model-making background. Now he uses computers to develop what he used to fabricate in clay.

As a Webmaster, Steve Buchsbaum created the award-winning Dodger Baseball Web site. He works in one of the fastest-growing professions in cyberspace.

As a computer software trainer, Pat Galagan is certainly on the cutting edge. The training he provides helps make many of the high-tech careers covered in this book possible.

In all, 50 careers are presented, from the unusual to the traditional to the high tech. And all are hot, in that they are careers readers want to know about in fields where opportunities abound.

Each career entry explores what it is like to work in a given field through the eyes of those engaged in it. Individuals in each career category provided insights as to how to get started, where to receive education and training, what makes for a great day, and what causes the inevitable downsides. You will hear, in their own words, these role models' excitement and, at times, frustration, at what they do for a living.

While many of these 50 careers require a college education, others do not. All, however, demand dedication, training, and hard work. You cannot, for example, become a successful voice-over actor just because you have a great voice. It takes practice and a financial commitment to training to make it, to actually earn a living in this extremely competitive field.

That personal trainers must be in top shape goes without saying. That they also need to have the personality to attract and retain clients is perhaps less well appreciated.

And today's stockbroker must, after passing a battery of grueling tests, spend years developing a client base. Many never make it past the first six months. Those who do, however, often reach six-figure incomes.

In addition to each career story itself, every chapter presents you with important hard facts.

- *What Will I Earn?* gives you the latest salary data, gleaned from U.S. Department of Labor statistics or association salary surveys.
- *For More Information* lists companies, associations, societies, and individuals you are encouraged to contact to further your career exploration.
- *What to Read* provides names of books and helpful publications in each field.
- *Cool Web Sites to Visit* identifies top sites I have found and explored. Of course, given the ephemeral nature of the Web, by the time you read this some may have changed or no longer be up. Others, however, are sure to have taken their places!

The Everything® Hot Careers Book was written with two kinds of readers in mind. If you're looking to explore varied career opportunities, either as a student starting out or as someone seeking a career change, you're going to find a range of exciting choices to explore. Alternatively, even if you're satisfied with your present occupation, getting to know and understanding what others in entirely different fields do, how they feel about their work, and what makes their day can be a real eye opener.

I trust that after reading *The Everything® Hot Careers Book* you will never look at a cartoon, play a computer game, engage the services of an interpreter/translator, listen to a commercial on the radio, observe an actor's unusual makeup, or stare at a zookeeper in quite the same way again.

Now, get ready to enjoy your investigations into the world of hot careers!

ADVERTISING SALES

Advertising in the United States is big business. Companies and institutions spend upward of $233 billion annually to get their message out on the products and services they are trying to promote. Someone has to sell all those ads.

*A*PG, or *Action Pursuit Games*, is the world's leading magazine for paintball sports. Published by CFW Enterprises, the 220-page, high-gloss monthly has a paid readership of 79,000. With 45-plus advertisers, this print exemplar of "extreme sports" explodes with four-color, full-page ads extolling all manner of paintball gear: long-barrel guns, tank pouches, anti-fog goggles, jerseys, neck pads, and the many-colored paintballs themselves. Catering to an audience that spends over $750 million annually on paintball products, the magazine has found its niche. "We may not be a *GQ*," says CFW's advertising director, Gabe Frimmel, "but we dominate in our field. Paintball is the fourth most popular 'extreme sport' in the U.S., behind skateboarding, mountain biking, and in-line skating."

It wasn't always that way—for the sport, or for *APG*. Yet the two have grown and matured together, finding a synergy that's made 2000 a banner year for both.

"When I came onboard as advertising sales director three years ago," says Gabe, "I suggested we position the fourteen-year-old magazine, with its then skimpy 118 pages, as the premier publication in the field by bringing paintball into the extreme sports category. I went to our advertisers with a five-year plan for growth, one that would target a younger, team-oriented player who wanted to move beyond the guns and ammo, out-in-the-woods crowd. The advertisers bought it. New markets for equipment opened up, and together we have prospered. Unlike the game itself, it's been a win-win situation."

Getting the Message Out

Advertising in the United States is big business. According to Jim English of *ADWEEK*, companies and institutions spend upward of $233 billion annually to get their message out on the products and services they are trying to promote.

Various communications media, be it radio, television, newspapers, magazines, outdoor signs, or the Internet, are eager to provide a vessel for an organization's message. And though economic conditions affect dollars spent, advertising expenditures are expected to grow significantly in the years to come.

Take just one media outlet, the Internet. As an advertising medium, it didn't even exist until the mid-1990s. By 1998, says Jupiter Communications' January 2000 report, advertisers were spending $3.3 billion a year on the World Wide Web. That figure is expected to explode ten-fold by 2004, to a whopping $33 billion.

Clearly the buying of advertising space, in virtually all media, continues to climb. And someone, of course, has to sell that ad space. Enter the advertising salesperson.

Multimedia

Stephen Russo is with *Consumer News*, an upscale weekly newspaper in Mansfield, Massachusetts. Circulation: 52,500. "Our readers have the ability to spend the dollars advertisers are looking for," Stephen says. "Yet, advertising for most firms is a difficult decision to make. Many don't put it in the right column. They see advertising as an expense, not an investment. As a result, our advertising sales force must sell the intangibles. The prospect must be made to visualize how he or she can benefit from advertising in *Consumer News*. It's the job of those soliciting ad dollars to draw a vivid, relevant picture for them."

Steve Raddock is vice president of production and communications at the Cable Television Advertising Bureau. "Cable ad sales are of two types," he says. "On the network level, you sell nationwide. On the systems level, you are contacting local retailers, offering them the opportunity to place advertising within one of the 'avails'—

What Will I Earn?

Advertising sales reps are paid strictly on commission or on a base plus commission basis. Salaries range from $20,000 to $70,000 or more per year depending on sales success, experience, employer, and location.

INFORMATION

For More Information

American Advertising Federation
1101 Vermont Avenue N.W.
Suite 500
Washington, DC 20005
(202) 898-0089

American Association of
Advertising Agencies
405 Lexington Avenue, 18th Flr.
New York, NY 10174
(212) 682-2500

the two to three minutes per hour allocated by the networks for local spots. Those entering the field as sales reps usually start at the systems level."

KFWB is an all-news radio station in Hollywood, California. With listenership up 20 to 30 percent in the last year, inventory—that is, time allocated for advertising—goes quickly. "We are sold out right now," says Melinda Haroutunian, the station's chief salesperson. "Yet, our twenty-three-person sales force is still dialing for dollars and knocking on doors. They sell for the future."

Steve Rau, the regional marketing manger in Los Angeles for the Pacific Bell Smart Yellow Pages admits turnover in his union shop is low. "With starting incomes at around $40,000 a year, we are an attractive place to work," he says. "All our sales reps work in-house; that is, they do the phones. Most of the time it's cold calling. Yet some think our media is dying. Not so. If you want to shop locally, you are not going to spend time surfing the Internet. You go to the Yellow Pages."

Judy Solomon of Judy Solomon Associates, in Bethesda, Maryland, is a publisher's rep. "We sell advertising space for numerous publications," she explains. "For example, we represent association magazines in the Washington, D.C. area. The magazines hire us to go out and get their ad space filled. It's cold calling, visiting trade shows, following up leads, and matching products and services with the appropriate magazine. Tenacity, likability, and attention to detail are minimum requirements for anyone wanting to sell advertising."

One-On-One

"Another requirement is the ability to hear 'no' a hundred times a day," says Gary Teitjen, the director of local advertising, sales, and marketing at the Cable Television Advertising Bureau. "It takes an average of five sales calls to close a deal," he adds. "That's from the time you pick up the phone, make an appointment, and finally close the deal."

"It is also about passion," declares Melinda of KFWB. "You must want to sell what you are offering. I believe in the product, that the station works for advertisers."

But how does she know, does she have the stats to prove it?

"The reason you're hearing more 800 numbers given out over the air, particularly on AM radio, is that they offer a direct response for the advertiser," she says. "Such advertisers can correlate success with how many people call in on the toll-free number. In many cases, there will be a separate number for each station used."

Like sales everywhere, success is usually based on strong relationships. In advertising, that means long-term associations. "We don't sell advertising by claiming a given ad will earn you a million dollars," says Stephen of *Consumer News*. "It takes a while for the client to get to know you, feel comfortable spending dollars with you. It's not often you make one call and get a sale."

"The ability to make intangible things exciting, at least when it comes to radio, is key," comments Bryan Farrish, an airplay promoter and broadcast time buyer for the music business who was also the creator and editor of the first newsletter to cover the topic of radio advertising. "With print, almost any advertiser can understand and see his or her efforts in a permanent printed form. With broadcast, once the commercial airs, it's gone. So you can't sell the commercial itself, you have to sell the impact instead."

Sales reps working at Pacific Bell Smart Yellow Pages differ in their approach from most in the field. They are not allowed to leave their desks to go out and meet the client face-to-face.

"It works for us, though it is still about relationships," Steve Rau assures me. "Our sales reps take a prospective client into his copy of the Yellow Pages and shows him sample ads. They grab him with a hook: cite a new fact relevant to their industry that immediately establishes credibility. Or they talk about the research we have done on Yellow Page usage in their particular market. You must dramatize it enough to get someone's attention. Then they'll talk to you."

What to Read

*25 Sales Habits of Highly
Successful Salespeople*
by Stephen Schiffman.
Adams Media Corporation, 1994.

*Advertising On the Internet;
2nd Edition*
by Robbin Lee Zeff
and Bad Aronson.
John Wiley & Sons, 1999.

*How to Sell Like a Natural-Born
Salesperson*
by Dr. Gary S. Goodman.
Adams Media Corporation, 1998.

*The Advertising Handbook
for Small Business*
by Dell Dennison.
Self-Counsel Press, 1994.

Gabe has no trouble getting his clients to talk to him. "It's about an ongoing relationship," he says. "Some of our advertisers have been with us for over a decade. To ensure that kind of loyalty, they must know that they can pick up the phone for a one-on-one any time."

First-Year Blues

So, what does it take to break in, to get started in advertising sales?

"When hiring someone without broadcast advertising experience, radio and TV stations look for a person with the ability to communicate well with many types of people," Bryan Farrish says. "This usually means hiring those who participated in many forms of clubs and activities in school. Good typing, good phone skills, and high energy are critical. For radio stations in particular, a knowledge of music is an asset [since music is the largest radio format in most radio companies]. Interestingly, no engineering knowledge is required to sell for TV or radio. But there are some key words you will have to pick up quickly, and this can be accomplished by either interning at a station or by taking a broadcast sales class at a college."

But what about experience? Are there openings for those with little or no background?

"You don't need any particular skill in the beginning," Bryan advises. "However, as you move up the qualifications ladder, you are expected to know about ownership groups, formats, national-versus-local clients, ratings, affidavits, signal coverage, and key words like LMA, CPP, ADI, AQH, dub, aircheck, spot, jock, PD, MD, traffic (not cars), stick, VO, Arbitron, diary, cume, cans, et cetera."

But surely you must be either technically savvy or entertainment-oriented to make it in radio or TV?

"Nope, "says Bryan. "Some of the best broadcast salespeople can't turn a dial. On top of that, they often have a booming, monotonous voice. Their simplistic approach works, however, because trying to woo a potential client with 'tech' or 'DJ' talk can often backfire."

Stephen of *Consumer News* prefers to hire individuals with a general sales background rather than those with advertising experience. "Everyone in advertising sales teaches their people different philosophies, motivations," he says. "To overcome the 'can't teach an old dog new tricks' phenomenon we prefer to train our sales people on our philosophy, motivate them our way, from within."

Melinda says, "Since we pay strictly on commission, we do have turnover. The first year is the roughest. People who succeed grow with the company or move on to another company. The ones who don't cut it, go. Those more established, with close ties to clients and agencies, have a base to stand on. But that takes time. Some of our younger hires are not always able to grasp that, develop good work habits, handle the rejection, and stay with it for the long haul. But for those who do, radio sales can be a great career, financially and otherwise."

To produce an effective sales force, the Pacific Bell Smart Yellow Pages offers an excellent training program. "Actually, I would like to see it expanded," comments Steve Rau. "Right now it's just five weeks. We teach our trainees how to interact with the technical system. But by the time they're through, there is little time to talk about sales strategies."

Thinking Like an Entrepreneur

Whether you're fresh out of college or switching careers, everyone in the business agrees, it helps to have some sales experience, even if it's in retail at the local food court. "Even with that," says Gary, "you must realize that starting out, you're going to be at the bottom. The company isn't about to say, 'Here's a half-million-dollar list, have fun.' No, they are going to say, 'Here's the phone book, enjoy yourself.' It is cold calling, building the business. Working on a commission, you are basically an entrepreneur."

Still, once you are established, and have a track record, it becomes easier, if not less work. As Gabe concludes: "I've seen companies grow with us. It's a satisfying feeling. When paintball exploded, a company well known in the jersey business asked me if I thought gamers would like their own jerseys, those designed especially for paintball tournaments. I felt it was a great idea and I encouraged them to pursue it. Today, they are a leading manufacturer in the field. Of course, they advertise that fact in *Action Pursuit Games.*"

Cool Web Sites to Visit

Advertising Sales Recruiting Network (ASFM)
www.asfm.com/ad.html

ADWEEK
www.adweek.com

Aviad
www.aviad.com

ANIMATOR

Pencilers, inkers, colorers, and cleanup artists are part of the "picture." So are today's hot 3-D computer animators. But don't throw away your sketchpad just yet, a traditional art background is still a must.

Hot Career

2

Though he's a good-looking guy, with a full head of brown curly hair, it isn't vanity that keeps Colm Duggan looking into a six-inch mirror, perched above his animation disc, a dozen times a day. Doing so is a job requirement.

As an animator for Rich Animation Studios in Burbank, California, Colm has to keep making faces in order to draw them. By contorting his mouth, squinting his eyes, thrusting his tongue out, and gritting his teeth, Colm sees in the mirror what he needs to draw on his light table. "You make a face, then caricature that shape," he says. "Everything in animation is exaggerated to get the right effect. This is particularly true with facial expressions. I can't help but look at myself."

Gotta Draw

With animation seen everywhere, as full-length feature films in theaters, as cartoons on television, and, increasingly, in educational and industrial enterprises, Colm is not only looking at himself, we're looking at him—or, more precisely, his work.

Led by Disney Animation, but also involving dozens of other animation companies, such as Rich Animation Studios, Creative Capers, Turner, Hanna-Barbera, and Steven Spielberg's DreamWorks SKG, the industry is animated, indeed.

"When you think of what it costs to pay actors today, in some cases it is cheaper to do full-length animation than live action," says Steve Fossati of Chuck Jones Productions. "And with related media—CD-ROM games and shockwave.com, for example—exploding, opportunities for animators have never been better."

As an animator, one who draws animated cartoons, whether with traditional pencil and paper or, increasingly, by computer, you're part of a diverse team:

- First, *scriptwriters* create the story line.
- Next, *art directors* design the characters, set the look and style.
- *Storyboard artists* then lay out animation cels, "frozen" images of selected scenes.
- Finally, *animators* draw each frame.

Animating, itself, has many parts:

- *Pencilers* draw each character for each frame.
- *Inkers* ink over the pencil drawings.
- *Colorers* fill in the inked drawings.
- *Cleanup artists* make sure items like the fairy princess's hair are consistent in style, shape, and color throughout.

"In many studios," Steve says, "animators do only certain kinds of scenes. For example, there are those that can only draw background, scenes with little animation. Or we have animators that just want to do action scenes: soaring flights, swinging off ropes, et cetera. Finally, effects animators draw splashes, smoke, mud flying, and objects exploding. It all depends on your expertise and interest."

What Will I Earn?

Since the U.S. Department of Labor does not separate out animators from visual artists in general, it is hard to identify an exact salary range. In the 2000-2001 *Occupational Outlook Handbook*, developed by the DOL, visual artists earn from $31,000 to $67,000 a year.

Beyond Disney

But don't you have to work for Disney and live in Los Angeles to do animation? Not according to these listings picked off the Internet:

- *AAC/TGWB*—Architectural firm develops photo-realistic animated walkthroughs and multimedia simulations of three-dimensional products and projects.

INFORMATION

For More Information

Motion Picture Screen Cartoonists
Local 839, (MPSC)
4729 Lankershim Boulevard
North Hollywood, CA 91602-1864

The Society of Illustrators
128 East 63rd Street
New York, NY 10021-7392

Contact your local community
college.

- *Abrakadabra Animations*—Offers cartoons and animations for the Web. Join the lend-a-loon program, check out animated Web games, and inspect the list of awards.
- *Acme Filmworks*—Offers cel, clay, stop motion, and computer animation for broadcast, the Web, and CD-ROMs. Review a list of directors, or work samples.
- *AMPnyc*—New York City studio combines digital technology with traditional animation techniques. Credits include work for MTV and The Cartoon Network.

And those are just a sampling from the *As*.

According to Patricia Ward Biederman, a *Los Angeles Times* staff writer, in 1999 it was clearly demonstrated that there was more to animation than just plain Disney. "In that year, we saw everything from the stately *The Prince of Egypt* to the rowdy *South Park*, from the wonderful *The Iron Giant* to Pixar's witty *A Bug's Life.*

"It was not so long ago," continues Patricia, "that audiences saw a new animated feature only when Disney produced one every four years or so. Now animated features are almost commonplace, utterly remarkable given how labor-intensive they are to make."

John Lasseter, the 42-year-old animation whiz at Pixar, in Northern California, directed the huge hit *Toy Story 2* and knows much work is involved in making a feature animated film. Hailed by many as the new Walt Disney, he told Kenneth Turan, *Los Angeles Times* film critic, "Animation is so expensive, you can't afford to do coverage, there's no editing in post-production. . . . Our rule is it has to play right in story reels, it has to give you the humor, the action, the heart, all the things that are important to us. Because what I've found in the past is that if it's not working and we say, 'Go ahead, it'll get saved once it gets in animation,' it never gets saved."

Animation has clearly arrived as a media for telling a great story. No longer considered a backwater industry, with the groundbreaking *Who Framed Roger Rabbit?* and the production of *Beauty and the Beast*, the first animated feature to win a Best Picture nomination, the genre has arrived.

Animation is being used in many forms of communication, for many purposes. And you don't have to live in Los Angeles to do it.

Computer Takeover?

Here's another ad worth reading:

> *Seeking two Flash animators to head up newly*
> *created FLASH services division of established*
> *animation house. In-house only, please, working*
> *off a studio lot in Hollywood. Must be familiar*
> *with traditional cel animation process and, above*
> *all, know how to translate tractional cel drawings*
> *into final flash files by scanning line art and using*
> *Adobe Streamline, Adobe Illustrator, etc., when*
> *appropriate. Must be familiar with optimal usages*
> *of various streaming audio formats and be able to*
> *create animations which are in sync with dialogue*
> *or other audio cues. An obsession with reducing*
> *file sizes wherever possible is key. Knowledge of*
> *higher workings such as Javascript/VBScript,*
> *FSCommands, TellTargets, etc., a plus.*

Wow! Are they looking for a programmer or an animator?
Is all animation being done on the computer now?

To find out, one need only visit Creative Capers in Glendale,
California. There we found Duane Loose, a 42-year-old "visioneer"
who is currently head of their 12-person product development team.

"Yes," he says, "a lot of games are developed with our high-end
computer modeling systems. To create environments, worlds that are
only in the mind of the developer, designer, or artist, you really
need a computer.

"But while we are heavy into computer animation," Duane continues, "we only hire animators with traditional backgrounds—those
that understand composition, sculpting, layout, color, form, and
function. "We don't want someone who can't do anything without
the computer. We need a person who can get out their pencils,
markers, and paints once in awhile.

What to Read

Getting Ready for a Career
as a Computer Animator
by Bill Lund.
Capstone Press, 1998.

"Remember, even if the entire project is done on a computer, the process of getting ideas across to the team involves traditional art. Everyone has to know how to sketch."

Perhaps John said it best when Kenneth asked him for his thoughts on CGI (Computer Generated Imagery).

"To me, CGI is a complete misnomer, because the computers are just tools. People generated the imagery using computers. Word processors don't write for you, but people assume the computers do a lot more than they really do. The exciting thing I'm looking forward to is getting this incredible medium into the hands of a lot of other filmmakers, because to me computer animation is like the Panavision camera. You put it in the hands of a great director and a great cinematographer and you're going to get something completely different from another director and cinematographer."

Competition Is Keen

OK, then, you have to know how to draw and use a computer to work as an animator. Yet, keep what the late designer Tibor Kalman had in mind when he said: "Animators shouldn't get hung up on software or technique, your design studio is really between your ears, not in your computer."

"Above all," Duane Loose says, "I need creative people, ones who can think. I can always teach a thinker to do, but I can't teach a doer to think."

Colm Duggan agrees. But for him, being able to act is almost as important as knowing how to draw. "You must act out every scene," he says. "It's tiring, hard work. After I have animated a scene I am physically exhausted. A good sword fight can wear me out."

Although job opportunities for animators are, according to the U.S. Department of Labor, expected to grow faster than average for occupations through the year 2005, competition will be fierce. In just a single week in early 2000, Creative Capers received 40 *unsolicited* resumes with portfolios.

Keep in mind that this is an industry, especially in reference to Hollywood, that has seen, and will see, many ups and downs. Steve Fossati's comment about it being cheaper to do full-length animation than live action aside, it took DreamWorks SKG five years, with 500 animators, at a cost of $100 million, to produce *The Road to El Dorado*. (Disney's *Dinosaur* reportedly cost twice that figure.) A month after release, the film had grossed only $42 million. DreamWorks acknowledged at the time that the film would struggle to reach $60 million at the domestic box office.

As one industry source said with regard to *El Dorado*, "Don't count on many *El Dorado* figurines, T-shirts, and lunch boxes being sold. Unlike in the mythical *El Dorado*, there's no gold to be found there."

Still, some animation films do succeed, of course, and in a big way. Two Disney blockbusters, *Toy Story 2* and *Tarzan*, reached $477 million and $446.7 million, respectively, worldwide. Go figure!

Nonetheless, if animation is what you want, go for it. How? Excellent schools abound. Parsons School of Design or the School of Visual Arts in New York City and the Art Center College of Design in Pasadena, California, are examples of the best. Of course, there are numerous four-year institutions and community colleges all across the country offering courses in animation.

Should you go to college to study animation? Won't talent alone get you there? "It is important to have native ability, inborn talent," says Duane. "But without training, that's all it ever is. It is scattered."

To see what schooling in animation consists of, you might peruse the Santa Monica City College Web site. The community college, a mile from the Pacific Ocean, offers another of the best animation programs in the country. As a student, you'll take courses in storyboarding, traditional animation, modeling, character animation, 3-D computer animation, and animatics. Of course, there's also interactive design for e-business and computer skills and software for animation and interactive media.

Yet, formal schooling isn't the only avenue to success. As Duane concludes, "Every artist I've ever read about has always had someone to point to as an influence in his or her life. To make it in this field, you must find an opportunity to put yourself in the hands of a mentor, someone who can channel and guide your passion for artistic expression."

Cool Web Sites to Visit

Animation Factory
www.eclipsed.com

Aviation Animation
www.asuspport.com/aviationgraphics

Danny's Collection of Animated Gifs
www.geocities.com/SoHo/3505

ANTIQUE APPRAISER

Hot Career

3

Once in awhile you find yourself in an Alice in Wonderland *world, with marvelous results. But it's not all visiting gorgeous homes, meeting famous people, and doing a quick appraisal. Often it is crawling around on your hands and knees, among typical garage sale items, shooing away spiders.*

Nancy Martin had never seen anything quite like it—and that's what bothered her. "It was beautiful, with an exquisite veneer in front," the accredited antique appraiser from Pasadena, California, says. "But its proportions were all wrong. The George II secretary bookcase was too tall. For me, that raised a red flag."

Brought in to appraise the "circa 1760 desk" for a client who had just paid a whopping $130,000 for it, Nancy concluded it was a recent fake, the true value a mere $20,000. "It was probably configured in England of five separate pieces," she explains. "I called in a conservator and together we tore into it. Spots of white paint, unmatched wood, irregular construction details, and odd stains indicating unexplained nail holes—such factors confirmed my suspicion. Eventually, with an additional scathing report from a London expert in hand, the client got his money back—and wound up keeping the secretary, too."

A Serious Business

Antique appraising is a subcategory within the personal property appraising field. According to Donna Chowning Reid, director of membership and public relations for the American Society of Appraisers (ASA), "Personal property is tangible, movable property that is utilitarian, collectible, decorative, or a combination of the three."

By witnessing, describing, and ranking various items in the marketplace and consulting with antique dealers, authors, experts, and collectors, antique appraisers estimate value. It is a serious business.

"If, for tax purposes, I overvalue an item, resulting in underpayment by the taxpayer, I can, under federal law, be fined $1,000 per item and disbarred from practice by the IRS," Nancy cautions. "Furthermore, if I say something is a fake, but it turns out to be authentic and is then sold as a fake, thus injuring the selling party, I can be sued."

Though antique appraisers are not state or federally licensed, three national societies certify qualified members and require adherence to the federal appraisal standards. "I have two certificates," Nancy explains. "I am certified as an appraiser of residential contents; that is, things found in the ordinary home. And I am qualified to appraise antiques and decorative arts from America and Europe. As a result, I identify and establish the value of furniture, silver, ceramics, glass, and decorations. I do not, however, deal in fine arts, paintings, sculpture, oriental rugs, stamps, jewelry, books, automobiles, and gems. Those are also specialized fields where experts spend, in many cases, a professional lifetime acquiring knowledge."

A Biochemist in Antiquity

Antique appraising wasn't Nancy's first career choice. After earning a bachelor's degree in biochemistry in 1975, she began working as an immunology research technician for the City of Hope Medical Center. Later she entered the field of pulmonary physiology. "But I wasn't happy doing clinical work," she says. "No intellectual stimulation whatsoever. My scientific training has helped me as an antique appraiser, however, in a field I truly love."

Nancy got started in the profession in a typical way. "There was something I needed to have appraised. And when I found out the appraiser charged $100, was booked months in advance, and spent his day surrounded by fascinating antiques, I was interested. Growing up around art and history, traveling to Europe and visiting the museums, and being fairly observant, I figured I had what it took to

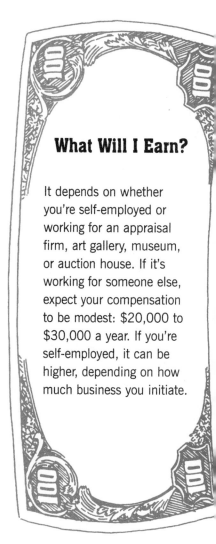

What Will I Earn?

It depends on whether you're self-employed or working for an appraisal firm, art gallery, museum, or auction house. If it's working for someone else, expect your compensation to be modest: $20,000 to $30,000 a year. If you're self-employed, it can be higher, depending on how much business you initiate.

INFORMATION

For More Information

American Society of Appraisers
555 Herndon Parkway
Suite 125
Herndon, VA 20170
(703) 733-2108
fax (703) 742-8471

Appraisers Association of
America, Inc.
386 Park Avenue South
New York, NY 10016
(212) 889-5404
fax (212) 889-5503

International Society of Appraisers
Riverview Plaza Office Park
Suite 320
16040 Christen Road
Seattle, WA 98188-2929
(206) 241-0359
fax (206) 241-0436

get started. Nonetheless, everyone I discussed my new interest with sought to discourage me. Yet, I was determined to proceed.

"So, I called the man who did my appraising and asked about getting into the field," Nancy continues. "He was very gruff. He gave me a pile of books to read two feet high. One was *The Dictionary of Decorative Arts*, a tome if there ever was one. Everyone was discouraging me: it doesn't pay well, liabilities are incredible, chances of being sued are high, it's lots of hard work. Yet, I didn't hear any of it.

"My former husband spent tens of thousands of dollars, thank you very much, sending me off to classes here and there—Sotheby's in Los Angeles, UCLA extension, and courses offered several times a year by appraisal societies on connoisseurship."

Finally, after all this study, and three-and-one-half years of an unpaid apprenticeship with the art appraiser, Nancy was ready, in 1983, to strike out on her own.

Down and Dirty

Whether examining pedestrian residential contents or fabulous eighteenth-century ceramics, as an antique appraiser you'll devote but a fraction of your time to actual fieldwork. Elizabeth Saveri, a researcher with degrees in architecture and fine arts, spends the majority of her time digging not among home furnishings but in auction catalogs, books, and on the Internet. "It's all about finding 'comps,' or comparable items," she says. "From photos and descriptions the appraiser gives me, I match objects. For the most part, that's how we estimate value."

Almost all antique appraisers agree that the public has serious misconceptions about what they do. "It appears so glamorous," observes Nancy. "We go to gorgeous homes, meet the rich and famous, and do a quick appraisal."

Yet, frequently Nancy and her colleagues travel to less impressive digs, where they crawl around on hands and knees while shooing away spiders. All to look for treasures among typical garage-sale items.

"To pay the bills, I do a lot of loss work: fire, flood, vandalism, sewage spill, and so on," Nancy says. "I am hired by lawyers, insurance companies, and private parties. We have seven lawsuits in-house right now.

"If I didn't do the residential contents cases, the lawsuits, the work for lawyers and large companies, I couldn't do the rest. The deal around here is that we do the jobs that are dreadfully boring so that we can do the fun, beautiful things."

And, people being what they are, items are not always what they seem to be. "Insurance companies hire me," Nancy says, "to check it all out. Often people will claim it is worth a great deal of money. It truth, usually it's very modest material, garage-sale stuff."

Research done, an appraisal report, usually with photographs, is prepared. All national appraisal societies provide strict guidelines for producing such a document. Victor Wiener, executive director of the Appraisers Association of America (AAA), says that "an appraisal report should read like a legal brief." He adds, "In addition to an in-depth knowledge of the subject, an antique appraiser must possess the ability to write clearly and accurately. The appraisal report is a critical document."

Can You Afford It?

Nancy's degree aside, most antique appraisers hold college diplomas in the arts and, in addition, take plenty of specialized seminars and workshops. For instance, the Appraisal Institute of America's 1997 national conference on "The Changing Aspects of Connoisseurship" offered seminars in "Mastering Comparative Analysis," "Antique and Period Jewelry," and "20th-Century Prints," as well as workshops on "Emerging Legal Issues" and "How to Create a Web Page." Such courses can, over a lifetime of work, run into tens of thousands of dollars. And for all your expertise, you'll command a modest

What to Read

*Green Guide to Antiquing
in the Midwest*
by John Fiske.
Globe Pequot Press, 1996.

*Guide to Evaluating Gold and
Silver Objects for Appraisers,
Collectors, Dealers*
by Scott V. Martin.
SM Publications, 1997.

salary. "Wherever you go in this field," Nancy says, "you're likely to be asked, 'Can you afford to work here?'"

In recognition of the public's need for professionally qualified appraisers, the ASA tests and accredits the personal property appraiser in one or more of 28 specialties. Are you an expert in any of the following?

- African Sculpture
- Antique Arms and Armor
- Antique Furniture
- Antique Glass
- Antique and Decorative Art
- Antique Guns
- Asian Art
- Automatic Musical Instruments
- Books
- Dolls and Toys
- Equines
- Ethnographic Art
- European China
- Fine Arts
- Fine Arts Photography
- Furs
- Japanese Prints
- Native American Art
- Manuscripts
- Numismatics
- Oriental Rugs
- Pre-Columbian Art
- Residential Contents, General
- Silver and Metalware
- Stamps
- Textiles
- Violins
- Wines, Fine and Rare

In addition, an accredited and tested ASA appraiser has specialized knowledge achieved through academic study and practical experience. This equips the appraiser to competently render appraisal for specific purposes, such as for:

- Insurance Value
- Sale Value
- Estate taxes
- Division of property in a divorce
- Donation to charity
- Equitable distribution

As Nancy said, it can take a lifetime to acquire the necessary knowledge. So why do it? Why put yourself though all this study when, for the same or less effort you could achieve higher financial rewards elsewhere?

Nancy smiles. "Because once in awhile you can find yourself in an Alice in Wonderland world, with marvelous results."

She explains: "Recently, I and two other professional appraisers, were called in by a movie studio to appraise their props. After tagging no less than 2,500 items, we began examining each one in detail. While I am forever keeping a wary eye out for reproductions, here I was surrounded by them: from plastic urns resembling antiques to spray-painted faux marble table tops. Then, all of a sudden, I glanced to my right—and let out a scream. Over in the corner was a bookcase that could only have been designed by Charles and Henry Greene. That circa 1910 treasure we wound up appraising for over $50,000. In a fortuitous reversal of fortunes, among all the reproductions I had found the genuine article."

Cool Web Sites to Visit

Ancient Times Story Tellers
www.hancockmd.com/ship/ a-times/

Assessors, Valuators and Appraisers
www.workfutures.bc.ca/text/ body/1235eb_t.htm

Search Arts> Fine Arts> Antiques
www.directory.netscape.com/ arts/fine_arts/antiques/

ATHLETIC TRAINER

They're not personal trainers, it's not about working out. Certified athletic trainers are the hub around which athletic health care takes place. All have at least a bachelor's degree, and all love sports.

It looks to be a promising season for safety Pat Perez, an Ayala High School junior. In its second game of a 10-game schedule, Ayala is playing rival Norco High School, on Norco's home turf in Chino Hills, California.

We're 10 minutes into the first quarter, field lights are shining, bleachers are crowded, and Mike West, Ayala's certified athletic trainer (ATC), paces the sidelines, chatting with head football coach Laing Stevens.

"I actually saw Pat go down," Mike declares. "And when he lay there, rolling on his back, obviously in pain, I knew we had a problem."

As an ATC, Mike is the first to provide medical assistance: "I rushed onto the field with my college aide, Christian. Our immediate job was to calm Pat down. We can't get information from an injured player who is anxious and confused.

"'I got hit on my left knee, then I heard a pop,' Pat finally uttered," says Mike. "With that important information, I examined the joint, searching for any deformity. If there were problems, I didn't want to go any further.

"Finding none, I placed stress on the knee," the 31-year-old ATC continues. "The results were positive, the joint moved in an abnormal way. My initial diagnosis, confirmed shortly afterward by our team physician, was for two torn ligaments: the interior cruciate and the medial collateral. Surgery? Definitely! Pat would be out for the season."

ATCs: Health Care Coordinators

Athletic training, recognized in 1990 by the American Medical Association as an allied health care profession, is charged with the art and science of athletic injury prevention, evaluation, management, and rehabilitation.

There are 18,300 certified athletic trainers nationwide, according to Eve Becker-Doyle, executive director of the National Athletic Trainers' Association (NATA). All possess at least a bachelor's degree, usually in athletic training, health, physical education, or exercise science. All pass a grueling all-day certification examination consisting of a written test, practical test, and a written simulation test. And all complete a minimum number of internship hours.

In some states, in addition to certification, athletic trainers are licensed.

ATCs work with the physically active, be they in regulated competitive sports or as weekend participants.

About 25 percent are employed in colleges/universities; 25 percent in high schools; and 34 percent in clinics, according to NATA figures. Of the remaining 16 percent, most are in the growing corporate field. A few, approximately 500, work at the supposed apex of the profession, professional sports. "Those folks have the bucks to hire ATCs for their million-dollar celebrity athletes," Eve states. "They are the most visible."

Often confused in the public's mind with personal trainers, ATCs are sensitive to the distinction.

"It's not about weight training, though there's nothing wrong with that," Geoff Schaadt, head athletic trainer and assistant athletic director at UCLA, says. "We act as a hub around which athlete health care takes place. The days of the bucket and sponge are long gone."

Geoff's colleague at USC, head athletic trainer Russ Romano, agrees. "The athletic trainer of old handled catastrophic injuries—period. Today, we coordinate health care. It's more complex than it was 30 years ago."

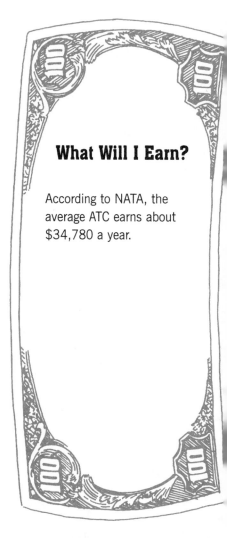

What Will I Earn?

According to NATA, the average ATC earns about $34,780 a year.

For More Information

The National Athletic Trainers'
Association (NATA)
2952 Stemmons Freeway
Dallas, TX 75247
(214) 637-6282
www.nata.org

Pure Athletics

That complexity is evident at the high school level, where Mike's nine- to ten-hour days are varied and active.

"I'll see a thousand student athletes this school year," he says, sitting in a crowded but well-equipped rehab room off the school's gym. Surrounded by the whirlpool bath, rehab trampoline, biomechanical ankle platform system, and warm-up bike, Mike explains what it's like.

"On a daily basis, but particularly at the beginning of any sports season, it's swimmers with sore shoulders, baseball players with bad elbows, and track athletes with shinsplints, to name but three sports. All have to be dealt with. For any athlete, even something as ordinary as shinsplints can be painful or uncomfortable."

It's when attending sporting events that Mike provides the health protection most needed, "yet few high schools can afford a full-time athletic trainer," he says. "If you want to work in this setting, be prepared to do something in addition. You need to be a teacher on staff or work in a clinic in the morning, then hire yourself out for high school coverage in the afternoon."

John Ryan, a licensed ATC at Bangor High School, in Bangor, Maine, is in the former category. "I teach three to four athletic training classes in the day, to about fifty students," he says. "I'm sure having a teaching credential in addition to my athletic trainer certification got me this job."

Mike and John both love what they do. "In high school," Mike says, "it's all about play. Few will get college scholarships, and they know it. Here it is pure athletics."

But what about the long hours?

"Compared to what?" questions John. "At least I'm home every night. You can't say that about Division I competition or the pros."

That's for sure.

"During football season," Geoff cautions, "It's a seventy-five-hour-a-week job. And I have nine athletic trainers under me [in all sports]."

Yet, long hours and games away from home aside, most certified athletic trainers at the college level are happy to be on the team.

"Yes, being with a winning program is great," says Geoff. "But unlike being a coach, wins and losses don't dictate an ATC's worth to the program. The joy in the profession comes from dealing with the student athlete."

Student Athletes Aside

Not all ATCs work in school settings. Sports clinics offer a growing outlet for athletic trainer services.

Jerry Whetstone supervises eight full-time and three part-time ATCs at the Franciscan Sports Medicine Center in Dayton, Ohio. "Beyond our work with the recreational athlete, we provide coverage for seventeen high schools, six middle schools, one community college, and two pro teams," he cites. "That works out to over a thousand event coverages a year."

In addition to employing ATCs, Jerry's center has physical therapists (PTs) on staff. "Yes, we've had turf battles," he admits. "But now our ATCs and PTs team up to share patient load. For ATCs, it's extremity injuries: joints, muscles, and bones. For PTs, it's more neural: the neck and back."

Crystal Saldivar, an ATC and PT assistant at the Riverside (California) Physical Therapy Center, sees the ATC/PT issue differently.

"In many states, insurance companies are not required to reimburse for services provided by an ATC in a physical therapy clinic. That nullifies our degree. Athletic trainers in a clinical setting often compete with physical therapist aids, working for $6 to $10 an hour.

"Everyone thinks we are in the gym working people out to get them fit. That's not it. We basically do a pre-med degree. It's injury prevention, rehabilitation, nutritional counseling. True, it's not so much the neck and back. That's more neural, for physical therapists. But for an extremity injury, we are the ones."

Still, clinics have their advantages. Even Crystal admits, "the hours, and salary, are fixed."

What to Read

Athletic Trainer
by Edward A. Voeller.
Capstone Press, 1999.

Yet, if she had to do it again, Crystal would shun the clinic work environment for the playing field or athletic court. "I'd much rather work with athletes," she says. "It is a much easier population because they have the desire to get better. In a clinic, it's 85 percent worker's compensation. Folks tend to linger. What's the hurry to get back to a crummy job? But if you are not in the starting lineup for next week's game, you might not get that scholarship because no one may see you. The incentive is there."

Another employment route for ATCs, beyond the student and recreational athlete, is in the corporate world.

"A while back I began receiving calls from headhunters representing various medical groups—hospitals, medical manufacturers, pharmaceuticals, etcetera," says Brian Berry, director of sales and marketing for Hely & Weber Body Glove Orthopedics. "They wanted someone who knows the medical community backwards and forwards, is good under pressure, has excellent human relations skills, and can teach technical subjects to technical and nontechnical audiences. I know thousands out there who can do that. They're called certified athletic trainers."

Routes to Certification

"In many states, anyone can call themselves an athletic trainer," Mark Gibson, head athletic trainer at the University of Wisconsin-LaCrosse, discloses. "Unfortunately, no certification is actually required."

But call yourself what you may, you'll find that in all but a few employment situations certification is demanded. NATA, through its Board of Certification (NATABOC), provides for such certification through two routes: curriculum and internship.

Educational institutions offering curriculum programs—there are nearly 100 accredited by the Commission on Accreditation of Allied Health Education Programs (CAAHEP)—require instruction in subjects such as therapeutic modalities and exercise, human anatomy and physiology, kinesiology/biomechanics, nutrition, and athletic injury/illness prevention and evaluation. In addition, you will need to complete at least 800 hours of supervised experience.

Doug Padron, an ATC graduate student at Michigan State University, went the curriculum route and wound up putting in over 3,000 hours. "I was always drawn to being involved in athletics," he says. "But I got to a point where my sports career took me as far as I could go. I didn't necessarily want to be a coach. So I took an athletic trainer introductory course at Ocean County Junior College in New Jersey and I have never looked back. I am where I want to be."

If you choose the internship road, you'll need, in addition to the bachelor's degree required of all ATCs, 1,500 hours of supervised experience. And you better hurry. NATA will be dropping interning as a route to certification in 2004.

According to Kent Falb, NATA's current president, "For athletic trainers to compete effectively in the arena of health care, we need to follow a single route to certification, one based on a curriculum, a course of study. Furthermore, some states have legislated that in order to work as an athletic trainer, even an ATC, you must have graduated from an approved curriculum program."

Once you complete either program, you're eligible to sit for the certification exam. If you pass, you are certified.

Is it worth it?

"I'd do it again in a heartbeat," Mike announces. "After all, much of the time I get paid for watching sporting events."

Cool Web Sites to Visit

The Athletic Trainer's Corner
www.nismat.org/transcor/index.html

Athletic Training Profession
http://coe.etsu.edu/department/pexs/index.htm

Career Search
www.careersearchinc.com/

As with an iceberg, most of what goes on is hidden from view. But when the auction begins, rapid-fire bid calling is a must. That, and great showmanship.

Hot Career

5

"Great bid calling, that is: *$35 bidder, now 40, would-a-give $40, $40 bidder, who's able-a-buy-'em at $50*, signals a terrific auctioneer," says Rick Machado. "But there's more to it. Clarity, voice quality, speed, ability to expedite the sale, bid-catching ability, and, of course, whether someone would actually hire you as their auctioneer are critical factors as well."

Rick ought to know. It's on such criteria that he and nine other finalists at the World Champion Livestock Auctioneer's annual competition in Asheville, North Carolina, are being judged.

Rick has been this far before, into the finals five times in seven years. "I was more relaxed this time," the affable, 37-year-old livestock auctioneer from Arroyo Grande, California, says. "I think that made a difference."

Yet, as the evening's banquet drags on, and the first runner up and reserved champion are announced, Rick still isn't sure. "I felt I'd done a good job earlier, selling my ten drafts of cattle at the live auction," he says. "But the sponsoring organization has a lot at stake in picking a winner. He will be their spokesperson for the next year."

Rick's anxiety is understandable, this is the Olympics of auctioneering. But his apprehension is misplaced.

"And now, ladies and gentlemen," the master of ceremonies and reigning world champion booms, "I give you the 1999 World Champion Livestock Auctioneer, Mr. Rick Machado!"

"In this field," the beaming Rick declares, "it doesn't get any better than this."

Free Enterprise to the Max

Auctioneers, six thousand of whom belong to the National Auctioneers Association (NAA), are a varied group, working in a unique industry. While not all are world champions at their calling, to succeed as professionals, in a tough, competitive business, they must be in top form.

"A professional auctioneer," according to the NAA, "is a marketing specialist. He or she must have a working knowledge of the value of items being offered, know how to attract people most interested in those items, and be able to present the items in a manner that creates excitement and stimulates competition."

It's not an all up-front business.

"About 90 percent of an auctioneer's work is behind the scenes," Forrest Mendenhall, cofounder of the Mendenhall School of Auctioneering and an auctioneer since 1953, says. "Preparation, organization, tagging, lotting, creating a buyer's guide, these are activities the public rarely sees. Chanting—announcing a series of numbers [bids or requested bids] connected by 'filler' words, which give the buyer time to think between bids—is but a small, though important, part."

The auctioneer, who is agent for the seller, must obtain the best price possible for an item. "It's the auctioneer's job to create an exciting, rhythmic, fast-paced selling atmosphere," says Larry Frederick, an auctioneer with four years' experience in farm and ranch, residential, and commercial properties, from South Coffeyville, Oklahoma, says. "You have to know your crowd, be able to put people at ease, and sell, sell, sell."

"When you think about it, most commodities are sold by auction," says David Berkstresser, a successful auto auctioneer from Arizona. "Treasury bills, all stock, tobacco, cattle, you name it. If you have to eat it, stock it, or bond it, it's auctioned. An auction is the greatest form of free enterprise there is."

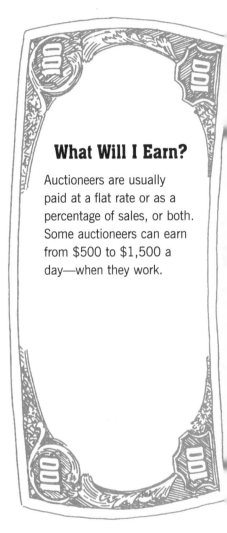

What Will I Earn?

Auctioneers are usually paid at a flat rate or as a percentage of sales, or both. Some auctioneers can earn from $500 to $1,500 a day—when they work.

People Business

Rick got rustled into that free enterprise zone at an early age: "My dad did a little auctioneering. He corralled me into helping him on the cattle truck when I was thirteen. Then, after hours, I would turn on the PA system and start playing auctioneer. I've been 'playing' ever since."

Growing up and working around cattle has paid off for Rick in the single most important factor for success as an auctioneer—product knowledge.

"You've got to know what you're selling," says Larry Frederick. "If you don't have a clue, you can't sell it, be it an antique desk, classic car, or commercial real estate."

"Integrity is right up there with product knowledge," volunteers Clint Sherman, of Lubbock, Texas, also a champion auctioneer, having won the Auto Auctioneers World Championship (with prize money of $7,500) early in 1999. "When you are asking a man to bid up from $29,000 to $30,000, he's got to trust you."

"Product knowledge and integrity, for sure. But I'd throw in tact and sensitivity," says Joe Keefhaver, executive vice president of the NAA. "Even when someone hasn't died, say they're just retiring and heading for Florida, they may be grieving as they see their business possessions sold to the highest bidder. You've got to handle the situation with care."

But in the end, when you're on the block, it's salesmanship and showmanship that make for a terrific auction event.

"When you are up there in front of the crowd, chanting, you're the man," Larry says. "I enjoy being in the spotlight."

Finding that Fine Line

$1 here, $2 where, $2 there, $3 now, $3 now, would you bid $4, now $5, 5 bucks and how about that. It's not your life, it's not your wife, it's only money.

Bookgrinders, an independent bookstore/cafe in Van Nuys, California, has succumbed to the superstore onslaught. Dan Dotson, a for-hire auctioneer for All States Auctions, is here to move everything out by day's end, including the kitchen sink.

Well over a hundred bidders mill around, eager to grab what All States, a successful auction firm specializing in small business liquidations, has shrewdly laid out in lots, starting with trinkets such as cookie jars, napkin holders, and dairy creamers, through mixers, blenders, and computers, to the cappuccino machine and huge oak bar which will have to be dismantled by a contractor to get it out the door.

"All States has done a great job bringing in local people," Dan says during a brief break off the block. "Through targeted advertising, the right people have showed up. Everything will go."

"Our job," says Marci Higer, cofounder of All States, "is to go into a place, set it up, lot it up, sell it, supervise the move out, collect the monies, sweep the place, and turn off the lights."

Brad, her partner, agrees. "We take what assets are there and quickly, sometimes within days, turn them into cash, clear it out."

Ultimately the job of doing that rests with the auctioneer. Dan, who's been at it since he turned 11, is fired up today.

The cookie jars go for $2, the blender for $100, and the bar, with its brass foot railing, for $450. "A good auctioneer can please both the seller and the buyer," Dan says in rapid-fire speech. "It's finding that fine line, establishing a price both can live with."

Cyberlots and Cattle TV

"It is the paramount issue facing us today, probably the biggest development in the history of auctioneering"—so declares Joe about online auctioneering. "Though there is apprehension among our membership, I find an amazing interest and receptiveness to the new technology."

"Online auctions have shaken the traditional auction house to its very foundation," Kevin Pursglove, director of communications for eBay, the San Jose, California, Internet auction company that is

What to Read

Country Auctioneer
by Thomas M. Martin.
Hamilton's, 1994.

both growing and making a profit, says. "We just purchased Butterfield and Butterfield," a traditional and well-known auction house based in Chicago.

Yet, Kevin sees the two auction worlds, traditional and online, coexisting.

"What will bring foot traffic to our Internet site will expose people to a live Butterfield auction, one they might not otherwise have attended," he says. "The two complement each other."

Dave, the auto auctioneer, isn't fighting the technology. "We put cars on our cyberlots, where buying and selling is done online. It is a small percentage, but growing."

"We now have satellite video auctions," Rick announces. "Cattle are filmed in their natural environment, the video is edited, then buyers go to a motel with phone banks set up and bid rapidly to the auctioneer through a phone bank representative. They never actually see the animals."

"Yes, the technology is working for certain items," Forrest Mendenhall cautions. "But the tire kickers will always be there. People want to look, touch, and feel. The auctioneer is here to stay."

"Rubber Baby Buggy Bumpers"

So, how to begin?

"Most auctioneers start out selling the smaller items," says Forrest. "Conducting benefit auctions, charity auctions, reruns at an automobile auction, calves or tack at a livestock auction, pots and pans at a household auction, et cetera. After practicing and practicing, they become popular and established. Their services grow in demand."

But everyone in the field agrees that even before you hit the block selling for a living, you should attend one of the many accredited auctioneering schools around the country.

"Most run eighty to one hundred twenty classroom hours," says Janet Scott, administrative coordinator at the South Carolina Auctioneers' Commission. "It's an intense two or three weeks."

Don't expect ivy-covered halls or a football team, however. What you will find is what Kimberly Marlowe, writing in the *Wall Street Journal*, says is "one of the few institutions of learning that gives credit to a student who can count backward from five hundred in a single breath."

The Mendenhall School of Auctioneering, with its 110-hour program, is perhaps typical. In an accelerated two weeks, you'll do drills for 40 hours and cover topics such as antiques, auto auctions, business liquidations, real estate auctions, farm sales, clerking and cashiering, tobacco auctions, general auction advertising, machinery and equipment auctions, and livestock auctioneering.

Throughout you must work to limber up your lips and tongue. "We do lots of tongue twisters," says Forrest. "You know, 'rubber baby buggy bumper' and 'around the rough and rugged road.' Tongue twisters are to an auctioneer what calisthenics are to an athlete."

Attending auctioneering school is a good idea for another reason. "About half the states require auctioneers to be licensed," Joe says. "In most of those states, having attended an accredited auctioneering school is an option that meets minimum requirements."

For Rick, auctioneering is more than a career, it's a way of life. "My dad forced me, at fifteen, to get up at a rodeo queen benefit auction," he remembers. "I've never looked back. I think the auctioneer's future is great. There is simply no other way of selling certain merchandise. It's the purest form—getting fair market value in an absolute sale."

Cool Web Sites to Visit

Auctioneer Job Profile
www.jobprofiles.com/ allauctioneer.htm

Auctioneering Colleges Gaining Popularity
www.globechat.com/ globedaily/content/ 012999_04.html

Internet Auction List
www.internetauctionlist.com/

Hot Concepts!

Informational Interviews

If you want to see what's going on in the "real world" and make valuable industry contacts at the same time, why not set up your own informational interview? Such an interview is just what the name indicates: a discussion with someone to find out about the job, the company, or the field in general. Remember, people love to talk about their work. Nearly everyone, if asked, will give you a 30-minute interview to discuss their favorite subject: themselves and what they do for a living.

Setting up an informational interview can work for you in two ways:

1. The most effective way to learn about occupations and the local job market is through personal contacts.
2. The confidence you gain while interviewing for career information will help when it's time for the real job interview.

Remember, in an informational interview, your purpose is to see but also to be seen; to hear but also to be heard; to be impressed but also to impress; and to discover but also to be discovered. In other words, while you want to learn all you can about a company, you want to let them know about you, too.

Make an appointment today.

CHEF

Wolfgang Puck and Alice Waters aside, they're not all celebrities. Twelve-hour days, standing in a cramped, hot, and greasy kitchen is how you'll spend your working hours. And that includes weekends and holidays. Still, if you love food, a chef's life it is.

B rad Toles knew the chef had a reputation, and not just for preparing the finest French cuisine in Lake Tahoe. "Everyone was aware of his disdain for American culinary expertise," Brad says. "In the true French chef tradition, he thought we were all lazy and incapable of learning the art of cooking."

Nonetheless, 18 and just a few months out of high school, Brad begged for a job. "I don't care where I have to begin," he pleaded. Immediately, he was thrown into the kitchen to wash dishes. A year and a half later, "the kid" had become an established cook and was ready to move on.

And move on—and up—he did. At 22, Brad became the youngest executive chef in the Red Lion Hotels and Resorts chain. Ten years later, after being promoted five times within Red Lion, he left to run four restaurants at the Queen Mary Hotel. It was then on to Hollywood Park where he was responsible for large-volume catering, serving up to 5,000 people. Today, a decade after first becoming an executive chef, Brad has started his own business, Savoury's Good Earth Cuisine, a multifaceted food company.

Not a 9-to-5 Job

Brad's meteoric rise to successful chef, in a tough, competitive profession that sees plenty of frustration and burnout, is the exception. Even after years of apprenticeship, few make it.

The apprenticeship—kitchen work—can be grueling.

"In this profession there's a high disparity between job perception and reality," says Paul Arenstam, owner and chef at Belon's in San Francisco. "It's long, hard, odd hours, almost all on your feet. Don't plan on weekends and holidays off, you'll work those so others may enjoy a meal out."

This theme is echoed by Bob Wemischner, certified chef and author of *The Vivid Flavors Cookbook*. "A hot kitchen, where you stand twelve hours a day, demands stamina—and commitment."

Yet, if you have a passion for cooking, there are rewards. "It's something tangible," Paul explains. "You succeed or fail in one single day. The great things don't linger, nor do the failures."

What, then, is required of a good cook or chef? According to Bob, three "ingredients" are necessary: "One, you need a good palate, which can be developed. Two, good hands: timing, coordination, a sense of rhythm. And, three, the ability to work with others and share responsibility."

The last characteristic is critical, particularly if you ever hope to move from chef to executive chef. As Brad describes it: "A good chef is good within him- or herself. A great chef is one who can execute through others."

That ability, to work through others, is what it takes to be an executive chef: one who manages and organizes the kitchen. "Cooking is maybe 20 percent of an executive chef's job," Brad explains. "I spent 60 percent of my time dealing with human relations problems, another 20 percent in working the numbers: the economics of the operation. People and management skills are what being an executive chef is all about."

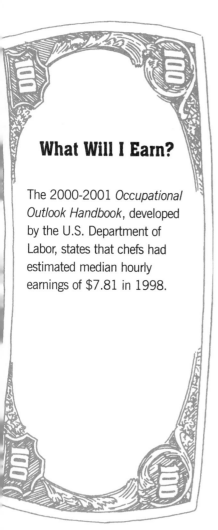

What Will I Earn?

The 2000-2001 *Occupational Outlook Handbook*, developed by the U.S. Department of Labor, states that chefs had estimated median hourly earnings of $7.81 in 1998.

How Do I Know Cooking Is for Me?

Answer: By working in a professional kitchen first. This is especially true if you plan to enroll in a culinary school.

All chefs interviewed were in agreement: "Get restaurant experience first," even if you have to do what Brad did, beg for it. Then, if after a few weeks or months immersed in food service you're still standing, and smiling, you might consider one of two ways of becoming a chef.

You could go the self-apprenticeship route, where you seek out great chefs as mentors. This was Brad's approach: moving from one recognized restaurant, and chef, to another, while learning from the masters. But there's a problem with this method. As Paul explains: "Such restaurants don't pay very well—they don't have to. After all, you're 'paying' for the experience."

Perhaps. Yet, the apprenticeship path has worked for Charlene Reis, pastry chef at Chez Panisse in Berkeley, California, consistently rated one of the top restaurants in America. "I left college in my junior year to work at the Canyon Ranch Spa in Tucson, Arizona," she says. "From there it was on to Los Angeles, San Francisco, and now, Berkeley. As long as you choose excellent restaurants to work at, and learn all you can, the apprenticeship approach is a good one."

The other route is through chef training at a culinary school.

Such institutions, public or private, usually require a two-year commitment. While none claim to turn out fully minted chefs, far from it, many will give you the basics and the sense of what it's like to move in a kitchen. As Bob comments, "The days of being trained exclusively on the job are passé. Schools, particularly those accredited by the American Culinary Federation, provide needed training in a controlled, protected environment."

Cooks for Hire: Personal Chefs

What if you don't want to work in a restaurant all day, all evening? What if you love to cook, but want to be your own boss? How about becoming a personal chef? Once the province of the rich and famous, personal chefs, who go to a client's home or corporate kitchens to prepare meals, are a growing service profession. According to the U.S. Personal Chef Association (USPCA), in Albuquerque, New Mexico, such folks charge from $8 to $20 per meal per person. Some hundred thousand Americans are now using such chefs on a regular basis, up from just a thousand in 1990. "It's no longer for the affluent," according to Jeffrey Shuman,

What to Read

Becoming a Chef
by Andrew Dornenburg
and Karen Page.
International Thompson
Publishing, 1997.

The Making of a Pastry Chef
by Andrew MacLauchlan.
John Wiley & Sons, 1999.

professor of entrepreneurship at Bentley College in Waltham, Massachusetts. "The service has moved down to the upper middle class, even the middle class."

The demand for such personal chefs is fueled not only by corporate executives with executive dining rooms but also by two-family workers who just don't have time to prepare their own meals. According to Juliet Schor, author of *The Overworked American*, in the last two decades of the twentieth century the average American has come to work an extra month a year. U.S. workers now labor longer than anyone in the industrialized world. According to a spokesperson the USPCA's four thousand members cater mainly to two-earner households with a combined income of at least $80,000.

Just what do such personal chefs do? According to Elizabeth Eckstein, writing in *Spirit* magazine, "A personal chef comes to your house loaded down with all the fixings for several entrees and side dishes that you selected from the chef's vast menu. After whipping up the meals in your kitchen, the culinary whiz stores the food in your refrigerator or freezer for you to heat and eat at your leisure, then cleans up the mess. As a bonus, a generous cook will leave behind a dessert, bottle of wine, or bunch of flowers for your table."

Such a service can be pricey, however. For a family of four, a workweek's worth of dinners can run from $160 to $400. Not exactly for the middle class, perhaps.

Does this sound like a cooking job for you? A typical personal chef is female, married, from 30 to 60, with more than 12 years of cooking experience, according to the USPCA. Each has 10 to 12 clients, on average.

If that doesn't fit your profile, at least with regard to cooking experience, not to worry. The USPCA offers training and certification. According to cofounder Sue Titcomb, "We offer correspondence courses that cover a variety of topics, from recipes that freeze well, to marketing techniques. We can link you up with a certified USPCA chef in your area for one-on-one mentoring. And every year we hold an international conference somewhere in the U.S."

What's it cost for all this training and information? According to USPCA, from as little as $500 to $2,000.

A Restaurant of Your Own

It seems the San Francisco culinary arbitrators just couldn't wait to file their assessments of the new restaurant in the Hotel Metropolis, at Turk and Mason. Open barely three months, reviews for Paul Arenstam's new Belon, named after a tasty, flat-shelled oyster with a crisp, slightly metallic flavor, are in. They're terrific—thank goodness.

"Belon is unique," says Patricia Unterman, in the *San Francisco Examiner*, "an important expression of San Francisco's ever-evolving culinary community. What was once a windowless Hofbrau has been transformed into a classic brasserie space with high ceilings and warm, wood paneling. . . ."

"Chef-owner Paul Arenstam is banking on the idea that people will travel anywhere for good food, and Belon has plenty of that to offer," says Michael Bauer, the *San Francisco Chronicle's* food editor. "In addition, it celebrates our seafood heritage with one of the best oyster bars in the city. Arenstam's food is still evolving, but even at this early stage he's cooking some of the most casual and delicious French-inspired food I've tasted in some time."

"Belon is a restaurant that cares, and if you take someone special there—a friend, a lover, a family member, yourself, a major campaign contributor, an adoring venture capitalist, that friendly clerk from the neighborhood store—he or she should get the impression you care as well," cheers Greg Hugunin, a city restaurant critic.

How important are such reviews for a new restaurant? Paul Arenstam says, "they're critical. Bad ones, even at this early stage, can set a devastating tone. When it comes to dining out, this city can be very discerning. I am thankful we are off to a good start."

It wasn't easy for 34-year-old Paul, a graduate of the Culinary Institute of America (CIA), to go into the restaurant business. "We had hopes of opening in April of 1999," he says. "What with all the delays—building permits, licenses, hiring

Cool Web Sites to Visit

Baking & Pastry Directory
www.pastrychef.com/ htmlpages/links.html

Great Chefs Online
www.greatchefs.com/

Star Chefs
www.starchefs.com/

good people, and, yes, financing—it wasn't until January 10, 2000, that we opened the doors."

And now, after over a year in planning, Paul has to shift his emphasis and expertise from what it took to open the restaurant to what it takes to run it. "Of course, I have a manager, one who handles the business end of things," he says. "I am the chef, the guy who spends his time in the kitchen. Still, I have to have some business sense, some feel for the business side of things. It isn't just about cooking great food, though that is critical. It is about people coming in and buying it."

For Paul, and for other chefs who decide to open their own restaurants, the first year is the toughest.

And San Francisco, where patrons have 3,600 restaurants to choose from, can be a brutal testing ground. Still, Paul is optimistic. "I have been working toward this all my professional life. With good food, great service, a congenial setting, and a sensible business operation, we will succeed. For me, it is a terrific, exciting time."

Go for It

Cooking at an eatery up the street, working as a personal chef, or someday perhaps opening your own restaurant—if food is what you love, go for it.

According to the U.S. Department of Labor, employment for chefs is expected to increase about as fast as the average for all occupations through the year 2005. Population growth, rising personal incomes, and increased leisure time will continue to produce growth in the number of meals consumed outside the home.

When Brad Toles was in high school, he thought about becoming a veterinarian. A chance job in a restaurant changed all that. He's never looked back.

COMMERCIAL REAL ESTATE AGENT

Time was, you had to pay your dues in residential sales before moving over to commercial sales. No more. In fact, an interesting phenomenon is taking place: new recruits are coming in right out of college.

It started with a "cold call," one of a hundred that 32-year-old Daron Campbell, of RE/MAX Commercial in Studio City, California, tries to make each day. "Yes," the landlord on the line said, "I want to sell my office building but I've already given an exclusive listing to your competitor." "Will you be looking to buy then?" Daron counters, not missing a beat. "Sure," the voice offers, "I'm in an acquisitions mode. If anything comes on the market, say in mid-Wilshire, let me know."

Not a week later, through his "underground" contacts, Daron gets wind that a 142,000-square-foot, 12-story office building owned by a Philippine bank, on Wilshire Boulevard, is for sale. Back on the phone to his potential buyer, Daron announces: "I've got a great property for you, I'll fax over specs: preliminary income, size, and condition. Why not drive by, take a look?"

Within an hour, an eager voice returns Daron's call. "I love it, let's make a deal."

The next 30 days are hectic, what with writing letters of intent, determining buyer qualification, drawing up a 75-page contract, doing inspections, and attorney meetings. In the end, the property changes hands—for $7.5 million. Since Daron is handling both sides on the deal, his commission is as high as the office building itself. "It was a six figure payday," Daron exults. "How I love commercial real estate!"

A Savvy and Aggressive Lot

Such enthusiasm is understandable. Composed of six distinct segments—office, retail, industrial, multifamily, hotel, and land—the commercial market is booming. Figures published by *Investment Trends*

Quarterly show a healthy second quarter 1999. Office sales, the accustomed leader, took 51 percent of the market, followed by multifamily (apartments) at 14 percent, hotels at 12 percent, retail at 11 percent, industrial at 6 percent, and land at 4 percent. Total investment volume: $7.55 billion.

Those handling the selling, buying, leasing, and managing of commercial property, known as commercial real estate sales agents and brokers, are a savvy and aggressive lot, prone to deal-making at its best. "Most have built their acumen in areas of business, finance, banking, and insurance," says Bruce Holmes, past president of the Maine Commercial Board of Realtors. "They already know the business end, now they work the flip side—real estate."

Time was, you had to pay your dues in residential sales before moving over to commercial. No more. "I don't know why that was ever the case," Cynthia Shelton, vice president of acquisitions for Commercial Net Lease Realty in Orlando, Florida, says. "You do not have to sell residential to be good at commercial—period. In fact, we are seeing an interesting phenomenon whereby people new to the profession are coming right out of college."

Of course, having sold homes for a living would be an asset for any commercial agent. Still, the knowledge base is different for the two. "You have to know construction," says Bruce. "Can you look at a block building and have a clue as to how it came together? Finance, codes, investment strategies, management—it's all in the mix."

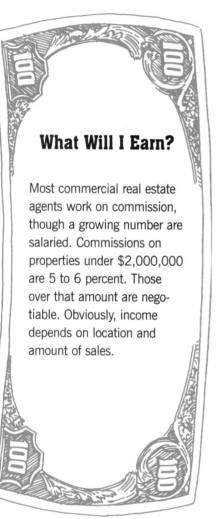

What Will I Earn?

Most commercial real estate agents work on commission, though a growing number are salaried. Commissions on properties under $2,000,000 are 5 to 6 percent. Those over that amount are negotiable. Obviously, income depends on location and amount of sales.

Working the Work Ethic

Armed with his B.A. in economics from UCLA in 1989, Daron says his first career choice wasn't commercial real estate. "I got into fund-raising after graduation. I was working with some big players willing to donate millions to capital campaigns. But I soon realized, no matter how hard I worked to raise money for someone else, it would not affect how much I earned. I needed to see a direct correlation between my work effort and income."

Within a year, Daron quit his fund-raising job and brashly approached Marcus & Millichap, one of the most successful real estate investment brokerage companies in Los Angeles. "I don't have a license and I've never sold anything," he told the human resource's manager. "Still, I think I belong with you. And let me tell you, I want to sell the big stuff."

Hired as a trainee in 1992, Daron began selling apartment buildings as soon as he got his California real estate license. Of the 26 rookies in his training class, eight months later only three were still at work. "There's high attrition, to be sure," he says. "Most last less than six months in the business. Not every day is a six-figure payday."

A similar motivation brought Daron's colleague at RE/MAX, Allen Levy, into the business a decade earlier. Teaching at a local junior high school, Allen, too, was looking to get paid for his efforts. During a six-month sabbatical from teaching, he decided to try commercial real estate—and never looked back. "I went from full insurance, a lunch I could purchase for eighty cents, and summers off, to the 'real world,'" he explains. "Talk about a shocking transition."

Working for the Haynes Company, selling apartment buildings, Allen did what he was told. "They said if I prospected, cold-called, on Monday, Tuesday, and Wednesday, 9:30 to 11:30, 1:30 to 3:30, and 6:30 to 8:30, I could make $100,000 a year. They were right. My first check, for $18,700, back in 1980, was more than my $16,000 annual teaching salary."

While both Daron and Allen brought from their previous jobs skills necessary to succeed in the hyper commercial real estate environment, new competencies were required. "It's a very demanding and complex profession," says Jim McDonald, Los Angeles chapter president of SIOR, the Society of Industrial and Office Realtors. "I have identified at least eleven core proficiencies I believe are necessary for those in my profession."

Here's the list:

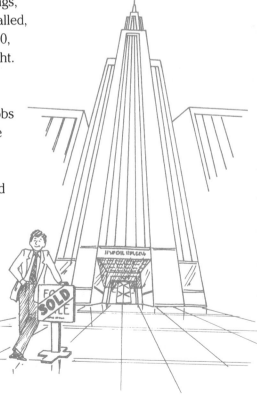

- Market Knowledge
- Marketing and Promotional Skills
- Negotiating Skills
- Command of Contracts
- Architecture/Building Knowledge
- Financial Expertise

INFORMATION

For More Information

Commercial Investment
Real Estate Institute (CIREI)
(312) 321-4440
www.naiop.org

National Association of Realtors®
430 N. Michigan Avenue
Chicago, IL 60611-4087
(312) 329-8458
www.realtormag.com

Society of Industrial and Office
Realtors (SIOR)
700 11th Street, NW, Suite 510
Washington, DC 20001
(202) 737-1150

- Interpersonal Skills
- Process Management
- Technological Currency
- General Business Competence
- Analytical Skills

"To the extent the above list represents what it takes to be an effective broker," Jim adds, "one would also expect each successful broker to be at least good enough at some and to excel at others."

"We're talking about a different mind-set," advises Allen. "I had no interest in working with an emotional mom and pop looking to make a buy decision based on the color of a living room carpet. I am more analytical. I prefer to look at the numbers, show the client the return he will get annually. Plus, the transactions are larger than in residential. You make more money."

Peaks and Valleys

Dirk Degraeve, director of leasing for Paramount Contractors & Developers, sits in his office at 6464 Sunset Boulevard, Hollywood, California, admiring the view of the famous Hollywood sign. "With worldwide name recognition, burgeoning high-profile retail and entertainment developments, and central location, Hollywood remains one of the city's prime leasing bargains," he declares. "Tinseltown is returning to prominence as a hot locale and rental rates are trending upwards, not down.

"There are trophy buildings here selling for $40 million," Dirk continues. "A year ago they went for $31 million, and three years ago, for only $19 million. This building has seen a 50 percent rent increase over the last year."

Dirk entered the commercial real estate business 10 years ago, leasing and managing buildings like the 110,000-square-foot one he occupies. Coming from a marketing background in Europe, where he handled clients such as Philip Morris, Dirk had the business savvy and people skills to segue easily into commercial real estate. "I knew how to meet people, develop

relationships, sell, and market," he explains. "This is a perfect profession for me."

While a tight office market and rising rents are great for management companies such as Paramount Contractors & Developers, that's not necessarily the case for real estate agents who live for the transaction.

"Volatility is what we all like," says Daron. "If the market is rising, I love it. If it's in the tank, I love that, too. A flat market is the worse. When values are steady, there is no movement, no action. Peaks and valleys, that's what it's all about."

Actually, peaks—or rising values—can also be a problem, Daron admits. "Yes, sellers feel they don't need agents as much during the good times. They figure they can simply run an ad in the paper and buyers will come. Right now we're all struggling for inventory."

Fax Broadcasting

In this profession, like almost all others, there's a technology issue. "It, technology, is an interesting thing," Cynthia Shelton observes. "I can now pull down demographics and environmental information at my desktop and have answers in minutes. Before computers, it could have taken a day or more. Yet, I am working harder now than ever. I guess the technology has allowed me to be more productive."

"We do what is called 'fax broadcasting,'" Allen explains. "When we procure a new listing, we immediately send out eight hundred faxes to principals and twice that many to brokers. The cost savings is tremendous: 4 cents a copy versus 50 cents per letter. Next, it is e-mail broadcasting, which is essentially free."

"For many brokers, adapting to the new technology is going to be a daunting task," says Jim. "Yet, powerful computer applications are available today to handle every brokerage task, from correspondence and contract preparation, desktop publishing, financial analysis, contact management, e-mail, faxing, lease analysis, to accounting and financial management, transaction management, and calendaring. The most effective brokers today have access to, and/or utilize, at least some of these programs."

What to Read

How to List and Sell Real Estate in the 21st Century by Danielle Kennedy and Warren Jamison. Simon & Schuster, 1998.

Real Estate License Examinations: Salesperson and Broker by Joseph H. Martin and Eve Steinberg. Prentice Hall Books, 1993.

Dialing for Dollars

So, how do you get started in a rewarding though strenuous and stressful career? "You better have at least nine months' salary put away," Allen advises. "The big bucks don't come in as quickly as you would like. If you start out as a junior agent, working for a senior agent, you'll receive a monthly salary and small commission. You'll coordinate all the efforts necessary to close an escrow: working with the termite inspection company, appraiser, engineers, lenders. And, of course, you'll prospect every day."

Cynthia adds, "Large companies will hire guys, and, more and more, thank goodness, gals, as apprentices to do research, spreadsheets, cold calling, and then turn it over to those who are better at meeting and doing the physical presentations. It's a team effort now."

"Typically, you'll start out on the streets, doing a little office and retail leasing," says Bruce. "You will work with contractors, dirty industrial buildings, and maybe, over time, move on to high-rises. It's learning the business: environmental issues, codes, and keeping an eye out for development opportunities."

While you're at it, you will need a thick skin, "a tolerance for pain," Daron says. "I am, for the most part, a telemarketer. I dial for dollars. And you know what people think of us telemarketers. You are going to get rejection."

Allen concurs. "Rejection is the biggest agent killer in my business," he says. "An agent will make ten calls and get ten no's. He then stops calling. I call ten more times and then keep calling until I get a yes. One yes can mean thousands. One good call can make an $80,000 payday."

That's why agents like Daron and Allen keep at it. "I have the best job in the world," Daron maintains. "When I come to work, no one can steal from me, I have no inventory on my shelf. I don't work nights or weekends. All I need is a telephone and a computer. I can go to work in any city in the world and be successful." Having said that, he leans over and places his headset on. Forty more cold calls to quitting time.

COMPUTER GAME DESIGNER

Loving to play games is important. But you must also like analyzing and tearing apart what you see on the screen. And keep in mind it's more than play, play, play. Designing the latest Dolphin, PlayStation 2, Dreamcast, and X-Box products is work, work, work.

L et's see, I want a monster with two heads and four arms. There were once two races, always fighting with each other, ravaging the land, destroying everything the gods had created. Fed up, a god comes down, grabs hold of both races and blends them into one new race—creating creatures with two heads and four arms.

Though now president of his own computer game development company, Liquid Entertainment, Ed Del Castillo still likes to hit the keyboard from time to time, conjuring up game fantasies and scenarios as he did while a computer game designer and producer on such hugely successful projects as Command and Conquer and Red Alert.

"Creating missions, characters, scenes, and stories is the part game designers love the most," thirty-year-old Ed says, as he sits surrounded by his 12-person development team in the company's Thousand Oaks, California, office.

"Writing down ideas, creating a story the company may some-day build into an actual game, with animation, textured models, and sound effects, is great. Empowering the page, that's what it means to be a game designer."

Hours of Idle Fun

If you're a gamer, with an interest—no, a passion—for what makes them work, then, as Sat Sharma, senior marketing manager for *Computer Gaming World*, declares, "Game development is definitely a good place to be."

The industry utilizes two broad hardware platforms, the home PC or a video game system (Sony's PlayStation 2, Nintendo's Dolphin, Sega's Dreamcast, and Microsoft's X-Box). And the industry is blasting out.

According to *PC Data*, 55 million PC-based game units and 71.5 million video game units were shipped in 1998. Mike Breslin, vice president of Ion Storm, a large game developer in Dallas, Texas, says, "In dollar amount, games surpassed theater attendance, $7 billion versus $5.5 billion, in 1999. What entertainment has ever outgrossed cinema in America?"

Made up of many genres: side scrollers, adventure games, parlor games, puzzle games, arcade games, and even "edutainment," electronic games of every kind are hot.

Colin Campbell, writing in the July 1, 1999, issue of *Games Business*, sums it up best when referring to the PC-based game market in particular: "Put frankly, as PC prices come down, the market is opening into an area that sees the PC primarily as a complex device for generating hours of idle fun."

Careers in this business vary, as in any collaborative enterprise. Seen as developers in the broad sense, the field breaks down into programmers, artists, musicians, producers, play testers, publishers, and game designers.

Design, according to Diana Gruber, author of *Becoming a Computer Game Developer*, "is a specific function in the game development field. Designers oversee the project and create the vision. There are people who excel at designing levels, puzzles, likable characters, and entertaining story lines."

Dave Leary, a game designer with Liquid Entertainment, explains it this way: "We define the game functionality. How is this character going to work in the game, what is this thing being drawn going to do?"

What Will I Earn?

From $25,000 to $60,000 per year, plus possible royalties and/or bonuses.

"A fantasy game designer," says Ed, "decides if archers will be in the game, if they fire every second, how much damage they do, and what armor they wear. An insane amount of detail encompasses each game play element. The designer understands how to create those elements and how to balance them to produce an interesting game."

Shower and Bed Provided

Though always a gamer, Ed gave little thought to designing games, at first. An economics major in college, it wasn't until after graduation that he began "play-testing" games his buddies were developing in their apartments. Next, it was on to writing manuals for Mindcraft and working as a level designer to create the 3-D worlds players run around in. But Ed's economics interest eventually came through for him as a producer.

"Many terms in this industry are taken from Hollywood," he says. "I worked for Sid Meier, a legend in our field, on his real-time strategy game, Gettysburg. What a challenging management experience!"

What are designers like, and what makes a good designer? "For a designer, the creative side promotes your inner child," Ed says. "The dark side, however, can manifest itself in immaturity, irresponsibility, and a lack of commitment and dedication. Designers can be incredibly temperamental. The trick is to find people with a strong inner child and the discipline and professionalism to do good work even when they don't want to."

Diana agrees. "A good designer works hard, is dedicated, and won't walk away when the going gets tough. The industry is crowded with people who don't want to put in the effort. They're going nowhere."

Putting in effort is key. It explains why most designers are young, often in their early twenties.

"If they're not in college," Diana continues, "they have the time to put into it. As you get older, family responsibilities keep you from fourteen-hour, seven-day-a-week efforts."

INFORMATION

For More Information

American Software Association
c/o ITAA
1616 N. Fort Myer Drive
Suite 1300
Arlington, VA 22209
www.arcat.com

"I know talented game designers in their twenties earning six-figure incomes," Mike says. "But they're laboring sixty to seventy hours a week. Here at Ion Storm we have showers and beds in the office. At times people simply do not leave."

Beyond Play

One such all-hours worker at Ion Storm is Stevie Case, the exuberant twenty-something game designer, also known as the "Cyber world's first chick game champ, or KillGreek" for having beaten her boss, John Romero, at his own game of Quake. How did she get started in what is acknowledged to be an overwhelmingly male domain?

"After college, I spent two years freelancing from my home in Dallas," she says. "I did level design, using tools I found on the Net for free, and nearly starved. Then, I saw an ad for a play tester at Ion Storm. Though an entry level job, it got me in the door where I could then play with their level editor."

Stevie has found her life's work, especially since being recently promoted to the Diakatana team as a level designer. "Having been a game fanatic all my life, making games is a perfect career for me," she says. "Yet don't expect to get rich quick. If your ultimate focus is to make money, money isn't why you want to do this. Instead, zero in on creating a fun game. Build your portfolio. Sacrificing the financial side first will pay off in the end."

How do you get started?

"The way to enter is as a play tester," says Ken Brown, editor of *Computer Gaming World*. "Game companies will hire you, often at minimum wage, to play games eight to ten hours a day. But it's not all fun and games. You're instructed to write down aberrations in the software, things you don't think work well. You have to interrupt your game play, take notes, tab out of Windows."

Another entree into the game design world is through programming. "If you know C++," says Ken, "you can simply hire yourself out as a programmer."

But programming for a game design company isn't programming for, say, an accounting firm.

"In every field, passion rules," Ken declares. "The ability to speak the language and display enthusiasm for what you're doing is critical. You've got to love games inside and out."

And, you must *write, write, write games.*

"You need to put a game in your head, and from there put the game in your computer," says Diana, who has done everything in this business, from programming to publishing. "Make it work. It doesn't have to be a great game. It doesn't even have to be a fun game. It can be Tic-Tac-Toe or Hangman. It can be ugly and hard to play. As long as it is a game, and as long as you wrote it.

"Your first game should be a learning experience. It should be a lesson you start, and finish, and move on from there. Try to do the best you can, but don't try to make Doom your first game."

"Game designer is the only job," adds Ed, "that you can get hired in because you are familiar with video games. All you need is a good work ethic, combined with the ability to write and communicate your ideas."

That said, if you're a college student in some parts of the country, you may soon be able to major in video game design. Read this, from an article entitled, "As If Students Didn't Already Waste Time on Video Games," by Shirley Leung, in the February 18, 2000, edition of the *Wall Street Journal:*

> *Playing Donkey Kong on Nintendo 64 may become homework if you're a student in the University of California-Irvine's newest concentration: the Interdisciplinary Gaming Studies Program. . . . The program will explore the growing role of video games as well as teach students the technical skills to program and design the computer pastimes.*

What to Read

Becoming a Computer Game Developer by Diana Gruber. Online at *www.makegames.com*

Fun Is Their Job

Though the computer game industry is growing—about 25 million homes in the United States had a video game machine of some sort at the end of 1999—game development is competitive and loaded with risks, financially and psychologically.

As an example of the financial risk, consider that in 2000, the average PC console game cost between $5 million and $10 million to create. Fantasy 7 reportedly cost Square Co. $30 million to develop.

"There are numerous ways to break in," says Diana Gruber, "all tough. As an employee, you work for the company, you own no part of the game, and you get paid the same whether the game succeeds or fails.

"As a contractor, if the game succeeds, you might receive royalties, and if it fails, you may have trouble finding work next year.

"Partnerships are OK, if you can make them work. Problems occur when you get sick and tired of your partner goofing off and sticking you with all the work.

"Finally, in a sole proprietorship you get all the rewards and take all the risks, both of which can be considerable."

Yet, as Ken says, "This is an exciting, fun, industry to be in. And game designers have the most fun because they come up with cool ideas to make games interesting and fun to play. That's their job."

"The future is bright," says Mike. "Cinema and games are merging. That's the next big step, a major shift in entertainment. Heck, two guys left me and went to work on the movie *Titanic*."

"I've thought of leaving this industry, too, though for different reasons," Ed concludes. "With Liquid Entertainment, I agreed to give it one last shot. It's turning out just fine. It is great working with programmers, 3-D artists, concept artists, managers, and, of course, computer game designers."

Cool Web Sites to Visit

Become a Computer Game Developer: Do You Have What it Takes?
www.makegames.com/ chap1.html

The Complete War Games Handbook
www.hyw.com/books/wargames Handbook/contents.htm

Making Animated GIFs
www6.unioui.es/gifanim/ gifmake.htm

COMPUTER SOFTWARE TRAINER

Whether you are a stand-up trainer delivering instruction in a classroom setting, an instructional designer putting together effective learning packages, or a training specialist involved in planning and program development, you're in demand.

Though the incident took place in the early '90s, Don Frozina, a Los Angeles-based Citicorp software trainer, remembers it to this day.

"I was to do a Monday-through-Friday Unix training seminar for our Chicago subsidiary," the affable 43-year-old operating systems specialist recounts. "For on-site training, my modus operandi is to arrive on the scene at least one business day early, just to check things out. In this case, was I glad I did.

"On the Friday before, I began setting up equipment, most of it rented. For two hours, I laid cables and ran power lines. Then, I stood up and flipped on the Sun 360 server. Nothing! I rocked the on-off switch a few times—zilch. The system was down. Friday, 4:00 P.M., in Chicago."

Don, with a B.S. degree in electronics technology, decided to dig deeper. He removed the server's case, fiddled with the motherboard and network cards, and scrutinized the hard drive. Though power was getting to the Sun 360, the hard drive wasn't spinning. A quick call to tech support elicited only bad news—a new server would be required. They could ship one out on Monday. "Too late," Don responded. "I'll see what I can do on my own."

What Don did next was simple, yet gutsy. "I lifted the entire server off the table, an inch or so," he says. "Then I dropped it. That broke the surface tension on the drive's bearings, freeing the disc to spin. I quickly taped the unit's on-off switch to 'on' and, on penalty of death, forbade anyone to touch it. Monday morning we were ready for business."

While hardware expertise is rarely mandatory for computer software trainers, a basic knowledge of disc drives, power supplies, connectors, I/O cards, and computer peripherals can't hurt. And that's just the beginning. Today's corporate trainers need varied skills to succeed, especially with technology-based training (TBT) exploding. Heck, such folks must not only provide training, they require a constant dose of it themselves.

Training—Critical to the Bottom Line

Though keeping abreast of new delivery technologies and learning methods is a challenge, there is good news for trainers, particularly computer software trainers. Pat Galagan, an American Society for Training & Development (ASTD) spokesperson, says, "There's never been a better time to be in training. It's a hot career."

In 1998, according to ASTD data, American corporations spent a whopping $55.3 billion to train employees. Of that amount, training in information technology skills received the most dollars, 13 percent. Knowing how to train workers to use the latest software, be it Microsoft's Windows 2000 or WinSPC's Statistical Process Control, Version 1.2, is obviously a skill much in demand.

"We're in a computer-based knowledge economy," says Pat. "Learning is essential to success. There's a demand for those who train others."

Given the complexity of the work environment, the rapid pace of organizational change, and the growing number of jobs in fields that constantly generate new knowledge, is it any wonder training is receiving renewed priority?

Whether you are a stand-up or "platform" trainer delivering instruction in a classroom setting, an instructional designer putting together effective learning packages, or a training specialist involved in planning and program development, you're in demand. "Time was," says Pat, "when trainers were the first out the door in an economic downturn. Not anymore. Training is critical to the bottom line."

As a trainer, you may work in-house, usually under the human resources umbrella, for a training specialty firm, such as ASK

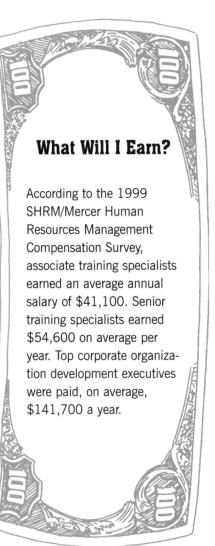

What Will I Earn?

According to the 1999 SHRM/Mercer Human Resources Management Compensation Survey, associate training specialists earned an average annual salary of $41,100. Senior training specialists earned $54,600 on average per year. Top corporate organization development executives were paid, on average, $141,700 a year.

International or CompUSA, Inc., or as a consultant, that is, a trainer for hire. Thomas J. Lenzo, a consultant specializing in software training, exemplifies the latter.

"You get called in as a consultant for one of two reasons," he declares. "The company doesn't have the internal training skills or they have them but they're over-whelmed. Either way, I've never been busier."

Where do trainers come from? How did they choose this career path?

"There are as many pathways to training expertise as there are to enlightenment," writes Chris Lee, in *Training* magazine. "Some people are lifelong practitioners who hold academic degrees in adult education or instructional design; others segued into work-place learning from technical or professional fields and discovered a new career; still others are subject-matter experts doing temporary duty as trainers." Varied backgrounds, varied entries into the field.

Stand and Deliver

Don beat a path to corporate training straight from high school, where he taught electronics. "The techniques I learned to charge up high school students also work with adults," says Don. "You just have to be careful that adults don't perceive you're talking down to them."

Being condescending wasn't the problem Don had with his Unix training group in Chicago—far from it. Nonetheless, they were still the most hostile audience he had ever encountered.

"Being COBOL programmers, they simply did not want to be there, learning a new language," Don confides. "I had to convince them it was in their interest to acquire the knowledge."

For trainees, gaining such knowledge is uppermost. "It's one thing to be in school where that's all the school does," Tom explains. "But in industry, the training has to be sharp and focused. You must teach exactly what they need to know. You mustn't waste anyone's time."

The lack of homogeneity in a corporate setting can also be a challenge to software instructors. Stuart Schlossberg, a self-employed

INFORMATION

For More Information

American Society for Training
& Development (ASTD)
1640 King Street, Box 1443
Alexandria, VA 22313-2043
(703) 683-8100
www.astd.org

The Society for Technical
Communication
P.O. Box 91400
Los Angeles, CA
(213) 896-2982

trainer specializing in statistical control software, has found varied participant skills frustrating at times. "With an audience, you're never sure what to expect," he says. "Some in the class may not understand how to click and drag an icon, while others are as good at roaming the electronic desktop as your twelve-year-old."

Keeping a sense of humor under such circumstance is a must for any trainer. "It's almost as important as product knowledge," says Stuart. "A trainer needs a high tolerance for frustration."

People skills aside, product knowledge is paramount. Kyle Kershau, a trainer with Engineering Geometry Systems (EGS), relates well to his machinist trainees because he's "been there."

"I'm the hands-on guy," he says. "In our company, the programmers who write software for CNC machines have never cut chips before. When I get in front of trainees, they know I've tasted oil. Basically, my training consists of 'tips and tricks' in question-and-answer format."

Even with excellent product knowledge and a dynamic, engaging platform style, trainers have their misses. Joe Perret, president of Executive Business Solutions in West Hills, California, recalls such a moment.

"I had a couple of people get up and march right out, totally frustrated with what I was trying to teach," he declares. "Unfortunately, in corporate training there's pressure—on the trainee. For the two who walked out, their peers in the class will spread the word on what happened."

Yet, if you're knowledgeable, can relate to your audience, and are comfortable with new delivery methods, computer software training has many rewards.

Virtual Training

"The Internet has changed everything" is the mantra of our time. Welcome to education and training in the twenty-first century.

"With 'virtual training,' opportunities for software trainers could wane, or at least change dramatically," say Dr. Eric Parks, founder and president of ASK International. "I'm currently working with a

company that has two thousand employees, in forty-six offices, on five continents. For them, the old training model, bringing groups together for classroom instruction, doesn't work anymore. Everything I do with that company is WBT, Web-based training."

"E-, or distance, learning, is altering the landscape for training," says Pat. "The learner is now in control. True, the stand-up trainer isn't dead. However, it would be wise for traditional trainers to pay close attention to what's happening and rethink their skill base. They need to get comfortable with learners being in control and technology being more and more the medium of choice."

To be sure, e-learning has raised some red flags, even among those in its vanguard. "With workstation training [CBT and WBT], you lose interaction with other students," comments Tom Gafford, a veteran CBT—computer-based training—trainer with Litton Industries, in Woodland Hills, California. "Brainstorming, camaraderie, and instant instructor feedback are often missing."

"Yet, if done well," counters Joe, "there can be tremendous interaction between instructor and student, and between students themselves. In the best of circumstances, the instructor takes on a more 'Socratic' role."

"Both traditional and distance learning have their place," says Stuart. "There's something to be said for the synergy created with people in a classroom. I've done corporate training where that classroom was the first place disparate groups involved in a project got together. Sometimes I think bringing people together was the main reason management called me in to do the training."

Nonetheless, online learning is here to stay, burning up the information superhighway.

According to International Data Corp., a research firm in Framingham, Massachusetts, spending on distance learning will reach $5.5 billion in 2002, up from $197 million in 1997—and that doesn't include growth in satellite-delivered and CD-ROM learning."

For computer software trainers, who should be as comfortable with e-learning as anyone, the message is clear: the virtual trainer has arrived.

What to Read

*Do It . . . and Understand!:
The Bottom Line on Corporate
Experiential Learning*
by Christopher C. Roland
and Richard J. Wagner, ed.
Robert J. Weigand.
Kendall/Hunt Publishing
Company, 1994.

Inside Technology Training
magazine

Training the Trainer

So how do you break into training as a career?

"Join ASTD," says, Pat, not surprisingly. "With over forty-six thousand members in one hundred and twenty countries, we're the largest, and oldest, organization of its kind in the industry."

ASTD chapters offer excellent "Train the Trainer" courses that provide the basic principles of adult learning and facilitation techniques. Here's an abbreviated course outline from such a seminar, available to Los Angeles chapter members:

- *Adult Learning Theory*: the adult learner, approaches, teaching styles, learning styles, student-centered learning
- *Systems Approach to Design*: identifying training needs, analyzing the job, setting objectives, measurement devices
- *Classroom Skills*: effective delivery skills, managing the classroom, making training happen, training aids
- *Managing Training*: selling training, implementation, internal consulting skills

Throughout the hands-on six-hour sessions, held on five Saturdays, participants make three stand-up presentations. Upon completion, they earn a certificate.

Speaking of certificates—or, more important, *certification*—the industry has been debating the pros and cons of trainer certification for years. Linda Montgomery of the Chauncey Group International Ltd., a subsidiary of the Educational Testing Service in Princeton, New Jersey, and issuers of the coveted certified technical trainer (CTT) certification, claims there is little to argue about: "Assessment of workplace skills is very important in this country right now. With so many professions and careers changing, there's a need to show the world you have appropriate training knowledge."

Whether you seek certification or not, as a trainer you should be able to demonstrate core competencies. Toward that end, the International Board of Standards for Training, Performance, and Instruction (IBSTPI) has published a list of competencies for training managers, instructional designers, and instructors. Here are a few skills an instructor needs:

- Analyze course materials and learner information.
- Establish and maintain instructor credibility.
- Demonstrate effective presentation skills.
- Respond appropriately to learners' needs for clarification or feedback.
- Provide positive reinforcement and motivational incentives.
- Use media effectively.
- Evaluate delivery of instruction.

You get the picture. Success in training, regardless of the medium, means today what it has always meant—good teaching, good learning. As an instructor, do you show enthusiasm for your subject? Do you understand that it isn't what teachers teach but what students learn that counts? And do you constantly strive never to forget what it means to be a novice?

In the end, you'll know success when you see the lights go on. "It's the 'ah' factor," says Kyle. "When a participant leans back from his computer, smiles, and says, 'Yes!'"

Though his Unix session started out on a difficult note, Don ended the five-day seminar in a good mood. "When we finished, one of the engineers took me aside. 'You know, I didn't want to be here at first,' he said. 'I figured I had better things to do. But I learned more in this class than any other I've ever taken—period. I want to thank you.' It doesn't get any better than that."

Cool Web Sites to Visit

The American Society for Training & Development
www.astd.org

Inside Technology Training
www.ittrain.com

Society for Technical Communication
www.stc.org/region8/lac/www/lahome.htm

COPYEDITOR

You need not work for a publishing enterprise to be a copyeditor. Any organization that produces documents needs copyeditors. Often such organizations farm out editorial work to freelancers, and copyediting is a natural function for companies to vendor out.

The textbook publisher pulled out all stops to make the new math book a bestseller. Copies by the thousands, 460 pages bound in hardcover, rolled off the presses. The book's textured, olive-green cover provided an elegant backdrop to the gold letters embossed squarely at its center. There, in 24-point type, ballooning a half-millimeter above the surface, the one-word title glistened forth, challenging the youthful reader: Algabra. ALGABRA! A-L-G-A-B-R-A!

True, algebra can be a tricky word to spell. But not for a copyeditor, a person whose job it is to prepare a manuscript for publication by finding and correcting errors in punctuation, spelling, grammar, and style. Heads—copyeditor's and proofreader's—would roll on this one. No way could a schoolbook go out with its title misspelled.

More Than Just the Details

Wendy Belcher, a former textbook copyeditor now working freelance, knows of such slip-ups. With 15 years in the profession, she's experienced minor ones of her own. "Still, finding a misspelled 'algabra' is the first order for any copyeditor," she says. "Good grammar, excellent spelling, a strong grasp of punctuation—such skills are a copyeditor's stock in trade.

"However, copyediting is more than just uncovering technical errors, about which there's little or no debate. You must also know different editorial styles, codified in such tomes as the *Chicago Manual of Style* and the *Associated Press Stylebook*. For instance, academic books place commas where newspapers don't. You need to know which style guide applies."

Beyond correcting technical mistakes, copyediting is the art of making something a little better—improvement. "But one must be careful," Wendy says. "copyeditors make a mistake when they try editing material as though it were their own, not the author's. The whole point of editing is to get into the author's head, help her to say what she intends to say, in her own voice."

"Editors determine the author's meaning and clarify it where possible," writes Mary Stoughton, in her excellent *Substance & Style: Instruction and Practice in Copyediting*, published by EEI Books. "They never change the meaning; where the meaning is ambiguous, they query. They bring problems or issues to the attention of the author or a supervisor. They attempt to make a manuscript be all that the author meant it to be."

Mary goes on to clarify the interdependence between author and editor this way: "The stereotype of the editor/author relationship was captured by a cartoon in the *New Yorker* that showed two men with muttonchop whiskers sitting at a table. One, holding a manuscript, is saying to the other, 'Come, come, Mr. Dickens, it was either the best of times or the worst of times. It could not have been both.' An author produces the perfect sentence and the editor quibbles over trifles; editors are 'comma people,' as opposed to authors, who are 'content people.' Like most stereotypes, this one contains a grain of truth. Authors in general are more concerned with content and editors with its expression. As a division of labor, this one is as valid as any other."

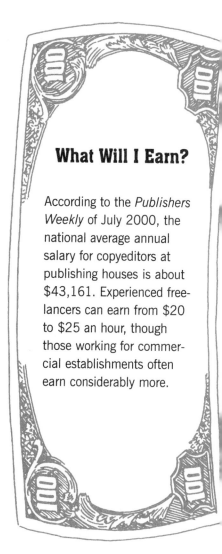

What Will I Earn?

According to the *Publishers Weekly* of July 2000, the national average annual salary for copyeditors at publishing houses is about $43,161. Experienced freelancers can earn from $20 to $25 an hour, though those working for commercial establishments often earn considerably more.

Enter the Diplomat

Staying true to that division by editing well demands a critical copyediting skill difficult to acquire in a class or seminar—diplomacy. "Authors don't always see copyediting as a helpful thing," Robin Cormier, vice president for design, editorial, and production services of EEI Communications, says. "When discussing changes, you must show the author how such modifications represent an improvement.

INFORMATION

For More Information

EEI Communications
66 Canal Center Plaza
Suite 200
Alexandria, VA 22314-5507
(703) 683-0683

The Society for Technical
Communications
P.O. Box 91400
Los Angeles, CA 90009
(213) 896-2982

You have to be able to explain changes, you can't just change something because it sounds better. You must have good, concrete reasons to do so."

Wendy agrees, adding, "It's all in how you word things. As for content, logic, I say: Don't tell, ask. 'Is this date correct, did the Korean War really happen in the 1930s?' You want to phrase everything as a question. Let's face it, writing is hard. You want the author to be open to your suggestions. I always include a cover letter with a returned manuscript in which I say something like, 'Best thing I have read lately. . . . A great contribution to the field. This section brought tears to my eyes.' That way, the author feels you are on his or her side. Bottom line—provide strong praise in the beginning."

Read Right

Ready to try a little copyediting? Prune the redundancy from the following sentence, which appears as an exercise in *Substance & Style*:

> *These various different agencies and offices that provide aid and assistance services to individual persons who participate in our program activities that we offer have reversed themselves back from the policy that they recently announced to return to the original policy they followed earlier.*

Though many solutions are possible, a well-trained copyeditor would come up with something like this:

> *The various agencies that assist participants in our program have reversed the recently announced policy to return to the original one.*

Well trained—that's the key. "Having good grammar, good spelling, and a love of the written word is not enough," Wendy says. "As with watchmaking and carpentry, success depends on gaining appropriate skills. In copyediting, you have to master proof marks, point sizes, indexing, internal fact checking, and querying. You must acquire and memorize a body of knowledge."

Computer Editor to the Rescue?

An e-mail:

> *I have a spelling checker, it came with my PC. It plane lee marks four my revue miss steaks aye can knot sea.*
> *Eye ran this poem threw it. Your sure reel glad two no Its very polished in it's weight. My checker tolled me sew.*
> *A checker is a bless sing. It freeze yew lodes of thyme. It helps me right awl stiles two reed and aides me when eye rime.*

Yet people ask: With word-processing programs complete with both spell and grammar checkers, aren't a copyeditor's days numbered?

"Not at all," says Linda Bayma, senior production editor for Prentice Hall in Columbus, Ohio. "It takes a human being to know whether it's to, too, or two. As for grammar checkers, we don't use them here."

But surely computer skills are important for today's copyeditor?

"Yes," says Robin. "Everything we do is online or on disk now."

Not so at Prentice Hall, however. "It depends on the type of manuscript," Linda says. "For example, given a symbol-laden math text, our copyeditors will attack it the old fashioned way, with blue pencil and pink slips."

"If it is any comfort, people have been predicting the end of editing and editors for as long as I can remember, certainly since the dawn of the computer age," writes Priscilla S. Taylor, in the *Editorial Eye*, EEI's

monthly newsletter for publications professionals. "How could any mere mortal compete with the mechanical wonder of spell-check, electronic thesauruses, and, later, grammar programs?

"Well, as we know, it's not that simple. Although nobody doubts that ignorance is increasing, it can be argued that this situation will dictate more emphasis on careful editing rather than less."

What to Read

Substance & Style: Instruction and Practice in Copyediting by Mary Stoughton. EEI Books, 1996.

Copyeditor for Hire

If copyediting sounds right for you, you might consider working first as an editorial assistant. "It's doing a lot of clerical functions," says Robin, "but it gets you in the door."

Or why not take a workshop if you are not quite ready to edit, even as an assistant? Here is the description for just such a seminar offered by EEI Training. It is typical of what you can expect:

> *Intensive Three-Day Introduction to Copyediting. For those entering the editing field or proofreaders who want to expand their skills, as well as editors who want a refresher. This hands-on course gives students a thorough grounding in the essentials of copyediting. Frequent exercises give students an opportunity to compare their solutions with those of expert editors. Students in Intensive Introduction to Copyediting should work with what they learn in this class for at least six months before continuing with any intermediate editing workshops.*

- *Editorial marks*
- *Grammar*
- *Government Printing Office and* Chicago Manual *styles*
- *Querying*
- *Wordiness*
- *Ambiguity*
- *Misuse of modifiers*
- *Tables and references*

Note that you need not work for a publishing house to be a copyeditor. "Any organization that produces documents demands copyeditors," Wendy explains. Furthermore, you don't have to do such work in-house. "Freelancing is perfect for copyeditors," Robin says. "Copyediting is a natural function for companies to vendor out."

To thrive as a copyeditor, having knowledge of a particular subject—engineering, science, or fine arts, for instance—also helps. "It's not essential," says Robin, "but it aids in establishing credibility with authors."

Nonetheless, "a great copyeditor can edit anything" is the famous claim. Fair enough. But what makes for a great copyeditor? "Bita Lanys, one such editor, said it best in what I call the 'Hippocratic Oath' for copyeditors," Wendy concludes. "Anyone can edit something 50 percent and improve it 50 percent. You're a great editor when you can change it 5 percent and improve it 50 percent."

Cool Web Sites to Visit

EEI Training
www.eeicom.com

Salon
www.salon.com

The Society for Technical Communications
www.stc.org/region8/lac/www/ lahome.htm

Hot Concepts!

Personnel

Job Shadowing

You've heard of Groundhog Day, but what about Groundhog Job Shadow Day? This is when you spend half a day at a leading local company or organization "shadowing" someone who has a job that interests you. While one can job-shadow any time of year, this nationally sponsored day drew one million students on February 2, 2000.

Basically, job shadowing is meant to:

- Demonstrate the connection between school and career, thereby making classroom work more relevant
- Build community partnerships between schools and businesses that enhance the educational experience
- Introduce students to the requirements of professions and industries to help them prepare to join the workforce
- Encourage an ongoing relationship between students and employers

When students visit organizations, some of the ideas discussed are:

- History of the career or field
- Roles and responsibilities of the job
- Personal attributes necessary for the job
- Career opportunities
- Education requirements

- Technology aspects of the career
- Related jobs and careers
- Where to learn more about the career
- Your experience
- Money questions

Sound intriguing? Contact your local community college for more information.

COURT REPORTER

Using a peculiar 14-key instrument first patented in 1879, an experienced court reporter can take testimony in excess of two hundred words per minute—and not just in court. Exciting avenues for court reporters' talents are opening up outside the courtroom—at football games, TV stations, in classrooms, and churches.

One potato, two potato, three potato, four; five potato, six potato, seven potato more. "Boring work," lamented Scott Sawyer, as he filled the produce bins at a Ralph's market in Sylmar, California. But the pay was good, seductively good. "I was caught in the supermarket trap," he says. "I had worked at grocery stores since graduating from high school and was now an assistant manager. But I hit a ceiling, you can go only so far. Besides, I wanted something more."

Four years at California State University, Northridge, majoring in pre-business and just going through the motions wasn't giving Scott any direction, however. "Then, school just fizzled," he says "I was twenty-five, no degree, and working at a dead-end job. I wanted a future—a good-paying one with a sense of accomplishment."

Today, Scott is a 29-year-old certified shorthand reporter (CSR). Though on the job only six months and not yet making the big money he's been assured is there, Scott definitely has a future. Nonetheless, the road from supermarket clerk to taking verbatim testimony at depositions, hearings, and trial proceedings has been a tough one. "There were times I wasn't sure it was worth the effort," he confesses.

Taking it all Down

Court reporters, of which there are fifty thousand nationwide, provide verbatim transcripts of official proceedings using a stenotype machine to record what is said. They're found in courtrooms, taking depositions in a lawyer's office, at government hearings, or at business or convention meetings. Rosalie Stevens, past president of the National Court Reporters Association (NCRA), says, "Court reporters are guardians of the record. They certify it is correct in every detail."

From the Lindbergh baby kidnapping case in 1932 to today's latest trial, court reporters were on the scene with their steno machines. Using the peculiar 14-key instrument, first patented in 1879, an experienced court reporter can take testimony in excess of two hundred words per minute.

Furthermore, with the latest computer-aided transcription (CAT) technology, verbatim records are taken, translated into English text, edited, and made available as a printed transcript almost immediately. Known as real-time transcription, CAT was in full operation during the O. J. Simpson trial, where more than one million lines of transcript were recorded. According to Benjamin M. Rogner, editor of the *Journal of Court Reporting*, "Ninety percent of all court reporters now use computers. The future is here."

Diane Saunar, a CSR, past president of the California Court Reporters Association, and owner of her own agency, Alexander & Saunar, has, in her 22 years in the profession, seen how the new technology alters the courtroom environment. "Lawyers don't have to take notes anymore," she says. "They connect their laptops to mine and have real-time transcription right in front of them. My records are their records."

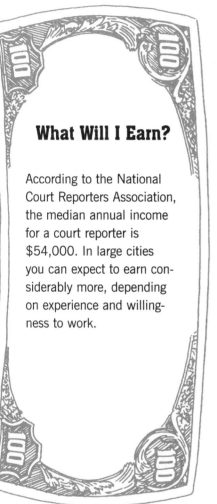

What Will I Earn?

According to the National Court Reporters Association, the median annual income for a court reporter is $54,000. In large cities you can expect to earn considerably more, depending on experience and willingness to work.

Captioning the Moment

Court reporters, the court title notwithstanding, also find exciting avenues for their talents outside the courtroom. How about football games, classrooms, churches, and television stations? Known as captioners, these reporters use CAT to display closed-caption text on TV monitors or computer screens, making the spoken word available to those who are deaf or hard or hearing.

"Basically, for broadcast work, the stenotype machine is connected to a state-of-the-art computer with special closed-captioning software," says Marshall Jorpeland of LegalVoice in Piscataway, New Jersey. "The software translates the strokes into English sentences that are automatically encoded in the broadcast signal and sent to the viewer's television screen in a matter of seconds."

"With the Americans with Disabilities Act," Rosalie explains, "people are realizing what they're entitled to. Everything from stockholder's meetings to classroom lectures are being closed-captioned."

Fausto Perez, a captioner for the deaf at California State University, Northridge, sits with his steno machine in front of a classroom. "Hard-of-hearing students have laptops in front of them," he explains. "As the instructor lectures, I take it all down. Immediately, his or her words appear on the students' laptop screens."

Yet, captioning isn't for every court reporter. "Captioning the news is . . . stressful," says Kevin Daniel, CSR, in a recent article in the *Contra Costa* (California) *Times.* "You have no control over the situation like you do in a courtroom. A court reporter can ask the judge to stop the proceedings for a moment to catch up. The news is happening and changing so fast . . . you can't control the flow."

INFORMATION

For More Information

Marshall Jorpeland,
Communications Director
National Court Reporters
Association (NCRA)
8224 Old Courthouse Road
Vienna, VA 22182-3808
(703) 556-6272
fax (703) 556-6291
71350.3433@compuserve.com

Contact your local community college.

What to Read

The Court and Free-Lance Reporter Profession: Improved Management Strategies
by David J. Saari.
Greenwood Publishing Group, 1997.

Read That Back, Please!: Memoirs of a Court Reporter
by John R. Reily.
Fithian Press, 1989.

It's Now the Law

As of January 1, 2000, closed-captioning is no longer a luxury, it's a federal requirement. Television broadcasters must now have at least five hours of program captioning each day. The need for real-time captioners has become acute.

According to Maureen McGuire, of LegalVoice, "With the first milestone of the Telecommunications Act of 1996, captioning companies and broadcasters now need qualified court reporters to caption thousands of hours of live programming every week. Specially trained court reporters provide 'stenocaptioning' services for television broadcasts through their skill, stenotype machine, and computers. With only a few hundred steno captioners nationwide, the demand will provide a surge of career opportunities as well as a need for more court reporting students."

How can all broadcasters possibly meet the demand? "The Act's deadline primarily affects [for now] the four major networks and their affiliates in the top twenty-five markets across the country," says Maureen. "Additional requirements over the next six years call for ten, fifteen, and then all hours of programming to be captioned in two-year increments. The Act provides additional time for broadcasters to caption programs that aired for the first time prior to 1998 and Spanish language programs."

Carl Sauceda, president of the National Court Reporters Association, sees demand for court reporters soaring. "Never before has our profession seen such an urgent need for our skill," he says. "For many years we've assisted deaf and hard-of-hearing persons in a variety of settings by captioning meetings, high school and college classes, religious services and other events. Television captioning is a natural extension of this work." Clearly, demand is there, right now.

Not for Everyone!

Just as captioning doesn't appeal to every court reporter, court reporting isn't for everyone. "To become a court reporter," Benjamin explains, "requires an indescribable element having to do with the ability to capture speech at very high rates of speed. No one knows what makes someone able to do that."

According to Marshall Jorpeland, communications director of NCRA, "Prospective students should be intelligent, disciplined, motivated, computer-literate, and possess above-average language skills. A court-reporting career requires two to four years of technical training as well as stringent state certification in many jurisdictions. Court reporting students also need to meet deadlines, work well under pressure, and concentrate for long periods of time."

Mike Bell, director at the Southern California College of Court Reporting (SCCCR) in Woodland Hills, California, concurs. "To pass the state examination, a requirement, and become a certified shorthand reporter, you must take down four voices at two hundred words per minute, for fifteen minutes, with 97.5 percent accuracy. It takes the average full-time student three years of constant application and practice to reach that level."

Iris Cooper, a dedicated student at SCCCR, knows about the stress. "There are ups and downs, like a roller coaster," she says. "You must pass speed tests at ten-word intervals, starting at sixty words per minute. Once you're over one speed bump, you start again, straining to reach the next level. At every test the anxiety is like at a rehearsal."

"Then there are the academics," Mike explains. "We have classes in English, vocabulary building, medical terminology, the law, and computer skills. Court reporting isn't for dummies."

"Students in court reporting education should expect to do college-level work," adds Marshall. "The level of intellect needed to complete a court reporting program is equal to that needed to earn a college degree. In fact, court reporting students learn a variety of subjects that are part of many different post-secondary school curriculums: including civil and criminal law, grammar, languages, legal terminology, anatomy, medical terminology, computer technology, keyboarding, and dictation."

Scott remembers all that. "It's the hardest schooling I ever went through," he states. "It takes tremendous focus, energy, and commitment."

Cool Web Sites to Visit

National Court Reporters Association
www.verbatimreporters.com

National Court Reporters Foundation
www.verbatimreporters.com/ncrf

National Verbatim Reporters Association
www.nvra.org/main.htm

Evidently he had what it takes, however. In November 1996, Scott sat for the two-day state exam. The day before Christmas he got his results. Scott was one of only 16 percent who passed.

Learning Every Day

Once licensed, you will work as an official court reporter (OCR) or, at least to start, freelance as a deposition reporter. Both have their advantages.

As an OCR, you'll have a steady job, set salary, and benefits. As a freelancer, usually working for an agency, your hours are more flexible but your income varies.

Speaking of income, according to the National Court Reporters Association, the median annual income is $54,000. However, in many large cities, you can expect to start at close to that amount. A lot depends upon how often you work. As Mike observes, "I know some court reporters in California making more than $100,000 a year."

Downsides exist, of course, as in every profession. Schooling is long and tuition, at a private college, high. You'll need anywhere from $10,000 to $15,000 for equipment before starting work (steno machine, computer, software). And then there are the repetitive-stress injuries. "It's an issue," says Benjamin, "though carpal tunnel syndrome isn't any more significant here than in other keyboard industries."

Yet, the rewards are considerable. You're a respected professional earning an excellent salary. And, as Scott puts it, "I'm no longer going to the grocery store day in and day out, putting up the same oranges. There is something new every day: new locations, new people, new things to learn. It keeps you intrigued."

DAY TRADER

Day traders rapidly buy and sell stocks throughout the day in the hope that the stock will continue climbing or falling in value during the seconds or minutes they own it, allowing them to lock in quick profits. It's a high-risk, exciting business.

Todd Benson of Dallas, Texas, an attorney turned full-time day trader, confesses that on only 10 days out of the year he generates 30 to 50 percent of his annual income. Today looks to be one of those 10 magic days.

As he fiddles behind a giant terminal at Momentum Securities, a brokerage firm providing super-fast access for serious day traders, a message flashes across the screen. The Federal Reserve Board is announcing, unscheduled, an interest rate reduction. Todd bolts upright, ready to take command. Trading quickly but methodically, his four and a half years of experience in evidence, Todd buys and sells like the expert day trader he has become. A mere 10 minutes later, this husband and father of a two-year-old is $8,000 richer. "It's been a nice day," he declares. "Who says you can't make money as a day trader? In fact, not to boast, I closed out last year with a seven-figure income."

A League of His Own

Actually, there are plenty of folks ready to question Todd's assertions of day-trading success. While they admit other "Todd Bensons" exist, such individuals are dwarfed, they claim, by those who habitually lose at this high-stakes game or have long ago been driven out entirely, their capital depleted like so much Wall Street confetti in a ticker-tape parade.

According to a recent study by the North American Securities Administrators Association, 77 percent of day traders lost money.

(However, there is some dispute as to whether that figure includes serious full-time day traders.) Of those who did make a profit, the average was just $22,000 over an eight-month period. Of the 124 accounts surveyed, only two traders netted $100,000 or better. The highest was $160,000. Todd, it seems, is clearly in a league all his own.

Furthermore, in early 2000, a U.S. Senate staff study turned up what it claimed was serious securities law violations at day-trading firms. "The firms themselves are racking up large profits, mainly via commissions paid by client day traders," the study said. "Cumulative profits at the top fifteen day-trading firms tripled in the last two years to more than $66 million. Yet, only a tiny fraction of novice day traders make money, and the majority of experienced traders lose money." Given such information, what's a would-be day trader to think or do?

Controlled Losses

"Day traders," as defined by the Securities and Exchange Commission (SEC), "rapidly buy and sell stocks throughout the day in the hope that their stocks will continue climbing or falling in value for the seconds to minutes they own the stock, allowing them to lock in quick profits. Day traders usually buy on borrowed money, hoping they will reap higher profits through leverage, but running the risk of high loss, too."

SEC Chairman Levitt, when asked about day trading, responded, "It is neither illegal nor is it unethical. But it is highly risky."

How many day traders are there? Ray Robbins of Pismo Beach, California, quipped in a letter to the *Los Angeles Times* in late 1999: "With this year's soaring stock market, it's no wonder there's a labor shortage in the U.S. Everyone's day-trading."

Not quite. According to Bill Lauderback of Momentum Securities, with offices in Dallas and Houston, "There are probably no more than seven thousand *serious* day traders out there, those with their own accounts at day-trading firms, conducting their business full-time."

What sort of people are they, these day traders? "He or she is a cross between an extrovert and an introvert with both characteristics in balance," says Mark D. Cook, in his online newsletter. "The introvert aspect is depicted by the disciplined workaholic with a reclusive concentration. The extrovert demeanor is shown by an aggressive, competitive, self-motivated individual striving to be the best in a selective profession."

"If we look at day traders working here at Momentum Securities," adds Bill, "We discover 98 percent are college educated, with 50 percent holding post-graduate degrees. An estimated 25 percent are former stockbrokers. That means, however, 75 percent did something else for a living first. We see lots of M.B.A.s and lawyers."

"It's not for everyone," admits Todd. "Even though a day trader hates to lose, he or she must be prepared to cut any losses. This is a game of controlled losses. Minimizing those losses, while letting profits run, is your key to longevity and success."

Don't Try This at Home

If you're going to day-trade, the best place to do it is at a brokerage firm set up to accommodate you as an independent trader. "Such firms," says Mark Ingebretsen, a frequent contributor to *Online Investor* magazine, "provide you with a seat, a terminal, a phone, maybe a separate office, and a catered lunch if you trade a lot. They make their money like any brokerage firm, off commissions on your trades."

The key service offered by all such firms is their high-speed access to the online market. Most have developed proprietary software to get you in and out of Wall Street in milliseconds—literally. "Many of the most successful day traders on the street are swarming to our office to use our technology," says Benjamin Weinger of Blackwood Trading in New York City. "Our system processes more than fifty thousand orders each day and we have invested tremendous resources making sure it is reliable."

"But can't I do this from home?" you ask. "Day trading seems such a perfect home office enterprise."

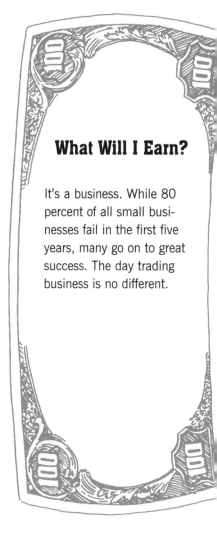

What Will I Earn?

It's a business. While 80 percent of all small businesses fail in the first five years, many go on to great success. The day trading business is no different.

INFORMATION

For More Information

Day Traders On-Line
P.O. Box 150
Pacific Grove, CA 93950-0150
www.daytraders.com

Securities Industry Association
120 Broadway, 35th Floor
New York, NY 10271

Wrong!

"The Internet for all its wonders, and continued improvement, is still too slow and unreliable as a day-trading option," says Bill. "If you get into a trade and your system crashes, or just slows a bit, you're in serious trouble. A day trader typically does forty-five trades a day. Some do over one hundred. You need reliable hardware and software, the kind you find at a day trading firm."

Still, as pointed out earlier, many such firms are coming under fire for less than professional practices. "It happens," says Dave Cathcart, of Day Traders On-Line, headquartered in Pacific Grove, California. "Some set up offices and lure people in with fantastic promises, overstating the profit potential. They give the good firms a bad name."

Risky Business

"It is suicidal to attempt day trading, risking thousands of dollars, unless you know what you're doing, read lots of books, and practice, practice, practice paper trading," says Mark, assessing the risks involved. "Many people are deceived into thinking all they need is a computer, a modem, an online account, and presto!—the megabucks will roll in. Remember, some of the brightest people in the world work on Wall Street. You are competing with them. No one would suggest you go out and play against the Celtics after shooting just a few hoops in the backyard. The bottom line? *Don't risk money you are not prepared to lose.*"

While we don't want to belabor the point or dwell on the difficulties inherent in succeeding as a day trader, it is necessary for all those contemplating such activity to understand the risks. Here, according to the SEC, are some facts everyone should know about day trading:

1. *Be prepared to suffer severe financial losses.* Many day traders typically suffer such losses in their first months of trading, and many never graduate to profit-making status.

2. *Day traders do not "invest."* True day traders do not own any stocks overnight because of the extreme risk that prices will change radically from one day to the next, leading to large losses.
3. *Day trading can be a stressful and expensive full-time job.* Stress in having to watch the market continuously, plus the cost of paying high commissions, are realities you must consider.
4. *Day traders depend heavily on borrowing money or buying stocks on margin.* Day traders should understand how margin works, how much time they'll have to meet a margin call, and the potential for getting in over their heads.
5. *Don't believe claims of easy profits.* Before you start trading with a firm, make sure you know how many clients have lost money and how many have made profits.
6. *Check out day-trading firms with your state securities regulator.* Like all broker-dealers, day-trading firms must register with the SEC and the states in which they do business.

"If you are actively engaged in making a living and enjoy what you're doing, you probably shouldn't consider day trading," Bill advises. "However, if you are not opposed to significant risk of your own capital, are an extremely disciplined person, and are willing to put in the hours, weeks, or months it takes to learn the mechanics of day trading, before you even get to the theory of it, then this could be a career for you. Those who are successful, and there are many, are doing very well indeed."

Serious Business

Day trading, as the SEC asserts, is not investing. It is a business. As such, you risk your capital, go to work every day, learn the ropes, and roll with the punches, hoping to make a profit for your labor.

What to Read

A Beginner's Guide to Day Trading Online
by Toni Turner.
Adams Media Corporation, 2000.

The Complete Day Trader: Trading Systems, Strategies, Timing Indicators, and Analytical Methods
by Jake Bernstein.
McGraw-Hill, 1995.

The Disciplined Trader
by Mark Douglas.
Prentice Hall, 1990.

The Tao of Trading: Discovering a Simpler Path to Success
by Robert Koppel.
Dearborn Trade, 1998.

OK, but how does it work? What do you do as a day trader?

"Your workstation will often resemble an air traffic control console," comments Mark. "You'll be scanning a bunch of stocks all at once, often on more than one monitor, the quotes will be changing constantly, colored candlestick charts will vie for your attention, and all the time you're trying to assess what major market makers are wishing to trade at the moment. For the uninitiated, it can seem quite complex."

But for committed day traders, this is heaven. "You can ask anyone in the office," says Todd. "They love every minute of it. Being in the market, on top of the game. It is private enterprise at its best."

Paul Ringel, 31, has been day trading but a year, with Blackwood Trading, and he is, he says, "making a ton of money." How so? "If you do it the right way, be conservative, learn before you take the gambles, you will succeed. You basically work the percentage plays. At the very beginning, you are just staring at numbers across the screen. But as time goes on, it all fits into place."

How much time? "It takes six to twelve months to become profitable," Paul says. "After that, though, there is no job like it."

To be a player, as Paul has indicated, you will need to invest—in yourself, in your business. And you can't do it on the cheap. "I'm afraid five to ten grand just won't cut it," cautions Dave. "Most day traders have at least $100,000 of their own capital invested. Many have several times that."

"I recommend putting away $100,000," Paul advises. "That would be $50,000 to invest and $50,000 to live on."

"Traders are entrepreneurs," Rob tells us to keep in mind. "They are independent business owners. With that independence comes responsibility. As such, they take credit for their gains and must accept responsibility for their losses."

What is the biggest mistake a novice tends to make? "All too often new traders want to start right off trading big, whether it be five hundred shares, one thousand, or even more," says Rob. "Why? Do parents throw their kids into the majors for their first baseball experience? No, and so we have Little League."

Cool Web Sites to Visit

Archives
www.topfive.com

Day-Trading: Not What You Think
www.futuresmag.com/library/daytrade97/day4.html

Day Traders On-Line
www.daytraders.com

"Above all, it involves a full-time commitment," says Todd. "And in the current environment, expect to take about six months to figure out whether you even have the ability to make it."

The Trading Life for Me

How do you get started in day trading? "You can't teach anyone to trade," says Todd. "You can teach them the tools, the techniques, the theory, yes. But how to trade profitably, no. They have to figure that out for themselves. I suggest you go to a firm that has the technology and is populated with successful traders. Watch what they do, note their style. Then you must find your own style, the one that works for you."

That style should encompass a stress level you can live with. Actually, Rob found out something interesting about his own stress test. "Everyone thought my gastrointestinal problems would be magnified once I entered the 'high-stress' environment of a trading floor. But it never happened. My health actually improved and I was able to get off the medication I was taking. In fact, I am most relaxed when sitting at my desk trading."

"If you feel too stressed day trading, you simply shouldn't be doing it," Todd concludes. "For me, practicing law was stressful: trying cases, having other people's lives in my hands. When I practiced law, I worked days, nights, and weekends. Now I work 8:30 to 3:00 and get a two-hour lunch— the market slows in midday. It's a job you can't take home with you even if you wanted to—remember, it is 'day' trading. Furthermore, my quality of life has never been better, not to mention my income. It's the trading life for me!"

EMERGENCY DISPATCHER

They turn chaos into comfort to help people in the most horrifying circumstances.

"My friend needs help," the nervous caller stammered. "Her step-dad is molesting her."

"I straightened up, clutching the phone," Donna Valdez, an emergency dispatcher with the Los Angeles County Sheriff's Department, says. "Not an everyday call. Five minutes into an intense, though sometimes confusing, exchange, the situation revealed itself. Christie, the fifteen-year old voice on the 911 line wasn't referring to a friend— she was talking about herself. And the stepfather in question was on his way to pick her up.

"With Christie now sobbing, I did my best to calm her down," says Donna." 'You know this is wrong, that's why it's been bothering you so much,' I assured the frightened girl. 'Yet, you did the right thing by telling someone, even a perfect stranger like me.' After our continuing back-and-forth, Christie agreed I should dispatch a police car to her home.

"Three deputies responded to the location. As one interviewed the female and took a report, others scrutinized the location while waiting for the suspect. Within an hour the stepfather was arrested and Christie taken into protective custody. The court case is pending."

Chaos into Comfort

Psychologist, nurse, teacher, disciplinarian, diplomat, and parent, emergency dispatchers, approximately 70,000 nationwide, provide a vital communication link in critical situations. As Randall Larson, senior public safety dispatcher for the San Jose Fire Department, and editor of *9-1-1* magazine says, "They turn chaos into comfort, to help people in the most horrifying circumstances."

Also known as police, fire, and ambulance dispatchers, these civilian and sworn voices are usually the first the public talks with when calling for emergency assistance. Sitting at a complex, computer-controlled console, often in a windowless basement, they carefully question a caller to determine the type, seriousness, and location of an emergency. They must then quickly decide on the kind and number of response units needed, locate the closest and most suitable ones available, and send them to the scene.

In a medical emergency, dispatchers not only keep in close touch with the dispatched units but also keep in touch with the caller, giving extensive pre-arrival first aid instructions while the caller waits for an ambulance. They serve to link the medical staff in a hospital and the emergency medical technicians in the vehicle.

What kind of person can accomplish all this?

"Someone who can do many things at once," says Randall. "Multitasking and prioritizing are key: simultaneously talking on the phone, carrying on a conversation with the sergeant behind you, and handling a radio channel or two. Talk about great communicators."

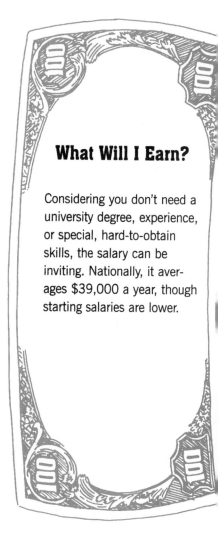

What Will I Earn?

Considering you don't need a university degree, experience, or special, hard-to-obtain skills, the salary can be inviting. Nationally, it averages $39,000 a year, though starting salaries are lower.

"Dispatcher Ear"

Communication was never Donna's problem. "I had just graduated from high school in 1986, when my dad, a sergeant with the Los Angeles Sheriff's Department, suggested I take the entrance exam for dispatcher," she explains. "He always thought of me as a chatty teenager, forever on the phone. I guess he figured I'd be a natural.

"Not quite! I failed the test on my first try," Donna concedes. "There were three parts. Part one covered vocabulary. No problem, I could break down a word, figure out what it meant. Part two involved comparing an original to a copy and finding all the mistakes. I had an eye for detail. That part was easy, too. But part three involved something I had never really fiddled with—listening. You had to listen to a recording and write down what was said. My handwriting couldn't keep up, I didn't know the abbreviations to use. I failed part three by one word."

Six months later, after extensive self-study, when she listened to commercial radio and practiced jotting down conversations, making up

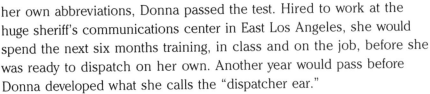

INFORMATION

For More Information

Associated Public Safety
Communications Officers
2040 South Ridgewood
South Daytona, FL 32119-8437
(904) 322-2500

Contact your local public safety
agencies.

her own abbreviations, Donna passed the test. Hired to work at the huge sheriff's communications center in East Los Angeles, she would spend the next six months training, in class and on the job, before she was ready to dispatch on her own. Another year would pass before Donna developed what she calls the "dispatcher ear."

"It's the ability to listen and process information, then repeat it almost as if you had a tape recorder in your head, but with only a second or two time delay," she explains. "I wasn't born with it, I had to learn how to talk and listen at the same time, something that in normal social situations is frowned upon."

Intense Training

Once hired as an emergency dispatcher, you'll likely be asked, in many states, to obtain your Peace Officers Standards in Training (POST) certificate. Doing so involves attending and passing a grueling three-week, eight-hour-a-day (plus three hours of homework) Basic Public Safety Dispatcher course.

In the class, you will take daily exams on the criminal justice system, communications technology, domestic violence, gang awareness, and stress management, to name but a few topics. "It opened up my world," says Nora Geller, dispatcher and office manager at Los Angeles Valley College. "I'd been sheltered. At times tears welled up in my eyes. People can be so mean."

"Intense is the word," adds Art Rodriques, supervising communications operator, Los Angeles Sheriff's Department. "You'll have zero social life for the time you're in class."

Not all emergency dispatchers receive training similar to a POST course, unfortunately. "Tremendous inconsistency exists in training levels throughout the country," says Randall. "In some places it's, 'Here's the radio, here's the phone, answer it.' Not good enough. You're left wide open for lawsuits."

"The Eddy Pollack incident in Philadelphia, back in 1992, was a watershed," Randall continues. "There was a gang fight, calls poured in, no one prioritized, dispatchers where rude to callers. Eddy was killed. Then they played the 911 tapes on the evening news. Good, professional dispatchers have had to live with that ever since."

Technology to the Rescue

New technology may help, though the price tag is high.

"In the old days, twenty-five years ago," says Gary Allen, editor of *DISPATCH Monthly* magazine, "clerical people were shanghaied for the job. They were told to answer the phone, write down what's wrong, and hand it to the radio person. Today, computers are in control.

"You gather information about an incident, put it in, and get it out to police and fire departments quickly. But now, thanks to new technology, we can do even more. Via the computer, past incidents at a given location can be called up. If I'm at Bob's Liquor Store, having responded to an alarm, the dispatcher can relay a history of that address. It's a tremendous help."

Captain Richard Gallen, Avalon City Dispatch Center, and author of *Become a 911 Dispatcher: Your Personal Career Guide,* agrees. "In the long term, technology is going to make the emergency dispatcher's job better, easier, faster, and higher paying," he says. "Heck, we are almost at the point where a GPS [Global Positioning System] can tell us where an officer is, even down to which floor in a building."

Self-Motivated

Yes, technology may help. But, as in any profession, there are still downsides to consider.

"When you start, you're at the bottom," says Gary, "Holidays, weekends, your family's birthdays, all will disappear."

"You'll sit in a chair all day, field calls, and when it's over, even if it is a horribly emotional experience, a lady witnessing the death of a child, you must handle the call perfectly, then a minute later go on to the next one," says Randall.

What to Read

Become a 911 Dispatcher: Your Personal Career Guide by Captain Richard L. Callen. Career Publishing, Inc., 1999.

"Essentially, you do all this for not a lot of money and virtually no recognition," Gary acknowledges. "Those who do well are self-motivated, self-congratulatory. They praise themselves because no one else will."

Lack of public recognition is, perhaps, understandable, people call while under tremendous pressure. "Yet, when officers and firefighters don't consider you part of the team, it's particularly rough," declares Randall. "In a large regional center, you may dispatch for a dozen different agencies, making it hard to develop rapport with those in the field."

And then there's the stress. "We are probably the only profession where everything you say is recorded, made a permanent record, which can appear on the six o'clock news," Randall observes. "That's stress."

Yet, as Gary is quick to point out, "It's generally a non-layoff type-job, benefits are good, and you are under no pressure to sell—the business comes to you. If you can leave it behind emotionally, you need take no work home. Every day is different; no two calls are alike. And, most important, you know you are doing something completely relevant. What you do affects—in some cases, saves—lives."

"You ask me why I get up in the morning, knowing I have to go to work?" Donna asks rhetorically. "As silly as it may sound, I go to work every day to help people. I am supportive to the deputies in their endeavors to enforce the law, reassuring to the victim of a crime, resourceful in my knowledge of referral numbers, and overall just plain caring about people. You have to be. I try to be considerate, understanding, productive, and improve whatever the situation is. Yet I try not to get so involved that I am rendered unable to assist, and sound interested and concerned in what is being presented to me. Believe me, that is not always easy. However, I find joking with my coworkers makes for an easygoing environment; it's a release. Yet I can certainly kick into a serious mode when things get hectic.

Having taken in every type of call in her nine years on the job, Donna has seen a lot. Fortunately, not all of it involves molestation, rape, or murder.

"I got a call recently from what turned out to be a five-year-old boy," she concludes. "Weeping, he said to me, 'My bestest friend just broke my favoritest toy.' Well, we're emergency dispatchers. I guess to the kid toy damage was an emergency. That call made my day."

FILM/TV MAKEUP ARTIST

Does slitting a wrist, balding a head, breaking a nose, or scaring someone for life appeal to you? Film and TV makeup artists do it all the time, in make-believe. It's not just about creating a pretty face.

Although a gunshot wound square to the forehead killed her, the middle-aged woman, slumped in an armchair, clearly had been beaten, thrashed, and dragged before that fatal wound occurred.

A blackish purple abrasion covers her left cheek, embedded with asphalt skid marks.

Her left earlobe has been sheared off, the stump swollen with coagulated blood.

Her lips are blistered, her skin sunburned orange.

From all appearances, the poor woman spent days wandering in a desert before her violent death.

Not to worry, it's all an act. Pam Smith is fine, even if spending the past hour getting made up was trying. Her makeup artist, Susan Cervantez, whose feature film credits include *Driven*, *The Feminine Touch*, and *In the Line of Fire*, knows exactly what she's doing.

With eyelash glue, latex, mortician's wax, styrotone, and FX (special effects) materials galore—spirit gum, black-tooth enamel, sculpting wax, and nicotine stain—Susan can do you in.

"My specialties are contact lenses, glamour, old age, body makeup, bullet and knife wounds, blood, burns, bruises, and tattoos," she says. "I can slit your wrists, bald your head, break your nose, and scar you for life. Furthermore, I'll age you fifty years, so that even your mother will pass you by."

Beyond Pretty Faces

"The entertainment makeup artist," according to Michael Key, editor-in-chief of *Makeup Artist* magazine, "is one who paints the script on the human canvas of an actor."

This means more than what we usually think of as makeup—lipstick and blush—it means creating old age, black eyes, and open wounds.

"In our industry, in addition to beauty makeup, you'll mainly do cuts, bruises, and beard work," says Jack Petty, a 38-year veteran who has worked on such films as *The Odd Couple*, *Seconds*, *The Godfather Part II*, and *Maverick*, and an instructor at the Learning Tree University (LTU) in Canoga Park, California.

Susan agrees: "In the movies there is always going to be conflict so someone's always being hit, slapped, stabbed, bruised, and shot. We're not just making people beautiful."

Indeed not. But in training at LTU, in a program typical of what you should expect in any makeup curriculum, you will start first learning beauty and glamour makeup for male and female performers. You'll do an intensive study of facial anatomy, including guidelines for identification and correction of facial flaws. Basic color and lighting theory and techniques for selection and application of professional materials is all part of your training. "Keep in mind," says Jack, "this is not street makeup, it's definitely a cut above Bullock's." After this, you'll then proceed to four subspecialties:

1. *Reverse aging.* Here you regress a performer's age—the most crucial element of contemporary motion picture and television makeup. The idea is to bring the actor or actress down in age, just using makeup.
2. *Balding.* You'll prepare a subject for a full bald cap and work with various adhesive applications. The safe use of toxic materials during application and removal is studied. Blending, coloring, and texturing principles are also covered. "This craft is one of the most difficult things to learn," says Jack. "I am still studying, after thirty-eight years."

What Will I Earn?

As in most entertainment jobs, it depends on experience and how often you work. Maurice Stein claims a makeup artist with 300 to 400 days' experience can earn from $175 to $400 a day. If you work on a weekly basis, expect from $600 to $1,500. Assistants starting out earn less: for the true masters, there is really no limit.

3. *Injuries.* Knowing how to apply black eyes, broken noses, burns, cuts and scars, blood and open wounds, as well as acne, warts, and bullet wounds are among the effects to master. You'll work with styrotone and gelatin to achieve these effects.

4. *Hair work.* According to Jack, this is "among the most demanding elements in professional makeup." You'll apply realistic beards, beard growth, sideburns, and mustaches. You learn to create a natural hairline on your subject using organic hair and synthetic materials. Preparation of hair and wool, as well as adhesive applications and removal techniques are covered. "It's mostly a mechanical, not artistic, act," Jack explains. "A director may want the talent [actor] in twenty minutes. You don't have time to be artistic."

In a final training module, you'll study techniques for creating the total look for a character using each of the makeup skills learned in previous modules. You'll learn to analyze a script and design a complete makeup based on a character description and key plot points.

Can one learn all this and be competent in so many specialties?

"Yes," says Maurice Stein, founder of Cinema Secrets, Inc., in Burbank, California, one of the largest suppliers of cosmetics, special effect makeup, and hair care products to the entertainment industry worldwide.

"One must do it all," he says. "It's the universal makeup artist who succeeds in our industry. The one who, when he or she is called, responds, 'When and where do you want me? I'll be there, I can do whatever is needed.' Unfortunately, too many in our industry now respond by saying, 'Oh, I don't do that.'"

Up Close and Personal

You don't become a makeup artist overnight. Susan, it might be said, began her "apprenticeship" at age seven.

"My mother saw this $5 beauty kit advertised in *TV Guide*," she explains. "Every month you'd send in $5 and get back perfume, lipstick, powder, and rouge. I saved my allowance, sent it in every month, and for years kept building my little beauty kit. I was fascinated—and hooked.

INFORMATION

For More Information

Maurice Stein
Cinema Secrets, Inc.
4400 Riverside Drive
Burbank, CA 91505
(818) 846-0579

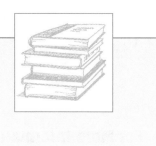

What to Read

Makeup Artist
by Kathryn A. Quinian.
Capstone Press, 1999.

In high school, Susan continued to develop her makeup skills. "I would do people for all kinds of occasions," she says. "On prom night I was a very busy girl. And on Halloween, well, it was an all-day affair."

Today, Susan concentrates on TV commercials. "It's straight beauty makeup, but it's also where the money is," she says. "No three weeks out of town. The client has lots of money to spend in a short period of time. There's a small crew, and usually only one makeup artist. I like it just fine."

Nevertheless, Susan's always looking around, learning about people, characters, and how makeup can be applied.

"My ex-boyfriend used to take me to wrestling matches," she says. "At first I couldn't watch. But then he told me to look at it from a makeup artist's point of view. All of sudden those bumps, bruises, and swelling faces enthralled me. I imagined replicating all that hurt on a talent's face."

Wrestling rings aren't the seediest places Susan has been, either.

Once on location under a freeway bridge in downtown Los Angeles, she saw a drug addict about to shoot up. "I went over, looked him in the face, and said, 'Before you shoot, can I examine your arm? I'm a makeup artist, I need to see what a needle-pocked arm looks like.' I never told my mother about that one."

"Basically, it's about studying people," says Jack. "The film director says, 'Age him five years.' You have to know how to do it. Next, he wants you to do an AIDs patient. Have you been with a person with AIDs, looked at him up close? You'll need to."

Just Part of the Crew

Show business is a business—a collaborative enterprise. So, being a film and television makeup artist means working with the entire crew. Susan explains what that's about: "You have to be able to do anything at a moment's notice. If the director has a new idea, you better be able to execute it. It means being creative and saying, in effect, 'It's not a problem, I can do it.'"

It also means reining in any starstruck tendencies you might have. "You are touching people, so you get personal with them really quick," Susan says. "Yet they are just working people like me. My work is as important as any. If I am putting on an old age and it doesn't look good,

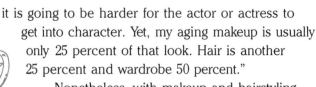

it is going to be harder for the actor or actress to get into character. Yet, my aging makeup is usually only 25 percent of that look. Hair is another 25 percent and wardrobe 50 percent."

Nonetheless, with makeup and hairstyling comprising half the "look," each is a key element. And both are finally getting the Hollywood recognition they deserve. On March 19, 2000, the first annual Georgie Awards, hosted by the International Alliance of Theatrical Stage Employees Local 706—made up of 1,550 makeup artists and hairstylists—were handed out at the Beverly Hilton Hotel in Beverly Hills. The awards are named after George Westmore, who organized the motion picture industry's first makeup and hairstyling department at the Selig Studios in 1917, and are designed to honor outstanding work in such categories as best contemporary makeup, best character makeup, best contemporary hairstyling, and innovative hairstyling.

Reality Check

"Georgie" recognition aside, it's still a tough profession.

"You'll work, minimum, twelve- to fourteen-hour-days," says Maurice Stein. "And rarely on an air-conditioned soundstage. Often, you'll wind up in the deserts of Arizona, snows of Alaska, or rains of Oregon."

Furthermore, the competition is fierce, and not just from other makeup artists.

"Computers," Michael explains, "are having a major impact on our field—as a design tool. Every design is now done by committee. To get visual agreement, we use a computer."

Yet, the makeup artists will always be needed. After all, someone must translate a director's whims into reality. Susan explains how she handles directors' idiosyncrasies.

"Once, after completing a grueling makeup, I went to the director for approval. 'I hate it, go back and do it again.' I took the actress into a trailer where we sat around for fifteen minutes, just talking. Then we walked out. 'I love it,' the director shouted. 'I knew you could do it, Susan.'"

Cool Web Sites to Visit

Beauty Buzz
www.beautybuzz.com/tips.asp

The Makeup Artists' Network
www.makeupartistnetwork.com

Makeup Man and the Monster
www.strangemag.com/chambers17.html

Forensic Artist

The forensic artist's skills were first used in nineteenth-century England to help solve the infamous Jack the Ripper murders. Today, such artists do everything from sketching courtroom dramas for TV to re-creating crime scenes, and making postmortem drawings and two- and three-dimensional facial reconstructions based on the skull. It is deadly serious work.

Hot Career

15

Her black-and-white morgue photograph, eyes shut, lips pursed, skin drawn, hair straggly, displayed full-screen on the 17-inch computer monitor, would make anyone squeamish. The 16- to 18-year-old had been fished from a drainage canal. The image of a life cut short was not easy to look at. No way could such a photo be published in newspapers or broadcast on TV in hope that someone would identify her. A facial reconstruction, to create a presentable and identifiable portrait, will have to be undertaken. That's what 41-year-old Michael Streed, a detective/forensic artist for the City of Orange (California) Police Department, is about to do as he hovers in front of his computer staring at the grainy, gray face.

Michael splits the screen vertically, leaving the dead girl's right side intact. With skill based on 20 years of forensic artwork experience, he painstakingly adds "life" to the girl's left side. Lips are reddened, an eye opened, hair combed, and the skin colored. "I have to be OK with the nose, lip shape, and eyebrows," Michael says. "Yet, I must remember, it's not about making her pretty, it's about making her identifiable." An hour later, as he completes the victim's right side, Michael leans back. "Hopefully we'll get a match that will aid in solving the murder." He sighs.

Bridging the Gap

Forensic artists have been doing just that, helping solve crimes, for over a hundred years. Composite sketches were used in the investigation of the infamous Jack the Ripper murders in nineteenth-century London.

According to the International Association for Identification, Forensic Art Subcommittee, forensic art is "any art used in the identification, apprehension, or conviction of offenders, or which aids in the location of victims or identification of unknown deceased persons."

The forensic artist, sometimes referred to by the more inclusive though less accurate term police artist, "does everything from sketching courtroom scenes for TV to re-creating crime scenes, and making postmortem drawings and two- and three-dimensional facial reconstructions based on the skull, to using computer graphics to depict the age-progression of missing children," Carrie Stuart Parks of Stuart Parks Forensic Consulting says. "Most often, however, they create composite imagery."

"Consisting of separate components, a composite may bridge the gap between the mental image of the police officer and the memory of the witness," Carrie declares. "Though usually remembered for their renderings of faces, they may be asked to draw literally anything: vehicles, weapons, tattoos, clothing, jewelry, or any other object described to the artist. Such composites may be generated from freehand drawings, a mechanical assembly kit, computer-generated image, or some combination of these systems."

Forensic artists come from a wide variety of backgrounds. Most, however, "work in law enforcement, whether civilian or sworn," says Steve Fusco, a detective with the Orange County Sheriff's Office in Orlando, Florida. One of only a handful of such artists working full-time, he knows how difficult it is to break in to the business. "Police administrators are tough nuts to crack," he advises. "They'll tell you there is no position in the budget, not enough workload to justify a full-time slot, or the chief may not believe in forensic artists. Still, I advise sticking with it. Perseverance, personal aptitude, and desire will pay off."

Do you have to be a cop? Karen T. Taylor, acknowledged by her colleagues to be a forensic artist's artist, was never on the force. Author of *Forensic Art and Illustration*, she says there are three skills needed in the composite imagery field: knowledge of art, knowledge of the criminal justice system, and a psychological sensitivity. "I have seen good forensic artists come from both ends, law enforcement and the artistic," she insists. "What's important is to place emphasis on all three skills."

What Will I Earn?

If you're lucky enough to work full-time, from $28,000 to $72,000 per year, depending on experience and employer. Freelancers may be paid per sketch.

INFORMATION

For More Information

Stephen A. Fusco
2450 West 33rd Street
Orlando, FL 32839
(407) 836-4020
ocsofusco@orlinter.com

International Association
for Identification
P.O. Box 2423
Alameda, CA 94501-0247

Christopher Simpson, a forensic artist with the Snohomish County Sheriff's Department in Everett, Washington, concurs: "I have no problem with civilians doing it. If the agency has the resources to train their own, they may be better off with their own. Still, by attending school, such as the Scottsdale Art School, you can break into the field no matter what your civilian background."

Face It

The 18-year-old girl, a rape victim, had sat, along with her mother, across from Michael's desk as he, sketch pad in hand, gently probed with questions. "I was talking to her, looking down as I drew," he recalls. "Then I glanced up. I saw the mother clutching 'her baby' in a fetal position. The girl had been reduced to a childlike state, a quivering mass of humanity.

"I never acknowledged the scene, I kept drawing," Michael continues. "To do so would have been humiliating and embarrassing to all. Besides, what purpose would it have served? Years of interviewing have taught me to be sensitive with trauma victims and witnesses."

"That ability to interview is key, the most underrated part of the forensic artist's job," says Karen. "Anyone can put together a face—heck, there are kits that allow a child to do just that. But is it the right face? Sensitively and correctly interviewing victims and witnesses of violent crime is what it takes to get a match."

"It's almost as though the interviewee invades my body and controls my hand," Michael says. "You're translating the verbal into the visual. If you don't listen, things get lost in the reconstruction."

Of course, if the subject is deceased and in a semi-skeletal state, interviewing skills are irrelevant.

"Using clay, I sculpt a face directly onto a skull," Betty Gatliff, the world's leading practitioner of the art, states. A former medical illustrator, she began her sculpting career while attempting to identify crash victims for the Federal Aviation Administration (FAA) in the 1960s. "It is a technical, mechanical, step-by-step process," she declares.

Betty Alice Finch, a forensic artist with the Kern County, California, Sheriff's Department, and a former student of Betty Gatliff, has sculpted her share of skulls. "I'd go to the coroner's office and remove the sticky, smelly things," she says. "In one case, before I could take photos, I had to wait for the beetles to crawl out of the eye sockets."

What to Read

Forensic Art and Illustration
by Karen T. Taylor.
CRC Press, 1999.

Lack of Intimacy

In the future forensic artists like Betty Finch probably won't have to worry about shooing bugs off skeletons, or even holding a sketch pad, what with all the new technology coming onboard.

"You might say technology began having an impact with the Identi-Kit, developed by Smith and Wesson, in the early 1950s," says Carrie. "The kit, consisting of acetate overlays of different facial features to arrive at 'composite look-alikes,' provides a generic-looking person, but lacks the versatility of adding unique characteristics to the face [that] could assist the investigating detective in identifying the suspect."

But with the computer, surely all that has changed? "We hope the computer will enhance what we do," says Karen. "Yet, it is a mistake to think you can go to the finished product with a few keys strokes. The computer is just another tool for the knowledgeable forensic artists to use."

Michael agrees, adding, "Take age progression. The software just isn't there yet. Besides, the market may not be large enough for vendors to develop it. The artist will always be needed."

Katherine Tushalski, a forensic artist with the Modesto, California, Police Department adds this cautionary note: "The computer can be a bit intimidating, intrusive. The victim or witness doesn't always relate well to this 'third party.' Sitting with your laptop at a patient's bedside doesn't lend itself to intimacy."

Freelancer

Robert Exter practically had to beg Betty Finch to let him prove what he could do. "Just to show you how capable I am," he told her, "I'll do a skull reconstruction for free." Betty took the bait and gave the freelance forensic artist an assignment. When the results came back, of a black female in her early twenties, exactly what the forensic pathologist had predicted the mangled body was, Betty was a bit surprised. She shouldn't have been; after all, Robert was the first to issue a composite of the Unabomber in 1987. So accurate was the drawing, it is credited by many in law enforcement for driving the terrorist into six years of hiding, during which he committed no further bombings.

"I have always been an artist," Robert says. "I always had an eye for portraits. I knew I had a knack."

Although such confidence suggests an egotist, with Robert that's not the case. He knows as well as any forensic artist that, when it comes to solving a crime, he plays a small role in the big picture.

"Yes, nine out of ten artists have huge egos," Michael explains. "The problem is, they tend to develop a style, a signature, to their work. Forensic art is not that kind of art. We're dealing with hard-core facts: eyes go here, nose goes here, full frontal—it's very clinical. You can't go in with a preconceived impression of how to draw something."

Or with the idea you're going to emerge the hero.

"You're just one small part," says Carrie. "In no way are you king of the universe. Your work isn't going to solve a case or be the deciding factor. Sometimes you'll help people, sometimes not. You must approach it as a collaborative effort. Remember, it is usually someone else's case. You must honor and respect that. You are not a junior cop."

"Like most artists, I've always drawn," concludes Michael. "You know, doodling in class when I was supposed to be paying attention. With my dad a police officer, becoming a cop was a logical choice for me. But I wanted to approach it differently. The way for me to do that was to use my art skills. I hunted around for good schools to attend. I found out who the best teachers were and sat at their feet. I became like a sponge absorbing everything. I have spent thousands of dollars in phone bills talking to colleagues around the country, picking their brains. But it's been worth it. It has made me a different kind of cop."

Cool Web Sites to Visit

American Academy of Forensic Sciences
www.aafs.org/index.htm

Forensic Science Web Page
www.users.aol.com/murrk/index.htm

OCSO Forensic Artists
www.ocsoartist.com/default.htm

Hot Concepts!

Computer Resumes

You can't help but notice that there are tons of books, mini-courses, and seminars to show you how to prepare a "killer resume," one "guaranteed" to land you a job interview. All this resume interest exists not only because workers are moving from job to job more frequently, but because preparing and sending out a resume has never been easier, thanks to the computer and the Internet. In fact, many large companies are so inundated with unsolicited resumes, they've resorted to using resume scanning software to search for key words in your document to make sure you're a candidate they're interested in.

In preparing a twenty-first century resume, it's best to assume it will be "read" by a computer first. Any number of resume-creation software programs are available; in fact, your word-processing program probably has several resume templates available. Here are some tips to keep in mind when preparing a computer-friendly, "plain vanilla" resume:

- Avoid unusual type faces, underlining, and italics.
- Use 10- and 14-point type.
- Use smooth white paper, black ink, and quality printing.
- Be sure your name is on the first line of the page.
- Provide white space.
- Avoid double columns.
- Use abbreviations carefully.

Remember, the purpose of the resume is to get you a job interview. But first you must get your resume past the computer!

FREELANCE WRITER

Basically, readers value magazines for the editing and selection process they perform. Editors decide which are the most appropriate pieces of information and how best to present them—and therein lies opportunity for freelancers.

It took the loss of her job—no, her business, actually, her livelihood—to propel Diana Saenger into the life she had always wanted—that of a full-time freelance writer. "In 1993 my husband and I purchased a food franchise that a year later went belly up," she says. "Since we'd already lost everything, we had nothing else to lose. I took the plunge. I decided to stay home and write—full-time."

Today, Diana is a well-respected freelancer specializing in the entertainment field. Having interviewed the likes of John Travolta, Richard Gere, and Sharon Stone, and written for magazines such as *Scr(i)pt, Intrinsic Romance,* and *Good Times*, Diana is, if not living, at least working, her dream.

Yet every day is a struggle, every week a 60- to 70-hour effort writing and marketing her product, her words, growing her business. "I have no life," she declares. "To succeed as a freelance writer requires a focused pursuit of your objective. If you write regularly for *Rolling Stone, Vanity Fair,* or *Vogue*, you have it made. Other than that, it's beating new paths every day."

Magazines—Alive and Well

There's no way of knowing how many full-time freelancers struggle to earn a living, but, like Diana, struggle they do. It's simply a matter of competition.

"The spectacular increase in the number of good freelance writers willing to write for fame, glory, and a dime a word means you will have to put in long hours just to have a byline or the chance to learn a new skill or develop a new contact," says Richard Cropp, coauthor of *Writing Magazine and Newspaper Articles.* "As a freelancer starting out, the pay you earn will probably just cover expenses—that is, if you receive any money at all."

"The word processor is at fault," adds Fred Blechman, author of over 750 magazine articles. "Sitting in front of a computer has made it so easy for people to write. Editors are inundated with product."

John M. Wilson, a long-time columnist for *Writer's Digest,* agrees: "Simply put, more print writers vie for fewer opportunities, often for decreasing pay and benefits. I no longer attempt to freelance as a nonfiction writer full-time."

Of course, magazines and newspapers aren't the only outlet for a freelancer's words, far from it. "In the quest to keep a steady stream of clients," says John F. Lauerman, a full-time freelancer specializing in the medical field, "I've written all kinds of things I'd had no experience writing before: market analyses, video scripts, slide shows, advertising copy, you name it."

Still, when one thinks of a freelance writer, magazines and newspapers come to mind. According to RCB's Media Research Report of Spring 1998, nearly 180 million magazines were being bought each month, through subscriptions and at newsstands. With over three hundred new publications launched in 1998, the magazine industry is alive and well. Furthermore, there are more than twenty-five hundred consumer titles alone. Clearly readers—and writers—have an abundance of choices.

Ah, but the Internet, surely it will affect reading habits, you may be thinking. Not yet it hasn't. According to NetSmart Research, magazine readers are not substituting online forms of reading for printed forms. "Exposure to the Internet may actually make the traditional magazine environment even more desirable," the report adds. Besides, with fifteen hundred online magazines as of mid-2000, led by giants such as *Salon* and *Slate,* freelancers have even more markets to go after. Some of those electronic publications pay pretty well, too. So it's worth it to be familiar with a computer.

What Will I Earn?

Since freelancers work for themselves, it's impossible to determine income. Most are content to earn what they could in a salaried writing position, about $35,000 a year.

INFORMATION

For More Information

American Society of Magazine
Editors
919 Third Avenue
New York, NY 10022
(212) 752-0055

Electronic Publishing Special
Interest Group
P.O. Box 25707
Alexandria, VA 22313-5707

Basically, readers value magazines for the editing and selection process they perform. Editors decide which are the most appropriate pieces of information and how best to present them—and therein lies opportunity for freelancers.

The Pro

From the two words, *free* and *lance*, the original freelancers where just that—knights of old who sold their services to a nobleman, party, state, or cause. With the job done, they were available for the next battle, or gig, to whomever offered the best deal.

Today's freelance writers operate in much the same way, with the lance replaced with a pen, or, more to the point, a computer. Magazine editors, reluctant to hire permanent staff writers, turn to freelancers to fill pages. Exactly what do these editors want?

"A minimum writing level," says Jose Fraguas, general manager of CFW Enterprises, publisher of four martial arts magazines, including *Martial Arts Illustrated*. "An editor, the name aside, can't spend a week editing a manuscript."

"We need a different edge to our articles," Sally Merlin, East Coast editor of *Scr(i)pt*, says. "We have done just about everything there is to do, so we need that special slant."

"Number one, I am looking for experience" says Michael Goldman, articles editor for *Boys' Life*. "If I want a writer to do a canoe trip with a bunch of kids, I am looking first for a canoeist who has also written, rather than a writer who can canoe."

OK, but what do writers do wrong? What are the mistakes even professional freelancers make?

"The professional," Jose says, "will do the research, dig down, get the details, the background, the facts. In conducting an interview he won't be happy with a simple answer."

"It's always the same," adds Sally. "The writer says too much. They are in love with their words. They think if they give you all the details, every little thing, somehow that is going to convince you."

"Most mistakes are made right in the query process," says Michael, referring to the letter or fax a writer sends to pitch an article

idea. "It's obvious when a writer is not familiar with our magazine. You have to know where you're trying to sell before you sell it."

Your Friend, the Post Office

"Selling yourself? Don't writers write?" you ask.

"I spend 50 percent of my time marketing," Diana says. "The post office and I are best friends.

"Once you get steady work, garner good relationships, you can send an e-mail with a couple of words and get a go or no-go answer from an editor. But still, I am querying new markets every single day. I send out thirty queries for one assignment. It's tough. The biggest mistake new freelancers make is thinking they don't have to put in the marketing work, that the business will succeed on the strength of their writing. It will not."

Actually, according to Richard, selling more than writing is where you want to be. "I don't write a lot," he says. "I have a stock of articles I can revise and sell to other markets. That's the key to success."

Fred agrees. "I am the king of recycling, though with the refusal of many editors to grant 'one-time rights,' that's becoming a problem. With such rights, you can use your stuff over and over again. With 'all rights,' demanded by more magazines, you lose control completely. They own your article to use throughout the universe and any other universes to be discovered."

"Many people make a living as freelancer writers," says Michael. "But to do so you have to have one or two good anchor jobs you can count on. I have a stable of several writers I know I can turn to at a moment's notice. From their point of view they know they'll get a call from me and, as a result, a fairly stable paycheck."

Kathleen Doheny, a Los Angeles-based full-time freelancer for 15 years, agrees, but adds: "I specialize in health reporting. Specialization has its advantages, especially if you are doing this full-time. You don't have to reinvent the wheel; you can spin off pieces. And you'll know a good story when you see it. It's worked for me."

What to Read

The $100,000 Writer
by Nancy Flynn.
Adams Media Corporation, 2000.

Writing Magazine and Newspaper Articles
by Barbara Braidwood.
Self-Counsel Press, 1999.

Writer's Market
by Kirsten C. Holm.
Writer's Digest Books,
published annually.

Low Pay Versus Slow Pay

A good, stable pay check is a rarity, however.

"I recently sold two articles for 75 cents per column inch," says Fred. "That works out to two and a half cents a word—terrible. But it's better than nothing. Those were two manuscripts I couldn't move anywhere else. Low pay is better than no pay."

True, but if low pay isn't bad enough, slow pay adds salt to the wound.

"Trouble is," writes David Petersen, in the July 1996 *Writer's Digest*, "even if you can earn enough to live on, month after month, you'll rarely know *when* those checks you've earned will appear in your mailbox. Budgeting will be difficult at best. Your days will revolve around the arrival of your mail. Disappointment will be your copilot."

"Publishing has changed," adds Fred. "Magazines either pay on acceptance or on publication. It's mostly the latter now. The lead time is awful. It could be six months to a year before you get paid for an article."

"That's why I counsel against plunging into full-time freelancing unless you have a bank account large enough to see you through those long and indefinite waits between paychecks," says David. "My advice is don't give up your day job until you're ready."

Nonetheless, giving up that day job is exactly what Diana has done. "I was earning $1,000 a week in corporate America. That was hard to forgo. Though I'm making nowhere near that now, as a freelancer I have doubled my income every year for the past five years. Besides, I'm a writer. This is what I do. I am always thinking and plotting what comes next, I miss freeway off-ramps. I hope to eventually cross that magic line where I don't have to work sixty hours a week. I will. It gets a little bit better and stronger each year. It doesn't come overnight."

FUND-RAISER

There are over ninety thousand full-time fund-raisers throughout the country. Whether you work as a sole developer, with others at a large institution, or as a consultant, there's work aplenty.

She was a cantankerous, downright irritable, old soul—not one to attract the affection of others. And frugal? *Cheap* would be a better term. Every time the vixen had a doctor's appointment at Good Samaritan Hospital in Hollywood, California, she'd call ahead to demand a free parking pass from Cheryl Bernstein Gurin, then director of development. "I traipsed downstairs with those parking passes, I don't know how many times," Cheryl recalls. "After a while I actually got to like the gal."

Indeed! A few years later, when the aging hellion ended up an admitted patient, Cheryl visited her every day, to the relief of overtaxed nurses. When she took a turn for the worse and became a recluse in her own home, Cheryl, and another fund-raiser in the office, would appear with candy and flowers. "We did it because we wanted to," says Cheryl. "The woman had no one in her life."

In death, nonetheless, the miserly charge was able to connect with the hospital that had ministered to her. With her late husband's Coca-Cola stock, she left "Good Sam," as the institution is affectionately called, a cool $1 million. "You never know what a little kindness all around can bring," says Cheryl.

Of course, unsolicited gifts are rare, and when they do occur, their stories delight us no end. But for nonprofit organizations to wait for such generosity to materialize out of the blue is unrealistic. These institutions, to support their good deeds, must solicit funds. They have to ask for what the average American finds uncomfortable even discussing—money. Enter today's professional fund-raiser.

Almsgiving to the Max

With nonprofits becoming a major economic sector, growing in the last two decades by 60 percent to nationally more than one million organizations, fund-raising is big business. Holly Hall, at the *Chronicle of Philanthropy*, reports that "in addition, government cutbacks have caused scores of institutions like public schools and libraries to go after private donations in earnest. Health charities, religious groups, environmental organizations, and others are moving away from fund-raising methods like direct mail and special events and starting major-gifts programs and capital or endowment campaigns. At institutions accustomed to seeking big gifts, particularly colleges and universities, the frequency—and monetary goals—of such campaigns has exploded."

Mary McNamara, *Los Angeles Times* staff writer, says, "What was once called 'almsgiving' has become a multibillion-dollar enterprise now experiencing an unprecedented boom: Last year, charitable giving in the United States alone generated $175 billion, a 9 percent annual increase."

It wasn't always this way. Though our country has a long philanthropic tradition, not until after World War II did fund-raising as an activity take off. "That is when higher education organizations began launching major capital endowment campaigns," says Michael Maude, president and founder of Partners in Philanthropy in Topeka, Kansas. "In the early 1950s, those with experience in such campaigns branched out, migrating to various nonprofits and, in many cases, becoming consultants."

Today, according to Dr. Kathleen Kelly, professor of communications, University of Louisiana, and author of *Effective Fund-Raising Management*, "there are over ninety thousand full-time, paid fund-raisers, also known as development professionals, throughout the country." Whether you work as the sole developer, with others at a large institution, or as a consultant, there's work a plenty. "Heck, when Stanford University went after a billion dollars, they had four hundred paid employees on staff to bring in the money," Kathleen declares.

Michael, whose company specializes in searching for fund raising professionals, says he has three major searches under way. In one position, the client is prepared to pay an $80,000 to $120,000 annual salary. So difficult is it to find qualified people at senior levels, says Richard Page Allen, president of RPA, Inc., an executive-search and consulting

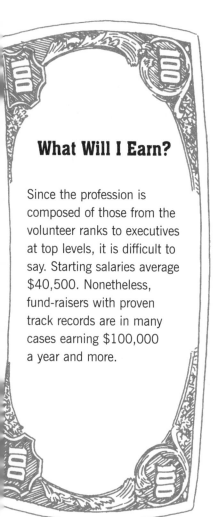

What Will I Earn?

Since the profession is composed of those from the volunteer ranks to executives at top levels, it is difficult to say. Starting salaries average $40,500. Nonetheless, fund-raisers with proven track records are in many cases earning $100,000 a year and more.

firm in Williamsport, Pennsylvania, that "today, we never have a search requiring fewer than five hundred phone calls. In one, we made twelve hundred calls."

The Rainmaker Cometh

"I've tried so many careers, but nothing seems to grab me. My sister told me about this fund-raising thing you do. . . ." As Cheryl relates the story, she sighs, having heard it so often. "They seem to want to 'try it on for size,'" she says. "They think the job is like a pair of shoes—you spy them on the rack and buy them, even if they don't exactly fit, because they're on sale, and after all, they're very cute."

Now director of major gifts and planned giving at the University of Judaism in Bel Air, California, Cheryl cautions, "Philanthropy is not just a job, it's a philosophy. It should touch your soul—not your sole. A successful fund-raiser must love helping people, have a sense of purpose and justice, cultivate the gift of gab, and develop just the right finesse to close the deal."

But all those parties, special events, and lunches with the rich and powerful sound like fun! "Sure, it looks like fun," says Cheryl. "But outsiders don't see the painstaking research and behind-the-scenes preparation going into each solicitation, not to mention the research, writing, and rewriting behind each successful—and unsuccessful—proposal. And, of course, there's pressure from the board and administration. They want results."

To be sure! Those six-figure salaries you'll earn—eventually—need to be, well, *earned*.

"If it's an astronomical salary, watch out," cautions Holly. "You will be expected to produce accordingly. In some cases the organization wants a 'rainmaker,' one who can deliver instant contributions from big companies and famous people with no link to the organization."

"Being a successful fund-raiser is no easy task," says Dr. Tim Seiler, director of the Fund-Raising School at Indiana University's Center on Philanthropy. "Hard work and dedication are required. You must martial resources and enlist volunteers for a cause."

INFORMATION

For More Information

Indiana University Center
on Philanthropy
(317) 684-8904

Nonprofit Management Program
University of Judaism
15600 Mulholland Drive
Bel Air, CA 90077
(310) 476-9777
www.uj.edu

National Society of Fundraising
Executives
1101 King Street, Suite 700
Alexandria, VA 22314-2967
(800) 666-FUND
www.nsfre.org

"It takes a person with balanced skills," advises Cheryl. "One must keep in mind the final goal is raising money, not just making friends."

Making Others Look Good

"Even our own mothers don't understand what we do," Deborah Strauss, executive director of the IT Resources Center in Chicago, Illinois, tells me. She gives some examples to help. Fund-raisers can be:

- The avuncular planned-giving specialist who visits older benefactors of a university to discuss bequests in the context of estate planning.
- The dynamic special-events expert whose attention-getting benefits feature clever centerpieces, celebrities, and society attendees.
- The experienced consultant who travels from client to client to orchestrate major capital campaigns.
- The energetic generalist who single-handedly carries all fund raising and public relations responsibility for an organization.

The list goes on: the academically oriented grant writer, the mathematically minded direct mail expert, and the vice president of development who supervises specialists.

"A relational, goal, and vision-oriented person who believes passionately in the cause makes the best fund-raiser," Pamela Autrey, vice president, Human Resources, at Ketchum, Inc., in Dallas, Texas, says. "They must take the opinions of others and consolidate them into one dream, one vision, and come up with the steps to execute that dream. All for little, or no, recognition."

That lack of recognition can be a problem for some. "The nonprofit board members, volunteers, committee leaders, and benefit chairs are out in front," says Deborah. "Making other people look good comes with the job."

If lack of recognition and knowledge as to what fund-raisers do are a concern, misperceptions are also an issue.

"People think it's something they can just go out and do," says Pamela. "They'll say, 'I helped my daughter's Girl Scout troop raise

money and I found I have fund-raising skills.' Truth is, those skills come from many years in the development field. Motivating people toward the parting of their monies for a bigger goal is a challenge."

When it comes to misperception, it is often the fundraiser's image that is mistaken. "At times we are seen as manipulative, dishonest, full of trickery," says Tim. "If you stop the man on the street, you'll get an earful: telemarketers calling at dinner time, direct mail overload, scandals in the paper, negative jargon such as 'begging' and 'arm twisting,' you know. That is not what ethical and effective fund-raisers do, however."

Let's Ask Bill Gates

So, then, how do fund-raisers bring in the big bucks?

Direct mailings, special events, annual campaigns, major gifts, and planned giving are all based on developing relationships. Ask any fund-raiser and he or she will tell you it all comes down to that. "People give to people, not organizations," is the mantra in the trade. So is the saying, "Asking a wealthy stranger to make a major gift is like asking a stranger to marry you just because he's single." Meeting someone is not enough; you have to get to know them, intimately.

"Working with volunteers, donors, boards, it's all about developing relationships," says Michael. "The most successful fund-raisers are sensitive to what the prospective donor is all about, what they value, ways they prefer being communicated with, the way they want to be involved in the organization. It does take a particular sensitivity. Giving large amounts of money is a major decision, arrived at over time. It doesn't always happen in the organization's time frame."

"People say, 'Why don't we just ask Bill Gates for money?'" says Kathleen. "OK, do we have a relationship with Mr. Gates? Have we been sending him our newsletter? Has he been to our organization to see the work we do? You do not solicit gifts from strangers."

"It takes courage to go out and talk to people, explore with them whether they share interests," says Tim. "Often you converse with people who don't share the same vision, then you get rejection."

Fund-raisers have been criticized for not sticking around long enough to develop these all-important relationships. According to Holly,

What to Read

Effective Fund-Raising Management
by Kathleen Kelly.
Lawrence Erlbaum Associates, 1999.

"Some nonprofit groups are so disillusioned with professional fund-raisers that they have started hiring people with little or no experience." High demand is given as the main reason development personnel remain, on average, only three and a half years on a job.

Kathleen is not so sure this criticism is justified. "I believe it's an unsubstantiated myth," she cautions. "Research by the National Society of Fund Raising Executives [NSFRE] shows that fund-raisers move from job to job no more often than others in high-demand professions."

An Accidental Profession?

It used to be called the "accidental profession," since one rarely set out in life to become a fund-raiser. That's still true to a certain degree. "Most who come into the field have had other work experience," says Michael. "There is a degree of maturity in that. For the most part, there is no direct pathway from educational institutions. Few go to college wanting to be fund-raisers."

That, however, is also changing. Now a myriad of institutions around the country offer seminars, certificates, and even degrees in fund-raising. "You can go the volunteer route," advises Tim, "that's OK. But we offer education and training in the subject across the United States and in thirty-five foreign countries. It is an excellent approach."

And there's the 20,000-member NSFRE. The organization is an invaluable resource for the fund-raising professional.

"Today, it is easy to find out exactly what the profession entails before ever applying for a job in fund-raising," says Cheryl. "Not-for-profit management courses abound, as do fund-raising courses, programs, and even degrees. We offer a nonprofit M.B.A. program here at the University of Judaism."

Would Cheryl do it again—that is, go into fund-raising? "Absolutely," she says. "I forgot to mention the other little old lady at Good Sam. She had given only $2,500 to the hospital over her entire life. A paltry sum in the fund-raising world. Then she ended up in the ER and, shortly afterward, died. She bequeathed a $51 million endowment to us. Yes, come to think of it, there is 'fun' in fund-raising!"

Cool Web Sites to Visit

Chronicle of Philanthropy
www.philanthropy.com

Fund-Raising Forum Library
www.raise-funds.com/library.html

Ketchum, Inc.
www.rsi-ketchum.com

Graphic Designer

With the computer as a design tool, it now seems that anyone can do graphic design. But you need to know composition, balance, color, layout—in other words, you need to know design.

Bert Johnson's Graphics Two design studio contains three drawing boards—and they're over in a corner gathering dust. "These days, we do almost no cut-and-paste," he says, referring to the old method of cutting out type and images and pasting them up for composition. Indeed not. Sitting at a Power PC, running Adobe Photoshop, is how Bert, a graphic designer for 35 years, does design work now. Today, he's "building" a brochure cover for a high-tech client.

The cover image, filling the 19-inch computer screen, is peppered with images of the space shuttle, a gearbox, an oil rig, a medical-imaging unit, and text in various fonts. "Each individual figure is layered," Bert explains. "Watch!" Reaching for his mouse, Bert plays what-if games as he repositions, sizes, and "paints" the oil rig. "Try that the old-fashioned way," he kids. "The computer has revolutionized the graphics industry, with profound impact on everyone in it."

An Industry in Upheaval

Although graphic designers, also known as graphic artists, still create packaging, promotional displays, and marketing brochures for new products, visual designs for annual reports and other corporate literature, or distinctive logos for products or businesses, the way they do it has undergone a sea change in the last few years. "I'm into my fifth technological change," Bert says. "After letterpress and then offset printing, I went on to photo composing, digital composing, and now, total-image assembly. The term 'camera ready' is passé. It's all disk to film, or even disk to print."

Val Cooper, art director, designer, and author of the *Instant Image: 1000+ Stationery Designs* source book, says it best: "Everything, the field, job titles, centuries of tradition, is being redefined. People who set type have disappeared overnight."

Fortunately, graphic designers are filling the void. With the design and production aspects of a graphic arts project merging, again thanks to the computer, the graphic designer can deliver final product at tremendous savings. "The technology today is at a point where we can generate a file, dial up a remote printing facility, image the file right onto the press, run ten thousand copies, and deliver them the next morning," Bert says. "It's called CTP, computer-to-plate imaging; it's one of the fastest growing areas of prepress."

With the increase in demand for graphic art, most of which now incorporates lower-cost, four-color graphics, graphic designers find plenty to do. Are they still working in the traditional ad agency or service bureau?

"No," says Bert. "The job market is fluid, work is moving from the traditional design agency office to the corporate office. Because firms produce enough marketing material, they're bringing graphic designers in-house, sidestepping the big agencies and, in some cases, service bureaus."

But Randy Ricker, manager of Mac Temps, an employment service for graphic designers in Los Angeles, isn't so sure: "True, the new technology makes possible in-house work. But the ad agency and service bureau business is growing. Everyone in the field is benefiting these days because more work is being done."

What type of work? Here are a few entry-level job titles open to those with knowledge and training in graphic design:

- Advertising Designer
- Art Director's Assistant
- Print Production Assistant
- 2-D, 3-D Animation
- Web Designer
- Service Bureau Specialist

- Photograph Manipulation, Color Correction Specialist
- Studio Designer
- Commercial Artist
- Digital Graphic Designer
- Illustrator
- Multimedia Designer
- Digital Colorist
- Mac Artist
- Production Designer
- Electronic Artist

That there is work to be done should come as no surprise. As *Time* magazine said in a recent cover article, "The Rebirth of Design": "Good design, communicating good services or products, is becoming the cornerstone of our society."

Designer First

Juliet Beynon, department chair, Graphic Design/Computer Graphics/Animation, at the Learning Tree University (LTU), stands ready to greet 60 eager faces as they line up for an open house on the Chatsworth, California, campus. As the potential students enter the lecture room, Juliet asks each in turn if they want the graphic design or computer graphics literature package. Over 80 percent opt for the latter. Only a handful select the graphic design brochures. Mistake! At least it is according to just about every working graphic designer.

"The biggest error people make," Juliet says, "is thinking the computer is more than just a tool—it is not. The computer will not draw for them."

Alissa Gould, manager for communications/public relations at the Graphic Arts Technical Foundation (GATF), concurs. "It now seems, on the surface, that anyone can do graphic design. 'I'll learn to use the software and that'll be it,' people think. But you need to know composition, balance, color, layout; in other words, you need to know design."

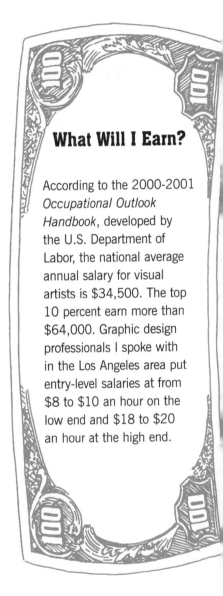

What Will I Earn?

According to the 2000-2001 *Occupational Outlook Handbook*, developed by the U.S. Department of Labor, the national average annual salary for visual artists is $34,500. The top 10 percent earn more than $64,000. Graphic design professionals I spoke with in the Los Angeles area put entry-level salaries at from $8 to $10 an hour on the low end and $18 to $20 an hour at the high end.

INFORMATION

For More Information

American Institute of Graphic Arts
1059 Third Avenue
New York, NY 10021
(212) 752-0813

The Society of Illustrators
128 East 63rd Street
New York, NY 10021-7392

"People who have computer experience but not the basic design background," Bert adds, "often design until they run out of time or stumble onto something. What a waste."

Mark Oldach, in his excellent book *Creativity for Graphic Designers*, sums up the need for both traditional knowledge and computer skills when referring to the computer and its role in design:

"The computer is both blessing and curse rolled into one expensive tool," he says. "Too many designers use it as their only tool or, worse, as a substitute for thinking. These designers use the computer as a sketching tool, thinking tool, writing tool, typesetting, and illustrating tool. Then the tool has mastered the designer, not the other way around, and the designer may have begun abdicating his responsibility to the computer."

Randy is even more emphatic: "Designers usually need a bachelor's degree in the arts," he says. "That, and a great portfolio."

Show Me

In graphic design, as in any art, it's not so much what you know, but what you can do. "Show don't tell" is the thing. Enter the portfolio.

"In this business," explains Juliet, "you are your portfolio. Resumes are fine, but how you represent yourself visually is key."

To gain the necessary design and computer graphics background to create a great portfolio, you'll want to attend classes, maybe with the ultimate goal of a certificate or even a degree. Although a degree is not always required, at least not for entry-level work. As Don Manganti, an academic counselor at Burbank High School in Burbank, California, puts it: "A bachelor's degree is always desirable. But today an associate's degree or a certificate program can work, too. In some cases, these shorter programs—two years for an associate degree, as few as six months for a certificate, are better for jump-starting your career because they offer specialized, focused skill training. Later on, once you're working, you can pursue a B.A. part-time."

What will you learn in these programs? From foundation courses to the latest course on creating Web pages with Flash, you will

cover the gamut. Here are the titles of a few courses listed in the Learning Tree University catalog for art and graphic design majors:

- Introduction to Graphic Design and Visual Communication
- Fundamentals of Design
- Color Theory
- Typography for Visual Communications and Web Design
- Introduction to the Macintosh
- Adobe Illustrator
- QuarkXPress Intensive Workshop
- Professional Opportunities in Web Design
- Digital Imaging with Adobe PhotoShop
- Advanced Web Design with Dreamweaver and Flash
- HTML for Designers

It comes down to traditional design theory plus use of the latest design tool—the computer.

As mentioned earlier, whatever education and training you acquire, be sure you emerge with a super portfolio. That portfolio is your entrance into an ad agency, large firm, or service bureau. Or, if you're ready, what you'll present to potential clients as you set up a freelance operation.

Fine, you say, you're the arty type anyway—drawing is your thing. It's just all the computer stuff—QuarkXPress, PhotoShop, Illustrator, and so on—that gets you nervous. But you can learn. Eight-year-old whizzes aside, no one is born with a mouse in his or her hand. In today's graphics environment, beyond design basics, computer know-how is a must. Actually, more than competence is required. As Randy puts it: "You must be both comfortable and curious about the new technology. A cursory knowledge is not enough."

Web Opportunities

It has been called the fastest-growing medium on earth. With an estimated four million Web sites as of mid-2000, with over a billion Web pages, that's an easy statement to accept. What does it mean

What to Read

Becoming a Graphic Designer: A Guide to Careers in Design by Steven Heller and Teresa Fernandes. John Wiley & Sons, 1997.

The Digital Designer: The Graphic Artist's Guide to the New Media by Steven Heller and Daniel Drennan. Watson-Guptill Publications, 1997.

for graphic designers? Plenty! The Web's interactivity, which includes text, graphics, animation, sound, and movies, offers a brand-new working world for artists and graphic designers. Using programs such as Dreamweaver to edit and Flash to create vector-based animation graphics, Web page designers are pushing the envelope in this, the most dynamic segment of the design industry. And, fortunately for designers, the Web is an ever-changing media.

"When I first started designing on the Web, I had to totally change my attitude about the work," says Sabine Messner, of *Hotwired*, as quoted in Darcy DiNucci's book, *Elements of Web Design*. "I was used to print, where I would get this moment of relief when I had the final product in my hands. But on the Web, you're never done."

Artists and graphic designers did not take quickly to the World Wide Web. As a design opportunity, it was seen initially as having limited possibilities. Born of the Internet in 1991, the Web began as a text-only tool for disseminating information. In 1993, with the creation of Mosaic, the first browser able to display graphics, that changed.

"Finally, information on the Internet could have color and personality," says Darcy. "Suddenly, the Internet became more than a way to exchange useful information and e-mail; it became an entertainment medium."

Thanks to great WYSIWYG (What-You-See-Is-What-You-Get) Web authorizing-design programs, such as Macromedia's Dreamweaver, Microsoft's FrontPage, GoLive's CyberStudio, and Adobe's PageMill, to mention only the more well known, you can design Web pages without writing a single line of HTML (Hypertext Markup Language). While computer programmers are still needed in the Web development world, artists and designers, thanks to WYSIWYG, are assuming the leading role.

In fact, any graphic designer not into Web design is limiting his or her options. "Most design firms are doing Web design," says Brent McMahan, of Sibley Peteet Design. "At least it is part of what they do. Some, of course, do nothing else."

"It's the way of the world," says Michael Lejeune, of KBDA, a 12-person design studio in Santa Monica, California. "Everyone needs a Web site. A design firm must be able to do it in conjunction with other aspects of a project."

The Client Rules

As in all professions, there's always a downside in a day's work. "The toughest part is in the lack of knowledge, even appreciation, in the customer base," Bert says. "You work on a project for days, then the client announces: 'My cousin Fred says we should do it this way.' You want to scream. On the other hand, graphic designers must understand they're not fine artists. We work to satisfy someone else's need, not our own. It isn't business's role to be a patron of the arts or an artist. The printed page should never be considered an art gallery."

Of course, working with creative, open-minded clients is every graphic designer's dream. But as Susan E. Davis, writing in the June 2000 issue of *How* magazine puts it, "Finding clients who value your creativity, actively participate in the creative process, and want to build long-term collaborations is no easy task."

Still, there is much to do and be thankful for in this exploding, varied, and satisfying profession. "Once in awhile," Bert reflects, "a great designer gets to work with a great client, one who has faith in him and his work. A client that lets the designer design." With that said, Bert turns, smiling, to face his computer. "Let's see," he murmurs, "maybe I'll move the gearbox over here."

Cool Web Sites to Visit

Digital Directions
www.lawler.com/directions

Graphic Artists Guild
www.gag.org/

Graphic Design Schools on the Web
www.sensebox.com/schools

HUMAN RESOURCE MANAGER

*It takes three things to succeed as a human
resource manager: patience, patience, patience.*

At the time, new to human resource management, Randy
Krzesinski was nonetheless stunned by the animosity ema-
nating from the two employees seated before him. Larry had
just completed his employee self-evaluation, and Linda, his supervisor,
her appraisal of him. They were light years apart. "Larry felt he was
doing a great job," Randy says, "and he rated himself accordingly.
Linda, on the other hand, was on the verge of asking for Larry's termination. In a situation like this, it usually comes down to a personality clash; facts fall away. I doubted Larry was ever going to view
Linda as fair, nor Linda see Larry as a good performer.

"I had to try to restore trust," Randy continues, recalling that
gloomy session. "If only each would give a little ground. I told Larry
the objective data pointed to a less than exemplary performance.
Linda, I cautioned, could have done more to rectify the situation
without waiting for evaluation day. In the end, movement occurred,
and respect, often the first thing to go, was restored. Such mediation,
however, takes psychology, patience, and understanding—skills, now
that I am a human resource director here at the Crippled Children's
Society of Southern California, that I am forever cultivating."

Up from Personnel

Human resource professionals, 544,000 in 1999, are employed in
every industry. They recruit and interview employees and advise on
hiring decisions. In an effort to improve morale and productivity
and limit job turnover, they also help their firms effectively use
employees' skills, provide training opportunities to enhance those
skills, and boost employees' satisfaction with their jobs and working

conditions. Frequent contact with people and attention to detail is a job requirement.

It wasn't always so. "In the old days, before the early 1980s," Randy explains, "Personnel was a department in the basement. People working there were record keepers. They didn't make people decisions: hiring, firing, performance reviews. Instead, they processed the paper associated with those decisions by department heads in other areas."

But as the 1980s progressed, employee disputes exploded. Complaints regarding sexual harassment, racial and ethnic insensitivity, and workplace grievances in general mushroomed. Arbitration was in order. Enter the human relations professional.

"HR, as human resources is often called, emerged in an attempt to put a softer, more human touch on what we do," Randy says. "The human, as opposed to the strictly clerical, function grew."

Sandra Deming, regional director of the Marquis Group, a human resources consulting firm, agrees: "The workplace changed. Diversity increased the demands on everyone to work closely with different people. The human resource responsibility expanded. Today, we are coaches, counselors, and liability preventers."

"Compliance became an issue, too," adds Tod Lipka, executive director of the Professionals in Human Resources Association (PIHRA), an affiliate of the National Society for Human Resource Management. "When a company gets above a certain number, say ten, compliance issues kick in. The result? Increased demand for human resource expertise."

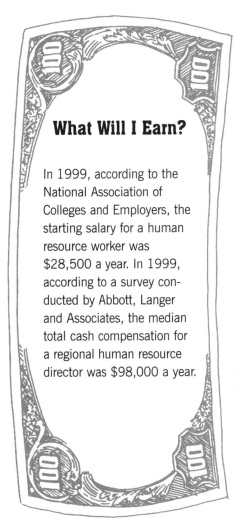

What Will I Earn?

In 1999, according to the National Association of Colleges and Employers, the starting salary for a human resource worker was $28,500 a year. In 1999, according to a survey conducted by Abbott, Langer and Associates, the median total cash compensation for a regional human resource director was $98,000 a year.

People Person—Not Quite

Randy didn't start out planning a career in human resources. "At sixteen I traveled to Washington to work as a congressional page," he says. "Eventually I graduated from American University with a major in political science. I then worked for Speaker of the House Tom Foley. But today, fifteen years later, I'm in HR. I've traded government politics for office politics."

His last comment pretty much sums up an HR person's environment. "It takes three things to succeed in this field," Randy continues, smiling, "patience, patience, patience. So much is stop and go, hurry up and wait. Because everything we do involves humans, it's not like working at a computer all day where if you press this key you'll get a predictable result. With human beings, you can say the same thing to three people and get three different interpretations.

"When people tell me they want to go into human resource management because they are people persons, a red flag goes up. It doesn't work that way. True, we get the joy and excitement of hiring someone, making a positive change in their lives. But we also experience the misery and drudgery of dealing with people who ultimately may be on the road to termination. In any organization you sometimes see the worst in people."

Firings! That's always got to be tough. "Yes, it is," responds Randy, "but California, like most states, is an 'at will employment state,' which means at my or your will we can end our working relationship—no notice required. In other words, it works both ways."

But is that actually done? "Well, it can be a problem," Randy says. "Many employers look at the monumental judgments jurists have made against others for wrongful termination, negligent hiring, and they get gunshy. Most take a more cautious approach.

"I tell our supervisors that they must come to us before they fire someone. Certain litmus tests must be passed. For example, stealing and dishonesty will not be tolerated, especially here. We want people to help the disadvantaged, not themselves."

Having to Let Them All Go

Gregory Sims, human resource director for International Medication Systems, knows something about employee termination—on a massive scale. In six months he administered the layoff of his company's entire work force: 400 people, including himself. "I've been there twice before, at other companies," he says. "It's no fun. I can deal with firing someone because they acted up, were disruptive. But when you're firing people for no cause of their own, that hurts.

"Everyone's aware of what's going on. Some had known for two years the plant would close. Still, when your name comes up, it has a real impact. If we had the time, we could have staggered the layoffs, we could have dealt with it better. But that wasn't to be. I prefer to give something to people that will add meaning, not take it away. Even though it wasn't me personally who let them go, I feel their pain."

When it was over, was Gregory fired, too? "Yes, I was," he says. "Actually, I'd been thinking of taking a few months off anyway. I needed downtime before I tackled the next human resource assignment."

Jobs for the Job Finders

Though any career has negative aspects, we needn't dwell on the downside. "A major advantage," Randy says, "is the recognition I receive. It is rewarding to know that the president or vice president routinely seeks my advice on various matters. The money is nice, but the sense of worth is key."

Speaking of money and opportunity, according to many human resource practitioners, prospects on both accounts have never been better. "A vice president of human resources in a large corporation can earn from $100,000 to $200,000; a human resource manager or director, $40,000 to $90,000; and an entry-level position pays $22,000 to $33,000," says Randy. But how's the competition?

INFORMATION

For More Information

Human Resource Management, UCLA Extension
(310) 825-2012

Professionals in Human Resources Association (PIHRA)
(213) 622-7472

"Jobs are going begging right now, particularly in Los Angeles. Organizations have seen the need and value of what we do—often the hard way. When they pay out big sums for worker's compensation, harassment, and so on, they discover they need someone to maintain those areas, keep a lid on things."

A Vast Field

Human resource management is a big field, encompassing areas of employment you may not have thought of. To get a better idea of just how broad it is, here is what Sandra's Marquis Group does:

For starters, the group provides:

- Recruiters—General and Technical
- Human Resource Generalists
- Human Resource Managers
- Compensation Analysts
- Employee Benefit Administrators
- Trainers—Program Development and Delivery
- Direct Sourcing and Internet Capabilities

Taking just one of these areas, compensation analysis, the group will design performance-based compensation programs that include:

- Base Pay Programs
- Variable Pay Programs
  - Incentive/Bonus Compensation
  - Competency/Knowledge Pay
  - Skill-Based Pay
  - Team Incentives
  - Gain-sharing
- Executive Compensation/Employee Ownership Plans
- Performance Evaluation and Management Systems
- Employee Recognition and Reward Programs
- Related Training and Communication Systems

If these areas of the working world interest you, consider human resource management.You'll wind up working in-house or for an outsourcing firm such as the Marquis Group. These firms, by the way, are booming.

According to a report in the April 4, 2000, issue of *MicroTimes*, in 1999 companies spent almost $14 billion on HR outsourcing. That number is expected to hit $37.7 billion in 2003. More than 70 percent of all businesses surveyed said they either outsourced HR now or are planning to do so. Of the types of services outsourced, benefits administration make up 20 percent; payroll services, 14.6 percent; education and training, 6.9 percent; and recruiting and staffing, 6 percent. "Soon," the report went on, "companies will be able to rent services like health and welfare benefits enrollments."

Routes to HR

One route into human resources is through a certification program. The University of California at Los Angeles (UCLA) offers a well-respected Professional Designation in Human Resource Management through adult extension classes. In the 10-course sequence, you'll cover employment, employee relations, training and development, compensation, benefits, and human resource information systems, among other subjects. The program provides a current and comprehensive grounding in the major areas of a personnel generalist.

Kansas State University offers a 30-hour distance learning program for students seeking a master's degree in industrial psychology.

Furthermore, PIHRA (see below) provides training for its membership. "You can join our organization as a student member," Catherine Haskett Hany, PIHRA marketing manager, says. "We have an extensive program for those coming from different backgrounds."

For example, here are a few seminar titles from the latest PIHRA conference guide:

- Awareness, Choice, and Change!
- Getting More "Yes!"
- Pay for Results

What to Read

Delivering Results: A New Mandate for Human Resource Professionals
by David Ulrich.
Harvard Business School Publications, 1998.

Human Resource Development: The New Trainer's Guide
by Les Donaldson
and Edward Scannell.
Addison Wesley Longman, 1987.

- Using Recognition to Motivate Employees
- Healthcare Access in the New Millennium
- Empowering Employees

Certification programs like those offered by UCLA Extension and the seminars provided by PIHRA are terrific. In the end, the bottom line is a relevant education in human resource management.

With all these great opportunities in human resource management, did Randy feel good about abandoning government for the corporate world? "When I first came here, to a nonprofit, charitable organization," he says, "I wanted to move away from a profit-minded, profit-driven environment, where people are perhaps a little too competitive and less sensitive to each other. Though I soon discovered people are much the same everywhere, with positive and negative motivation—hearts aren't always ahead of egos—to a large degree I found what I was looking for here. At the Crippled Children's Society of Southern California we have wonderful, dedicated people. Though I had aspirations for all sorts of things when growing up, this is the profession I fell into. Yes, I'd do it again, in a minute."

Cool Web Sites to Visit

HR Job Opportunities
www.hrplaza.com/
hrcareercenter/hrjobs.html

Human Resource Management Basics
www.members.aol.com/
hrmbasics/

Human Resources Development Network
www.mcb.co.uk/htl

INDEPENDENT COLLEGE COUNSELOR

In 1990 one percent of entering first-year students used independent counselors in planning their college path. By 1999, that number had climbed to 12 percent.

Brandon, a senior at Liberty High School in Colorado Springs, desperately wanted to attend Colorado State University, the state's flagship public institution of higher education. Problem was, that for the past two years he had been making some rather poor choices. With lousy study habits, inappropriate classes, lack of commitment, and a rebellious nature, Brandon found himself entering the 12th grade with a 2.2 grade-point average. No way was the lanky teenager going directly on to CSU with a GPA like that.

Yet, Brandon was lucky, he had an ally on the Liberty High campus, someone who believed in him, sensed a growing maturity, and was disinclined to dwell on his past mistakes. But most of all, Margo McCoy Howe, the school's college counselor, honored as Secondary School Counselor of the Year by the Colorado Counseling Association, had an idea.

"I brought in an admissions officer from the university and the three of us sat down for a long, hard talk," she says. "The university representative sensed a readiness in Brandon to grow up and accept responsibility for where he found himself. He offered Brandon a great opportunity."

Since the senior had passed all his classes and was on track to graduate, the trio put together a plan that would place Brandon at Pike's Peak Community College, full-time, for the last semester of his senior year. If Brandon took the right courses and got good grades, he would earn the right to enter CSU on time in the fall. "Today," says Margo, "Brandon is at the university, majoring in business, and doing just great."

Personal Guidance

Unfortunately, few high school students are blessed with counseling services such as those offered by Liberty High.

"Most high school counselors are severely overextended," says Lila Beavans, of Academic Directions, an independent counseling service in Villa Park, California. "They are dedicated, yet overworked, being required to spend time on scheduling, disciplinary problems—you name it. Often they have little time for college counseling."

Mark Sklarow, executive director of the Independent Educational Consultants Association (IECA), agrees. "Public high schools are reducing counseling services across the board, particularly college counseling. Some feel that if they set up a computer in the career center, they won't need a counselor."

Hence, a growing desire for independent counselors, or educational consultants, who will, for a fee, counsel students and their families in selecting an appropriate post-secondary educational institution.

Specifically, independent counselors such as Lila offer professional consultation, admission strategies, assessment of strengths, direction in filling out applications, guidance in writing essays,

exploration of college options, advice for handling interviews, showcasing of abilities, tips for recommendations, and personal follow-through. "What we're providing is time, attention to detail, and individuality," she says. "Students should receive personal guidance in matching their unique strengths to a college's specific requirements."

Evidently many parents and students believe so, too—the demand for independent counselors, who generally charge from $200 to $2,000, or more, is exploding.

"Social changes are driving the increase," advises Mark. "With Mom and Dad working, families have more expendable income, yet time is at a premium. Bringing in an independent counselor fits with what we're seeing in general—people hiring service workers to make their lives a little easier."

According to IECA data, in 1990, 1 percent of entering first-year students used independent counselors to plan their college path. By

1999, the number had climbed to 12 percent. "We expect one percent growth each year for at least the next five years," says Mark.

Getting to Know You

While Steve Armamino, an independent counselor in Tarzana, California, provides a full range of services for his clients, he usually starts them off with curriculum planning and guidance, interest exploration, and assessment testing. "It's reality-check time, too," he explains. "With over six hundred college majors to choose from, there's plenty for a student to explore."

Harriet Gershman, of Academic Counseling Services, Inc., in Evanston, Illinois, first meets with the family as a whole, encouraging parents to talk about the child, and his or her strengths and weaknesses. "Often, for the student, it is the first time he's ever heard his parents talk about him," she says.

"In the initial meeting we meet with the family and get to know the student," says Diane Geller, of DeFlice & Geller, Inc., educational consultants, in Los Angeles. "We ask questions, review transcripts, examine extracurricular activities, do personality assessment, and begin to make suggestions about options. Our job is to help families sort out appropriate college choices."

Aqueela Jeffer, of San Marino, California, works primarily with students from Asia—India, Pakistan, Saudi Arabia, or Singapore—who wish to come to a university in the United States. She also works with those already here on the secondary level. "It's often a process of bringing everyone involved down to earth," she says. "I cannot get a kid into Harvard. The student must do it. I provide encouragement and guidance, but, essentially the GPA, school records, test scores, extra-curricular activities, and essays are the determining factors."

How Much Help?

Guidance, encouragement, information, assessment, tips, planning— all to the good, most would agree. But is there such a thing as too

What Will I Earn?

Most independent counselors charge flat fees for their services. If fees average $500 per student, per year, and you counsel 100 students annually, you'll earn $50,000.

INFORMATION

For More Information

Certificated Program in College
Counseling, UCLA Extension
(818) 784-7006

Higher Education Consultants
Association (HECA)
*www.collegehelp.org/join/
index.cfm*

Independent Educational
Consultants Association (IECA)
(703) 591-4850
www.educationalconsulting.org

much help? Can a counselor cross the line—wind up doing all the work for a client?

"Independent counselors should offer help and advice only," says Mike McDonnell, of UCLA-GSE&IS, on the College Choice Web site. "They should not write essays for you or fill out your college applications."

Ah, yes, that essay . . . required by more and more colleges, public and private, elite and utilitarian, never has 500 words meant so much. "Its purpose," says Lila, "is to tell the college what you will bring to the institution and what you expect to get from it. It lets the admissions officer know the who, what, when, where, and why about you, the student."

Should one get help in writing the essay? Lila offers a telling incident:

"A couple of years ago a conference at the University of California was held for high school counselors, and a counselor asked, 'When a student comes to us and asks for help on his essay, what should we tell him?' The large auditorium, filled with school counselors, suddenly became utterly silent. All counselors are constantly fearful that if they tell students to get help with their essay, they will have someone else write it for them. There was a collective sigh as UCLA's director of admissions answered, 'At UCLA we say if a student isn't smart enough to get help when he needs it, he's not smart enough for UCLA.'"

Maybe the essay issue is overblown. After all, you can get sample essays galore on the Internet. Aqueela points out, "Colleges know if you have written it. They don't just ask for one essay. There is always a mini-essay on the application itself to be compared, in terms of style and content, with the more involved essay to come. Furthermore, students, being quite independent, write what they want anyway, even if it means being their own worst enemy."

Dealing with Parents

Though technically the client is the high school student, the whole family gets involved in the wearisome selection process,

particularly the parents paying the bill. Often they are more stressed than the student.

"Parents are the anguished ones," says Mark. "Kids just want to get on with it. I had a parent call the other day in a panic: 'What color ink do I use to sign my name on the application form, black or blue?'"

"I spend lots of time talking to parents, in person and on the phone," says Lila. "They need solace and encouragement just as much as their kid does."

"I love dealing with parents, the whole family," says Steve. "Sure, some cases go smoothly, others less so. I get in the middle, help the family dynamic play itself out. Everyone's interested in the same thing, the best choice for the kid."

"Some parents, however, can be difficult," confesses Aqueela. "Many I deal with have high expectations for their son or daughter. Some will say it outright: 'Get my kid into MIT, period.' It doesn't work that way. I have to calm them down."

What to Read

Counselor Preparation 1999-2001: Programs, Faculty, Trends by Joseph W. Hollis and Thomas A. Dodson. Accelerated Development, 1999.

Path to Counseling

So, where do independent counselors come from, what is their background?

"Our data shows that a third were college admissions representatives; they've come over from the other side," says Mark. "Another third have high school counseling experience. And the last third were English teachers, speech therapists, nurses—those from the helping professions."

"Regardless of background, you must like and understand kids, be honest with everyone, and be able to stand up and voice an opinion without caving in to families that are often very powerful," advises Harriet.

"You must also have patience on the business end," says Mark. "The phone isn't going to ring that often the first year or two. Our studies indicate it takes a good three years before you can make a living at this."

Diane agrees, and adds: "The clients don't just magically appear. Much of it is word-of-mouth. You have to be willing to go out and make it happen."

"It's a challenge to break in," says Steve. "Independent counseling is a game of connections and relationships. It's not something a Mom can do. Those who went through the process with their kids got a great start, but to be effective and successful, you must take it many layers deeper. Even when starting out, independent counselors must have all the resources to do the job they know has to be done."

Making a Difference

Fortunately, organizations, associations, and continuing education programs abound to help individuals enter the profession and grow professionally once they're in.

"The IECA is the national association representing counselors who work in private practice," says Mark. "The National Association for College Admission Counseling [NACAC], a fine organization, is primarily for those in the public schools."

Being admitted to IECA is difficult; requirements are stringent. "You must have been doing admissions work for at least three years, including one year as an independent," advises Mark. "In addition, you will have had to visit a hundred campuses and do assessments. And you must have worked with at least seventy-five client families." Even with these requirements, or perhaps because of them, the IECA receives 100 to 120 membership inquiries a month.

Pepper McCullough is an active member and champion of another association devoted to the needs of independent counselors, the Higher Education Consultants Association (HECA). "While we are mostly in the West, we are open to all," she says. "It's a great, growing organization, particularly for those transitioning from the school counseling profession to the private sector."

Frank Azzariti is the program representative for the Certificated Program in College Counseling run by UCLA Extension. "The six-course program covers everything from 'Counseling the College-Bound Student' to a 'Practicum in College Counseling,'" he says. "Best of all, you don't have to live in Los Angeles to take the courses—they're all taught online."

In the end, whether you work in the private sector, as an independent counselor, or as a counselor in a high school, it comes down to making a difference in kids' lives.

"Many students come to me feeling lost, put down by the school system," says Harriet. "They think they won't be able to go to college. But you work with them, and you find a way. Then to be with them on the day they receive an acceptance or two—well, there's nothing like it. Their whole personality changes; they now have a world to conquer."

Aqueela remembers a poignant example illustrating lack of faith in a great potential: "A Hispanic girl from Alhambra High School came to see me. I agreed to help her pro bono, something a lot of us in the profession do. No one in her family had ever attended college, yet she was clearly a superstar. The best advice she had received was to head straight to a nearby state college. Nothing wrong with that. Yet I felt she could do better. I worked with her one-on-one for weeks on end. She was a jewel. Last fall she entered Stanford University with a full scholarship. A *perfect* match."

Cool Web Sites to Visit

National Association for College Admission Counseling
www.nacac.com/index.html

Hot Concepts!

Interning

Interning is hot. More than one-third of all students intern before graduating. In fact, in many fields, particularly art and entertainment, it is all but mandatory. Interns work for nothing, but in return they're getting experience that can get them jobs later on.

For employers, interns represent a three-fold benefit:

- First, they may become future employees.
- Second, interns can mean free labor, a plus for many companies, particularly nonprofit agencies.
- Third, many employers view interns as energy boosters.

"They bring new ideas, heightened energy, real excitement," says Salina Yoon, art director at Intervisual Books, Inc. "Interns pump up the volume by charging everyone up."

Of course, interning can and should be as valuable for the intern as it is for the employer. Above all, an internship should allow you to see all aspects of the work environment: the good, the bad, and the boring.

As a student intern, be sure you are doing meaningful work. You must avoid getting stuck in narrowly defined and repetitive tasks. Your employer should not view you as free labor to be exploited. Your immediate supervisor should take an active interest in your learning on the job.

If these components are met, an internship program can add to your education and training in almost any field. It's worth looking into!

INTERIOR DESIGNER

Demand for interior designers has never been better. Small, medium, and large firms are so desperate for competent staff that they are raiding each other for talented designers.

Nicki Jackson rendezvoused with the client, her first, on a lonely stretch of Pacific Coast Highway five miles north of Malibu. After entering a roadside gate, the two drove up rugged, picturesque hills, the blue-green ocean shimmering below. About a half-mile in, the road ended. Continuing on foot, the pair cut through underbrush and over clear-water streams. "What was I getting into?" Nicki asked rhetorically. "Was my contact, the one now leading me to a mountaintop retreat, the member of some bizarre cult looking for its latest sacrificial lamb?"

Actually, Nicki needn't have worried. As she soon discovered, the Santa Monica Mountain Conservancy Foundation, then in its infancy, was no hideaway for the occult. On the contrary, the dwelling, being used as a temporary office, had a soft, seductive charm. "My job, as it turned out," says the exuberant proprietor of Nicki J. Interiors, "was to transform the structure's interior into a captivating visitors bureau. Yes, my first assignment as an interior designer, twelve years ago, meant refurbish a humble, Mexican land-grant adobe." Nicki has been into interiors ever since.

An Inside Job

Interior designers, approximately 55,000 of them nationwide, go into an empty room and figure out how to fill the space. In doing so, they analyze a client's needs, goals, and safety requirements; develop design concepts that are appropriate, functional, and pleasing to the eye; select materials, finishes, furnishings, fixtures, and equipment; prepare working drawings and specifications for non-load-bearing interior construction; and administer bids and contract documents as the client's agent. Interior designers specialize in areas such as homes, offices, shopping malls, hospitals, hotels, restaurants, childcare centers, museums, theaters, schools, industrial facilities, and even movie and theatrical sets. Their purpose is not only to make interiors look better—the status-based approach—but to make them more functional—the task-based approach.

Mayer Rus, editor-in-chief of *Interior Design*, the leading practitioner-oriented magazine in the field, says, "Demand for interior designers has never been better. All firms, small, medium, and large, are desperate for competent staff. Poaching is even going on," he says, "design firms raid each other."

Desi Kovacs, interior design department chair at Learning Tree University (LTU) in Chatsworth, California, agrees: "Consumer interest in their living environments is soaring. People want to create environments that say something about themselves, how they want to live and work."

In addition to doing interior design, practitioners work as furniture designers, model home consultants, manufacturer's representatives, showroom managers, and color consultants.

Many interior designers find employment in design firms such as Hirsch Bedner Associates, Santa Monica; Barry Design Associates, Los Angeles; and Design Development, Tarzana, to name just three in California. Such firms, according to *Interior Design* magazine, specialize in offices, 51 percent; hotels and restaurants, 11 percent; medical facilities, 8 percent; and residential, 4 percent. While the residential category represents only a tiny percentage of the design firm business, home interior work is what the majority of single-proprietor interior designers do. According to Jerry Harke, marketing manager for the American Society of Interior Designers (ASID), "More than 70 percent of our twenty thousand professional designers own or manage their design firms."

Nicki owns her own design firm. "I was pushing forty and needed a career to fall back on," she explains. "I enrolled at LTU and the rest is history, so to speak."

How did she get so successful? "If there is a key to success in the business," Nicki says, "it's in the interview process. I'm a

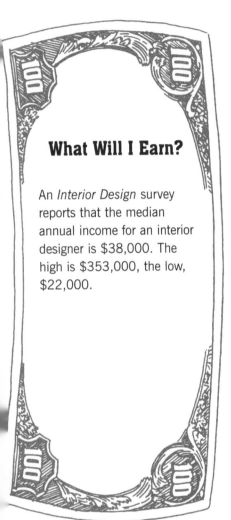

What Will I Earn?

An *Interior Design* survey reports that the median annual income for an interior designer is $38,000. The high is $353,000, the low, $22,000.

probing person, able to find out who the client is and what they want. It's being a good listener."

Desi agrees. "Interior design is a people business. It's intensely personal. You are bringing to your clients some level of ability to tell them how to live their lives. You must help them create their vision, not yours."

"Designer-client relations, that's what it's all about," Nicki interjects. "Are you someone the client can trust, someone they want in their house? After all, the client often gives you a key to their home; you're in there when they're not. You're working with their money."

However, design skill and personality will carry you only so far. "Business skills are also vital," Jerry emphasizes. "Our membership's number one request is, 'Help us with marketing, selling ourselves, and running our own business.'"

Interestingly, emphasis on business goes beyond operating your own. "Firms surviving, even flourishing, in the last recession," Mayer explains, "became business partners with their clients rather than just service providers. Everyone in the organization needs a business sense."

The Educated Designer

Certificate, two-year, and four-year programs in design abound. Be sure you select an accredited program, one recognized by the Foundation for Interior Design Education Research (FIDER) or the National Association of Schools of Art and Design (NASAD), two respected certifying bodies. According to Kayel Dunn, FIDER's executive director, "The professional programs we accredit are at three-, four-, and five-year schools. At two-year schools we accredit design assistant programs."

INFORMATION

For More Information

The American Society of Interior
Designers (ASID)
608 Massachusetts Avenue N.W.
Washington, DC 20002
(202) 546-3480
www.wp.com/asid

Foundation for Interior Design
Education Research (FIDER)
60 Monroe Center N.W., Ste. 300
Grand Rapids, MI 49503-2920
(616) 458-0400
www.fider.org

The International Interior Design
Association (IIDA)
341 Merchandise Mart
Chicago, IL 60654
(312) 467-1950
www.iida.com

The National Council for Interior
Design Qualification (NCIDQ)
1200 18th Street, N.W.,
Suite 1001
Washington, DC 20036-2506
(202) 721-0220
www.ncidq.org

One such program accredited by FIDER is the UCLA Extension Professional Designation in Interior Design, a 38-course sequence that instills equal parts practical theory and creative training. According to the catalog, "Traditional skills and artistry are taught alongside new technologies and an awareness of emerging socioeconomic and environmental issues. Curriculum areas include history, theory, and culture; design communications, including drawing, drafting, and CAD; space planning, construction details, and lighting; and professional practices, research, and career preparation."

This course is indicative of the rigor required to succeed as an interior design student. No matter where you train, the bottom line is simple, you'll study traditional design, computer-aided-design (CAD), business, and, at four-year institutions, the liberal arts.

CAD is critical. "Being able to design on a computer is essential today," says Mayer. "Not as an alternative to traditional design methods, but as a necessary complement. This is true in residential as well as commercial design."

And don't be too quick to dismiss those general education courses. "A need exists for interior designers with broad background plus specific knowledge," Kayel says. "Remember, interior designers work with an educated customer, they relate to the client on many levels."

Certification as a Professional

Then there's certification. Many state and national organizations provide certification in the interior design field. The National Council for Interior Design Qualification (NCIDQ) is one such association. You don't need to be certified by NCIDQ, or any other organization for that matter, to practice as an interior designer. Nevertheless, after passing the NCIDQ exam and meeting specific experience qualifications, you may call yourself a certified interior designer (CID), a big plus.

The International Interior Design Association (IIDA) is another association offering certification and training. Defining a professional interior designer as one who is "qualified by education, experience,

and examination to enhance the function and quality of interior spaces," they are committed to providing education to their members. Their continuing education options are instructive. With IIDA, CEU courses are available in many venues and formats. Some options include:

- Courses sponsored by IIDA chapters and forums at the local level
- Home-study courses available to the IIDA Education Department
- Travel/study tours
- Courses available via CD-ROM and the Internet
- Courses approved by affiliated organizations—ASID, IDC, IDEC, IFMA, NKBA
- Courses taught by professional consultants.
- Courses at trade shows, in industry publications, and in *Perspective* magazine

In the home study department, a plethora of courses are offered:

- Interior Design and the Law
- Interior Design and Technology
- Developments in Facilities Management
- Developments in Residential Interior Design
- Developments in Retail Interior Design
- Interior Design and Practice Management
- Developments in Hospitality Interior Design

Taking the last course as an example, it includes, "Articles on opportunities for the hospitality industry resulting from the NAFTA agreement; implications of the growing trend of 'working on the road'; aspects of cruise ship interior design; how to achieve customer satisfaction in guestroom lighting; and traditional marketing methods applied to hospitality interior design."

Clearly, today's interior designer has come a long way from the interior decorator of old.

What to Read

Design and Decorate Kitchens
by Lesley Taylor.
Adams Media Corporation, 1998.

Design and Decorate Living Rooms
by Lesley Taylor.
Adams Media Corporation, 1998.

How to Prosper as an Interior Designer: A Business and Legal Guide
by Robert L. Aldeman.
John Wiley & Sons, 1997.

The Ultimate Interior Designer
by Ruth Pretty.
Sterling Publishing Company, 1998.

Up from Decorator

"The public thinks we do nothing but pick colors and fluff pillows," Doug Stead, executive vice president of the California Council of Interior Design Certification, told the *Los Angeles Times* in early 2000. "They don't understand that when they walk into a restaurant or hotel, it has been designed by an interior designer. It's not only comfortable, but it's a safe environment."

Today, interior designers in California and in many other parts of the country are attempting to raise the standards and credibility of their profession by seeking state-authorized registration or licensing. Architects, for the most part, are opposed to their efforts, believing that interior designers lack the training for such status and are incapable of enforcing professional standards.

This dispute, which promises to get nasty—since it involves turf battles, economic interests, and maybe even gender issues—is unfortunate. However, it does serve to illustrate the profession's need to rise above the age-old "decorator" image. "We are not trying to do architecture," says interior designer Rosalyn Cama. "We are just trying to do what we have been trained to do."

With the increase in more complex regulations—from the Americans With Disabilities Act to local fire codes—interior designers argue that higher standards are more important than ever. Those standards can only be clarified through some form of registration or state licensing, they say. So far, interior designers are registered in 20 states. In Nevada, only licensed individuals are allowed to practice interior design. The fight continues.

For now, however, such battles are not on Nicki's mind. Speaking of her profession in general, she concludes: "The right training and education are important. Knowing how to run a business is essential. But in the end, it's about ability. Do you have a flair, even love, for interior design? You must make clients feel your passion—and then absorb it."

Cool Web Sites to Visit

Design Times magazine
www.tiac.net/users/bdr/destime/destimetop.html

International Interior Design Association
www.iida.com/

National Council for Interior Design Qualification
www.ncidq.org

INTERPRETER/TRANSLATOR

Law and medicine aren't the only areas where interpreters and translators are needed. The film and TV industries, with their need for captions, subtitles, dubbing, and simultaneous interpretation of news are wide open to those with the right skills.

W as she guilty of murder or involuntary manslaughter, or innocent by self-defense? It depends on your interpretation. Or, if not yours, certainly that of a professional, court-certified interpreter.

Here are the facts:

A Cuban waitress in a bar meets a Mexican drug dealer and moves in with him. After a year of beatings and fights, she goes into her bathroom, retrieves a sawed-off 12-gauge shotgun, and shoots him. The man dies on the spot.

The women is arrested and interrogated by a police officer. The interrogation, conducted in Spanish, is taped. Key passages, however, are in dispute. As a result, the prosecution, which is seeking a second-degree murder verdict, brings in two court-certified interpreters. The defense, which is hoping for involuntary manslaughter, or better, self-defense, has its own interpreter. Even though the interpreters are well trained, highly educated, and certified, differences exist in their interpretation of important passages. What is meant by a given word or phrase can determine whether the defendant spends her productive years in prison or resumes her waitressing.

Enter for the defense, Dr. Alexander Rainof, Ph.D., head of the Translation and Interpretation Certificate Program at UCLA/UNEX and, for 11 years, the official translator for all election materials into Spanish for the city of Los Angeles. "I listened to one key passage on the tape one hundred and forty times," he says. "I played it at different speeds, on different machines, and in the end did a complete dialectal analysis of the Cuban dialect spoken by the defendant. It came down to this question: 'Was the gun moving forward or backward when the trigger was pulled?' The answer to that in turn rested with the Spanish word for finger, *dedo*."

In the end, the jury sided with Alex's interpretation of *dedo*. The verdict? Involuntary manslaughter. The defendant walked. Had it gone the other way, the woman could have faced 15 years of kitchen duty in prison.

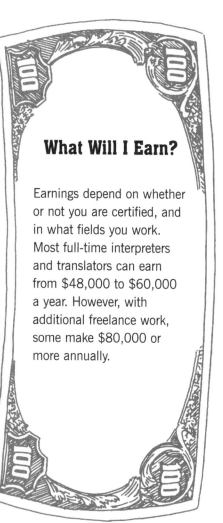

What Will I Earn?

Earnings depend on whether or not you are certified, and in what fields you work. Most full-time interpreters and translators can earn from $48,000 to $60,000 a year. However, with additional freelance work, some make $80,000 or more annually.

Speaking in Tongues

The professional interpreter or translator, "attempts," according to George Rimalower, CEO of Interpreting Services International, "to bridge the oral and written language barriers. The former deals with the spoken word, the latter with the written word." Though the difference is perhaps obvious, misinterpretation exists as to the level of translation. "Some think translation is accurate and precise, whereas with interpretation you can say whatever you want," says Analia Sarno Riggle, the simulcast interpreter for Los Angeles television station KTLA. "Not true. In both cases, you're taking concepts and ideas from one language to another, in the best possible way."

Five types of translation/interpretation are recognized:

1. *Sight translation.* In this form, you look at text in one language and, according to Alex, "just start translating." It has to be done smoothly, however. "An excellent sight translation is one in which you do not know the person is translating or reading the original," he says.
2. *Written translation.* In this style, the quality has to be higher. "You sit at a desk with glossaries and dictionaries," Analia explains. "You have time."
3. *Consecutive interpretation.* "This is the interpretation of an utterance as it has been completed." Alex says. In other words, you wait for a person to stop speaking, then you interpret. "At state level exams, you must be able to handle sentences ranging from thirty-five to forty words. With the federal exam, it's sixty-five to seventy words."

4. *Simultaneous interpretation.* The interpretation of an utterance while in progress is demanding. You must speak as the speaker speaks. It involves, according to Alex, five steps: (1) listening; (2) decoding; (3) encoding; (4) uttering; and (5) storing. "You listen, understand, transpose into the target language, you speak, and you store it," he explains. Hey! No one said this was easy.

5. *Summary interpretation.* This type is often done at conferences. "When speaking is rapid, you're allowed to summarize," Alex explains. "You don't interpret every word; you're free to edit as long as the meaning of the utterance is preserved."

Just Say the Word

Michael Buss, staff writer for *Career Watch*, reports that "with the growing 'global village' born by the growth of computers and, more specifically, the Internet, there has been an upswing in the demand for translators and interpreters." Indeed, to Muriel M. Jerome-O'Keeffe, president of the American Translators Association (ATA), "It has gone from a cottage industry to big business." How big? According to the market research firm Allied Business Intelligence, Inc., in Oyster Bay, New York, the worldwide market for translation services hit $10.4 billion in early 1999 and will reach $17.2 billion by 2003.

Just who are these interpreters and translators? "Of ATA's seven thousand members, 70 percent are independent contractors, split almost evenly between full- and part-time," Walter Bacak Jr., CEO of the 40-year old organization, explains. "The most common native languages of ATA members are English and Spanish, followed by German, French, and Russian. Furthermore, our members have expertise in one hundred and forty specialties, from art to zoology. Every business or technical field requires interpretation and translation."

While court interpretation is well known, and medical translation is a fast-growing field, these aren't the only areas where interpretation and translation are required. The film and TV industries, with their need for captions, subtitles, dubbing, and simultaneous

INFORMATION

For More Information

American Translators Association (ATA)
1800 Diagonal Road, Ste. 220
Alexandria, VA 22314-2840
(703) 683-6100
www.atancet.org

Legal Interpretation and Translation Program,
UCLA/UNEX
(310) 825-9082

Dr. Alex Rainof, California State University, Long Beach
(562) 985-4310
arainof@ucla.edu

interpretation of news, represent a strong opportunity for those with interpreting and translating skills. State agencies, such as the Department of Social Services, Department of Motor Vehicles, Housing Authority, and Agricultural Labor Relations Board, are another source for jobs. And there are museums, think tanks, schools, and industry. As Carlos Cerecedo, president of the California Court Interpreters Association (CCIA), says, "America Online has just signed a deal with Latin America. Think of what that means for interpreters and translators."

KTLA Español

For nontraditional (as opposed to law and medicine) interpretation, we need look no further than Analia's career. Although she has done both court and medical interpretation, and as a freelancer, still does it on occasion, Analia has for the past 10 years been the Spanish voice of KTLA television news, a full-time job. "Through the use of their SAP [Second Audio Program] sets, my Spanish-speaking audience hears only my voice when newscasters Hal Fishman, Terry Anzur, or Walter Richards speak," she declares. "This is also true for reporters in the field, weather, sports—the whole thing.

"I have developed a style, an identity. This is different than being in court. In court, you impersonate the speaker. On television I do not."

Things can get tricky in the TV news environment, however. "If news reporter Stan Chambers is out there live at a fire, and he says 'Right behind me you can see a building burning,' I obviously can't say that," Analia explains. "Instead, I say, 'Stan Chambers tells us that right behind him . . .'"

Analia is under the same legal and ethical broadcast restrictions as newscasters, and she is a member of the American Federation of Radio and Television Actors. As such, she assumes full

responsibility for what she says. "If I wish to elaborate on a point, add a little detail to a story, that's OK. If I say the wrong thing, however, or make an inappropriate statement, I can be called to account."

Bilingual Is Not Enough

Ask any interpreter/translator what misperceptions they labor under and chances are all will agree with Analia when she says, "Many people think that knowledge of two languages is enough, that simply knowing how to speak English and Spanish, for example, automatically makes you an interpreter or translator. Bilingual is not enough. It is the foundation, the raw material. But to be bilingual is not to be an interpreter or translator."

Alex puts it this way: "It's like saying because you have two hands you're a concert pianist. It is not having two hands, it's what you do with them, how you train them."

Furthermore, to be an interpreter is not necessarily to be a translator, and vice versa. "Two different mentalities are operative," Alex says. "Often the translator is a perfectionist, picky, introverted. He or she works alone, surrounded with dictionaries and glossaries. An interpreter, on the other hand, is more outgoing, highly gregarious."

"Interpreters must think quickly on their feet," adds Walter. "They are people people."

"Translators have an area of expertise: medicine, insurance, computers, et cetera," says George. "For interpreters, that's not necessarily the case."

Referring to the field in general, Elisabeth Brooks, director of the Legal Interpretation and Translation program at UCLA/UNEX, offers this insight: "Some are better in one than the other. Something goes on in the brain that makes this possible. For example, in simultaneous interpretation, interpreters go into an almost trancelike state. They go on automatic pilot. Some can do that, other can't."

What to Read

Basic Concepts and Models for Interpreting and Translator Training
by Daniel Gile.
Benjamins Translation Library, 2000.

Cool Web Sites to Visit

Aquarius Directory of Translators and Interpreters
www.aquarius.net

NAJIT
www.najit.org/

Spoken Language Interpreter & Translator Area
*www.pieinc.com/
spoken_language_interpreter.htm*

Certified or Registered?

If you plan to do court interpretation in, say, California, to cite one state as an example, you will with minor exceptions need to be certified or registered. The two are not the same.

Certified court interpreters, according to the Judicial Council of California, are those who have passed exams administered for the following designated (tested) languages: Arabic, Cantonese, Japanese, Korean, Portuguese, Spanish, Tagalog, and Vietnamese. Registered interpreters include those interpreters for all other nondesignated (nontested) foreign languages. To become a registered interpreter, you take an exam designed to test your ability to comprehend and speak the English language correctly, and display a knowledge of the Judicial Council Standards for Court Interpreters. The exam does not assess the applicant's ability to perform the three modes of interpretation nor does it measure the applicant's foreign language fluency.

Thus, to quote the Judicial Council, "Because the Registered Interpreter exam is significantly different from the certification exam, it is important to remind applicants and interested parties that Registered Interpreters cannot use the title Certified Interpreter or Certified Court Interpreter."

Are there jobs to be had? "If you are state-certified, you will work, full-time," George declares. "And if you possess the more demanding federal certification, allowing you to work in federal court, you won't have time to do anything else."

Where to get the training, then? In Southern California, the Legal Interpretation and Translation program at UCLA/UNEX, mentioned earlier, is a good place to investigate. Of course, there are numerous such programs across the country, some offering programs online.

Furthermore, Alex adds, "As an assistant professor at California State University, Long Beach, I have been working to establish a bachelor of arts degree program in interpretation and translation." Hardly able to contain his excitement, he elaborates, "We'll be able to send people out educated and trained for good jobs, well-paying careers. I am talking about $75,000 to $80,000 a year. But money is only part of the story. In what other profession can you meet such eclectic colleagues and do good at the same time?"

LITERARY AGENT

It's not all being surrounded by great literature. You'll have to cull through piles of query letters, proposals, and manuscripts to find that "diamond in the rough." But who knows, you may just discover the next Frank McCourt!

Having had thirteen literary agents reject her manuscript, first-time novelist Lalita Tademy began to despair. "I was passionate about mapping my genealogy back five generations to a Creole slave woman," the Sun Microsystems vice president declares. "I needed a literary agent who shared my passion and enthusiasm, and could resonate with the work on a commercial as well as a personal level."

With agent number fourteen, Jillian W. Manus, of the Manus & Associates Literary Agency, in Palo Alto, California, Lalita could rejoice. Jillian, a savvy, well-connected industry veteran, poring over the 700-page tome on a Memorial Day weekend, phoned a nail-biting Lalita to announce: "I love it, I want it, let's meet and talk."

The rest, as they say, is history. Already being hailed as the "women's *Roots* for the new millennium," the now 480-page novel, titled *Cane River,* is due out from Warner Books in the spring of 2001. A TV movie is being discussed, Oprah's producer loves it, and the work will be translated into French and Italian. Best of all, thanks to Jillian's business acumen, ability to work closely with the author, and extensive pre-presentation editing, the publisher paid a cool half-million dollars as an advance for the property.

Diamond in the Rough

Literary agents interested in fiction and nonfiction manuscripts are also known as "authors' representatives," which is an apt description. A writer or wannabe writer finds an agent to represent his or her interests to the publishing industry. According to Lori Perkins, founding partner in New York literary agency Lori Perkins and author of *The Insider's Guide to Finding and Keeping an Agent*, these representatives will do the following for a writer:

- Know which editor to send the writer's work to
- Help the writer choose the right publisher/editor
- Negotiate the terms of a contract
- Represent foreign and subsidiary rights to a book
- Make sure the publisher keeps the writer informed as to the book's progress before and after publication
- Prepare future projects for submission and negotiate terms
- Keep on top of financial and legal matters related to a book after publication
- Give the writer career guidance, for both the long and short term

Whether one works for a literary agency or for himself or herself, being an agent in today's publishing environment of mergers, acquisitions, layoffs, mega-book stores and mega-authors is grueling. This is especially so when many writers think their agent is, as Lori facetiously puts it, "their editor, business manager, lawyer, publicist, banker, therapist, groupie, mother, new best friend, and fairy godmother."

Some agents do indeed take on such roles. But that is after they have a client, which doesn't happen until the agent, or the agent's readers and assistants, cull through piles of query letters, proposals, and manuscripts to find that "diamond in the rough."

"I am looking at query letters a foot high," says Julie Castiglia of the Julie Castiglia Literary Agency in Del Mar, California. "I see synopses and chapter outlines twice that high in addition to a shelf of requested manuscripts. If an agent is well known, she's inundated. Yet, I'm always afraid if I don't go through it all, I'll miss that jewel waiting to be discovered."

For all their work, acting for the most part as filters for publishers, what are agents compensated? "Not a penny," says Julie, "until we sell something. Then it's usually 15 percent."

Words for Sale

With 10-plus years in book publishing in New York and Beverly Hills, from assistant editor to editor-in-chief, Jane Jordan Browne was ready to strike out on her own, work for herself. But to do what? "I didn't particularly like agents," she confides, "so when a friend asked me to sell her book, I was reluctant to take on that role. But that's how I got started, with a typewriter on my dining room table, looking to sell one book.

"I thought it would be a piece of cake. As an editor I had been the one buying books; now I had to sell them. It took ten months into my little business to make my first sale. I was getting a dose of what I'd been handing out—rejection. I had to have my first success before I could be seen as someone with something to sell." Jane is now the owner of Multimedia Product Development, Inc., in Chicago.

An editor for 15 years and a writer herself, Julie got her start responding to an ad for a literary agent assistant. "Actually, the position was taken," she says, "but the agent gave me a manuscript to read anyway. I knew I could sell the book, a historical romance written by a twenty-six-year-old, and I did. From a two-hour-a-day job I went on to selling books like crazy, full-time."

Linda Allen, of Linda Allen Literary Agency in San Francisco, unlike most agents, doesn't come from publishing. "I learned my apprenticeship probably without realizing it," she says. "I was married to a writer for fifteen years, so I knew the publishing world vicariously. Having met my husband's editors, I took the plunge and went into the business. I've never looked back."

What Will I Earn?

It is difficult to say, since agents work strictly on a commission, 10 to 20 percent. Mega-buck signings result in mega-buck incomes. More commonly, a $20,000 advance for an author yields an agent only two to three thousand dollars. Keep in mind that few authors command million-dollar advances.

Reading for a Living

While many seasoned literary agents were editors for New York publishing houses, today the route in can be more direct. One often begins as a reader working for an agent. Jill Maverick, of Manus & Associates, exemplifies the trend.

"I started here as an unpaid intern, or reader," the exuberant, articulate Princeton University graduate enthuses. "But in making the transition to assistant, I learned to read less. Readers can get hung

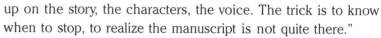

INFORMATION

For More Information

The Association of Author's
Representatives, Inc.
Ten Astor Place, 3rd Floor
New York, NY 10003
(212) 252-3695
www.publishersweekly.com/aar/

up on the story, the characters, the voice. The trick is to know when to stop, to realize the manuscript is not quite there."

Now that Jill has became a full-fledged agent, she's working a typical literary agent day. "In the office I do fifty to sixty hours a week," she explains. "At home I add another two to three. And on vacation, I lug along manuscripts. I make frequent trips to the optometrist to update my prescription."

Still, Jill isn't complaining. "In the end, I get paid for reading fabulous books before they come out. I have a hand in getting them to the public."

East Coast/West Coast

Though coming from publishing is not required for agent success, it helps. "If you're serious about this," Betsy Amster, of Betsy Amster Literary Enterprises in Los Angeles, cautions, "you might want to move to New York, at least for a while. I'm not saying every agent on the West Coast comes from New York, but they do have something in their background that lends itself to this field: writing, editing, and so forth. There is just so much more of it back east."

Today's technology being what it is, however, you won't have to settle permanently in New York to do your job. "It's useful for an agent to come to New York two or three times a year," advises Ruth Cavin, senior editor/associate publisher at Thomas Dunne Books, an imprint of St. Martin's Press. "You'll want to meet people face-to-face if you don't do so at conferences. However, I have dealt with agents in other cities that I didn't meet for several years after starting work with them. The same is true with authors."

"It comes down to the writing you represent, the authors," says Linda. "It doesn't matter where you live. One editor told me she sees her agents in Los Angeles more than her editors across town in Manhattan."

Jill clarifies it best: "Agents in New York spend all their time on the phone anyway, so what does it matter where you live? You

need a phone, fax, e-mail, and a UPS man to deliver manuscripts. You're then good to go."

Indeed, literary agents, it seems, can work anywhere. The bottom line is the author. Even though publishing houses are concentrated in the Big Apple, authors are everywhere.

Like a Spouse

All the agents, assistants, and even interns in Jillian's Palo Alto office are women. "It's not that I don't like men," she says, "I love them. It's just that 82 percent of all book purchasers are women. And from an agenting viewpoint, I think women tend to be a bit more nurturing, more the psychologist. In publishing today, an agent is more than a salesperson."

Elaborating, Jillian explains: "Agents aren't just part of the sales process, they are in charge of the process. Publishers are essentially printing houses. All other responsibilities, including editing, positioning, marketing, and, yes, hand-holding, are up to the literary agent. I, and others here, edit everything going out the door, from rewriting to actually writing proposals.

"When I sell a book, it's not just to the editor," she continues. "It is to the publisher's marketing team. In the old days the process was editorially driven. Not anymore. Now it's marketing, the publicity teams, and the sales force making the decisions."

And then there's that all important agent/author relationship. "An agent is like a spouse, almost," says Lisa Huang Fleischman, author of *Dream of the Walled City*, published by Pocket Books, an imprint of Simon & Schuster. "You can spend years with an agent; he or she has to be someone you like."

Unfortunately, some agent/author marriages end in divorce, however. "I made an author a million dollars and he up and left me," says Julie. "His editor got laid off, became an agent, and took the author with him."

What to Read

The Everything® Get Published Book
by Peter Rubie.
Adams Media Corporation, 2000.

The Insider's Guide to Finding and Keeping an Agent
by Lori Perkins.
Writer's Digest Books, 1999.

Literary Agents: What They Do, How They Do it, and How to Find and Work With the Right One for You
by Michael Larson.
John Wiley & Sons, 1996.

Passion All Around

So, what makes a good literary agent in the ever-changing publishing world? "A critical eye and excellent literary instincts," says Lisa. "An agent should be picky, too, not just take on anything."

Lalita agrees, and adds, "The agent has to have a realistic assessment of what will sell, be savvy and believable, and in the end have some style, be a genuine, high-energy person who is passionate about his or her work."

"Two things are critical," says Julie. "First, you must have the talent to find good material, something that is marketable. Second, you need the right personality. That means being on top of things. You're sending out all this stuff, following up, collecting money, checking contracts, it's pretty hands-on."

Although the hours are long and the remuneration, though good at times, can be a while in coming, most literary agents can't imagine doing anything else.

"I love good literature," Julie confesses. "That's why I am in this business. The biggest high is when I read an unsolicited manuscript and it's absolutely wonderful. Good writing *is* still out there."

"They are flocking to us in droves, those wanting a career as a literary agent," concludes Jillian. "We had fifty-three interns last year alone. Publishing is still a wonderful place to be, surrounded by all that literature."

Cool Web Sites to Visit

The Evan Marshall Agency
www.thenovelist.com

Literary Agent Resource Guide
www.grantguides.com/literaryagents.html

LOBBYIST

As a lobbyist, you must be persistent and diplomatic, and be able to build coalitions. Some lobbyists thrive on the interaction, the dealing, the fight. For others, it's a passionate belief in the cause they serve.

If being politically connected is a lobbyist's "signature characteristic," Robert Burke, of Rose & Kindel, Public Affairs Advocacy, is the lobbyist role-model. In his spacious, 10th-story office at the Wilshire Grand in downtown Los Angeles, eyes scan the requisite photos pairing the attorney with a political who's who.

Atop his credenza, one spies pictures showing Robert arm-in-arm with Senator Barbara Boxer, standing next to Governor Gray Davis, shaking hands with Mayor Willie Brown, chatting with Vice President Al Gore, making small talk with Hillary Clinton, and, yes, kibitzing with the president himself.

In addition, two large black and white action photos, grainy from overenlarging, hang on a wall. Though Robert is in neither, the pictures of Robert Kennedy, taken during his ill-fated 1968 presidential campaign, recall a bittersweet relationship. "It was my first political activity after graduating from law school," he says. "I had always been interested in public affairs. Sadly, Kennedy's similar concern was cut short, right here in Los Angeles."

Such relationships—connections, if you will—are something Robert, 30 years later, is still developing. They are, for lobbyists, crucial, though access is not the only story. Nonetheless, being able to mobilize "friends" on the city council, airport commission, and at the FAA in Washington, was a big help when Rose & Kindel represented the Air Transport Association (ATA) in 1997. Mayor Richard Riordan had wanted to divert $31 million in airport landing fees to the general city fund. According to John Ek, ATA spokesman, such a move was clearly prohibited by law. Through the lobbying efforts of Rose & Kindel, the mayor and city council backed down. "This is not the one we want to go to the mat for," said Councilwoman Ruth Galanter. "We ought to be entitled to the money, but we have bigger fish to fry."

"We consider the ATA issue a successful lobbying effort," says Robert. "We got our facts in order, presented our case, built coalitions, and talked, talked, talked. We did what lobbyists do, represent their clients' interests."

No Cigars

The right to represent clients' interests, it should be noted, is guaranteed by the First Amendment to the Constitution. Lobbying, the practice of attempting to influence legislation, has a history dating back to our founding, when those representing various groups hung out in capital lobbies hoping to pigeonhole legislators. The lobbying profession has grown dramatically since those early years. According to the National Lobbyist Directory, "There are now an average of 900 lobbyists per state, with more than 40,000 registered lobbyists across the country. This number does not include the more than 4,000 federal government lobbyists registered in Washington, D.C. Some list as many as 100,000 persons involved in legislative advocacy, as it is often referred to, nationwide."

Lobbyists represent interests as diverse as JERICHO, in Sacramento, which lobbies on behalf of the poor and homeless, to Microsoft, the world's largest corporation fighting to prevent its breakup under antitrust laws. Some are strictly volunteers, like those working for the Parent Teacher Student Association. Others are well paid, representing clients on the Fortune 500 list. Many lobbyists work in-house, that is, solely for a particular organization or cause. Others are "contract lobbyists," employed at firms that represent varied clients at the local, state, and national level.

As would be expected, many lobbyists are former legislators or those who have held staff positions to such persons. "Most lobbyists are people who have at one time or another worked for an elected official or worked in the legislature," says Robert. "They know their way around a city hall or state capital."

Surprisingly, lobbying is not a licensed profession in any state. According to the Council for Ethics in Legislative Advocacy, "For the most part, there aren't even minimal qualifications for an individual to register as a lobbyist. Generally, no classification of lobbyist exists to distinguish between citizens who merely volunteer to 'lobby' their legislator versus professional lobbyists paid to advocate on behalf of others."

Does this mean lobbyists are no more than cigar-smoking cons, as the media would have us believe? Far from it. Today's legislative advocate is a politically savvy, well-educated technocrat, for whom research skills are as important as any ability to schmooze. "In essence, we work much like lawyers," says Robert. "We do research and analysis, prepare fact sheets and briefings, talk to legislators, and make our case. Essentially, we are asking the legislator to be a judge without the circumstance of a courtroom."

Gift Giving at Its Worst

The public's perception of what lobbyists do or how the process works is not a good one. Legislators acting as impartial judges basing their decisions solely on what's best for the "people"? Consider this report in *Campaign Central*, by Jeff Pillets, February 1999:

> *From Tokyo to Dublin, New Jersey legislators were wined and dined around the world last year by lobbyists who doled out more than $91,500 in gifts to lawmakers, their family members, and staffers, state records show.*

You get the picture: TV clips of senators and House members frolicking with lobbyists on all-expense paid trips to the Caribbean. "Fact-finding" trips to sunny destinations.

Then there's this report by *Washington Post* staff writer Rajiv Chandrasekaran, November 11, 1999:

> *On Friday evening, just minutes after a federal judge declared Microsoft Corp. an out-of-control monopolist that has smothered innovation and stifled competition, the software giant's newfound allies on Capitol Hill kicked into high gear. . . .*

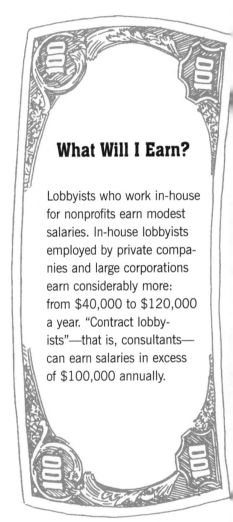

What Will I Earn?

Lobbyists who work in-house for nonprofits earn modest salaries. In-house lobbyists employed by private companies and large corporations earn considerably more: from $40,000 to $120,000 a year. "Contract lobbyists"—that is, consultants—can earn salaries in excess of $100,000 annually.

INFORMATION

For More Information

Council for Ethics in Legislative
Advocacy
P.O. Box 1846
Capitol Hill Station
Denver, CO 80218-0416

JERICHO
926 J Street, Suite 410
Sacramento, CA 95814-2706
(916) 441-0387

Microsoft—which almost doubled its lobbying spending last year to $3.7 million—also has retained some of Washington's top political consultants, among them . . .

Again, the same image. And there are more misperceptions. Take this headline from the Daily News, Los Angeles, on February 18, 2000: "Lobbyists Shelled Out Cool Cash on Hot Issues." It implies that lobbyists are conduits for bribe money sent by clients to be delivered to legislators. Actually, reporter Rick Orlov got it correct in the article itself, when he said, referring to a theater renovation contract deal: "More than $243,000 was hurled into the lobbying battle by the various factions." Yes, lobbyists get paid for what they do, they earn fees and salaries.

Let's face it, serious misconceptions exist as to just what lobbyists are supposed to do, even by those who should know better. Referring to the New Jersey lobbying efforts cited above, Pamela Garfield, a spokeswoman for New Jersey Common Cause, said, "We are opposed to all gifts because lawmakers are supposed to be doing the people's bidding, not the bidding of private interests."

Setting aside the issue of just who "the people" are, private groups, from conservationists to those representing the professions, such as law and medicine, are guaranteed the right to "petition government and seek redress of grievances."

"Gifts," of course, are another matter. But as Thomas Flintoft, of Rose & Kindel, explains, "Anyone out there who thinks that raising $5,000 to $10,000 for an elected official is enough, when even local campaigns can cost a million dollars or more, should have their head examined. A $500 check isn't going to mean much."

A Higher Calling

Checks, payouts, and "gift giving" certainly isn't how Sister Sheila Walsh, the only nun lobbying in Sacramento, conducts business. In work she does as founder and lobbyist for JERICHO, Sister Sheila responds to a higher calling. "With some people, the fact that I am a Catholic nun puts me in a box," she declares. "A box they don't want to open. On the

other hand, there is no question it gives me access that I might not otherwise get. People see me as having a conscience."

For Assemblywoman Deborah Ortiz, D-Sacramento, more than morality is at issue here. As she told *Sacramento Bee* staff writer Andrea Lampros, "For those of us who are Catholic, can you imagine saying no to a nun?"

Considered a shrewd, no-nonsense advocate by friends and foes, Sister Sheila is willing to go to the wall on issues she believes in. "Big-monied interests have plenty of people here," she explains. "Poor people don't."

Tirelessly, Sister Sheila reviews hundreds of bills each legislative session, looking to see how they will affect the poor and lead to systemic change. Through a dogged approach, built on 31 years of experience in the capital, she has obtained what every lobbyist seeks: unprecedented access. "Relationships are extremely important," she advises. "And with term limits, it's becoming more difficult to develop those long term. Knowing staff people, many of whom are carryovers, is key."

That, and getting your facts straight. "You need knowledge and integrity," she says. "Legislators have to trust your information and your principles."

Stacie Hiramoto, an in-house lobbyist for the National Association of Social Workers, California Chapter, agrees: "Us 'good-guy' lobbyists have little or no money to give. What we do try to provide is information relevant to how an issue will affect a legislator's constituents. It can't be mumbo-jumbo or meaningless statistics. It has to be accessible and meaningful to them."

So, just what are the skills necessary to succeed as a lobbyist? "You must be persistent and diplomatic, and be able to build coalitions," Stacie advises. What about belief in the cause, is there any room for that? "Some just love to do the job for the job's sake," she says. "They thrive on the interaction, the dealing, the fight, if you will. Which client they represent isn't all that important. For others, it is a passionate belief in the cause they serve."

There's little doubt which category Sister Sheila falls into. "Senator Burton, the other day, introduced me as the 'last of the bleeding heart liberals,'" she says. "I considered it an honor."

What to Read

The Lobbyist: How Influence Peddlers Work Their Way in Washington by Jeffrey H. Birnbaum. Times Books, 1994.

Not Strictly for AT&T

Belief in causes and the desire to be involved in public policy are what brought Samantha Ziskind to Rose & Kindel in 1996 as an intern. A former White House intern, 1993–1994, she holds a master's degree in international relations from the University of Southern California. "It's strange," she says, "having earned my graduate degree, I never thought I'd want to work on local issues. But here I am, and loving every minute."

In her year as an intern, Samantha researched clients, tracked issues, kept tabs on media coverage, developed bios on elected officials, and worked on various events. "It was learning the ropes: strategy, issues, local politics, you name it," she says. "Then, when I got my master's, they offered me a job full-time: half administrative, half backup lobbyist."

Today, Samantha is a junior lobbyist with the firm. "All the senior lobbyists here had government or public policy experience before arriving," she says. "I can't say I was any of that. Still, I believe I fit in well."

What Samantha loves about her work is the variety. "I couldn't be a lobbyist strictly for AT&T, one of our clients. I'm a generalist. I like covering a range of issues: the Internet, telecommunications, education, safety, health."

Samantha gives an example: "When I first started here, we were representing the pipe-fitters' union in an attempt to better their health and safety conditions. We were instrumental in getting mitigation language in their contract. It was gratifying to see that work out."

Committed to Making Things Better

Samantha's formal education and commitment exemplify, in many respects, the "new lobbyist." Although experience in government will always be important, additional skills are required for today's practitioners. Today, lobbying is highly technical and fact- and information-based. In addition to being technically astute, a lobbyist must have the ability to relate knowledge to clients and legislators.

Cool Web Sites to Visit

Georgia Lobbyist Online
www.georgialobbyist.com

National Lobbyist Directory
www.ss.ca.gov/prd/ld.frm/
f20990.htm

New York State's Lobby Data
www.nylobby.state.ny.us/
lobby_data.html

MARTIAL ARTS INSTRUCTOR

Martial arts is the art of stopping conflict. Being a martial arts instructor, however, is more than knowing quick moves to defend yourself.

Hot Career

25

Anyone hoping to understand today's martial arts phenomenon in America, must experience a seminal work that burst forth from Hong Kong a quarter-century ago. Almost all martial arts practitioners agree, Bruce Lee's *Enter the Dragon* heightened awareness in the West, as no other event had, of the combative arts—hap ki do, judo, karate, kung fu, tai chi, kick-boxing, and tae kwon do.

Though predictable in plot and, with its bellbottoms and Elvis sideburns, dated, it's easy to see why this Warner Bros. movie generated enthusiasm for the martial arts, particularly among the young.

Fight scenes are everywhere, with rapid punches, kicks to the face, back flips, somersaults, and wrestling. Bruce Lee, who sadly and mysteriously never lived to see *Enter the Dragon's* commercial release in August, 1973, is fearless, concentrated, skilled, and determined. Credited not only with great technique, his insights are respected to this day.

"A martial artist," he said, "is not tense, but ready. When an opponent contracts, I expand; when the opponent expands, I contract. When an opportunity presents itself, I do not hit with my fist, it hits all by itself."

Fight or Flight

Enter the Dragon aside, many within the martial arts community feel Hollywood gives a false image of an ancient and honorable art.

"In the public media, it's all about fighting," Edward Sell, the highest ranked—Ninth Degree Black Belt—non-Asian in the world, says. "They even have video games with guys beating up on women."

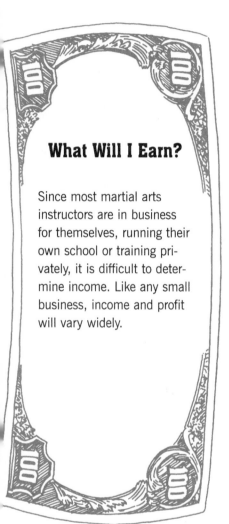

What Will I Earn?

Since most martial arts instructors are in business for themselves, running their own school or training privately, it is difficult to determine income. Like any small business, income and profit will vary widely.

"That's not what it should be about," says Robert Chu, a traditionalist in the martial arts world. "'Make savage the body, make civilized the mind,' is an ancient Greek ideal," he says. "Take the Chinese characters *Wu Shu* for martial arts. *Wu* means 'to stop conflict.' *Shu* means the 'art or science.' Martial arts is the art of stopping conflict."

While self-defense is key to the martial arts appeal, watch out—a little knowledge can be dangerous.

"Self-protection has more to do with common sense," Jose Fraguas, general manager of CFW Enterprises, publisher of magazines such as *Inside Kung-Fu* and *Martial Arts Illustrated*, declares. "A man with a knife is dangerous. Oftentimes, flight is better than fight."

Alan Lamb, a win ching instructor, who studied for years in Hong Kong, agrees.

"Martial arts is the last line of defense," he says. "Often it's best to just start running."

"The opponent in the ring is not the same as the opponent on the street," Francis Fong, *Inside Kung-Fu's* "instructor of the year," reminds us. "Those who fight on the street aren't disciplined to be martial artists."

From Self-Defense to Self-Awareness

Self-defense is but one aspect of martial arts, though it is the most sought after.

Edward explains, "Many martial artists never made the team, never had any athletic inclination or skill level. Little Johnny, who has been beat up by neighborhood bullies all his life, trips over his own feet. That kind of guy thrives on martial arts."

But there are more benefits than that one.

"Many techniques in martial arts were developed to bring health to the body," says Jose. "Keeping your spine straight, stretching your limbs, placing your pelvis in the right position, and breathing exercises. It's not all about fighting."

Nor about physical health, either.

"Though martial arts gives you a 100 percent body workout," Grandmaster Hee Il Cho explains, "improving your attitude and under-

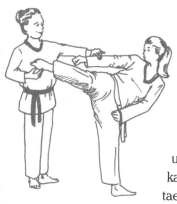

standing the deeper self are more important than just defending yourself. Martial arts is about self-awareness."

To get from here to there, one must choose a style, or system, to develop and concentrate on.

For example, there are the more strenuous forms of martial arts such as judo and karate from Japan, kung fu from China, and tae kwon do from Korea. Or, there are the gentler arts, tai chi chuan and aikido, the former from China, the latter from Japan. Each has its own forms, substance.

A trend lately is to mix various styles to, as Francis says, "make your own style that represents yourself. Then you represent a system."

Dojo on Every Corner

Kane Hodder, the beaming father of four-year-old Jace, stands observing the younger Hodder, along with 10 classmates, all dressed in loose white pants and jackets, go through their jabbing exercises at Tim Connolly's U.S. Tae Kwon Do Center in Calabasas, California.

"I'm hoping for a little discipline, concentration, and some physical capacity to defend himself," says Kane, in response to an inquiry as to what he expects for Jace. "The competitions and belt-rating system act as incentives. And the instructors are great. It's the right mix of discipline and fun."

Tim, owner of the center, has been providing that combination for two years.

Blond, buffed, and 34 years old, he would be as much at home on a Malibu beach as in any martial arts dojo. And though owning such a school may not be Tim's last career stop, you can say he has been heading here since junior high school.

"I was a track star at fourteen, never lost a race," Tim says. "Then this kid beat me because of flexibility he had gained in martial arts training. I investigated and got hooked. I've never looked back. Martial arts became my life."

INFORMATION

For More Information

Action International Martial Arts Association (AIMAA)
4217 San Mateo Boulevard, N.E.
Albuquerque, NM 87110
(888) 388-1884
www.AIMAA.com

What to Read

Instructor: Teaching Martial Arts by Robert Sprackland. Young Forest Company, 1998.

In the following years, Tim continued to train and, eventually, coach and teach.

World Silver Medalist, four-time U.S. Olympic team member, and athlete representative to the U.S. Olympic Committee, Tim's a man who loves his sport. But, as owner/operator of a tae kwon do center, whose job is to make a profit, his day is anything but all fun and games. Both teacher and businessman, it's a tough mix in a competitive market.

According to *Tae Kwon Do Times*, tae kwon do is the most practiced martial art in the world. In the United States, participation has risen eight times in the last 10 years, to seven million practitioners. No wonder there seems to be a tae kwon do school on every corner, what Tim calls a "McDojo."

The Competitive Spirit

What brings students, customers, into such places varies. "The ranking system helps," says Tim.

The World Tae Kwon Do Federation in Seoul, Korea, recognizes a 10-grade system going backwards from tenth to first grade, with a multitude of colored belts marking the grades. Then, it's on to your first degree (dan) Black Belt.

With a lifetime of dedication, work, and accomplishment, you could go as high as ninth degree, though there are probably less than a dozen such belts in the United States.

Do not think, however, that martial arts, even tae kwon do, is just about sports.

"If it were," Tim explains, "we would all be out of business. Perhaps only 20 percent of our clients are here for the competitions, tournaments, and trophies. Though tae kwon do is a medal sport in the 2000 Olympics, that can't be what it's all about."

Just as well.

As Shihan Fumio Demura, chief instructor, Japan Karate-Do Itosu-Kai, says, "If martial arts instructors try to turn out champions, it's a mistake. Then it's just like football or soccer. They are teaching how to win. I teach how to be successful in life. Those are two different things."

Tim agrees. "With an overemphasis on sports, you can get into the Little League syndrome. You try to develop respect, discipline, a positive atmosphere, what martial arts should be about, and parents are up in the stands complaining about a bad call. You must be careful, since you can lose what you are trying to teach in class. Some instructors think that taking students to competitions hurts what they are trying to accomplish in class. There's a lot of truth to that. Heck, kids are more than happy to have fun."

A Changed Life

While an instructor ranking of master or grandmaster is, if legitimately obtained, a respected prerequisite to teaching the martial arts, those just heading in that direction can still get valuable teacher training.

For Chris Macedo, a 20-year-old community college student and stunt double in such movies as *Mighty Morphin Power Rangers* and *Big Bad Beetleborgs*, that's what's happening at the Chul Jin Martial Arts studio in Van Nuys, California, under Myung S. Kim, master.

"A lot of movie people, actors, and particularly stunt people, are into martial arts," he says. "But for the most part for them it is all about techniques, skills. On the other hand, younger students are more contest and tournament oriented. It gives them a chance to compare themselves with those beyond the class where they train.

"For me, I started training, and now it's my job. For kids, I try to build concentration, self-esteem, and confidence. For adults, it's great exercise, a total body workout, and increased mental focus."

It seems to be working for Patricia Olmos, a student who will, in a few weeks hence, be testing for her first degree Black Belt.

"When I started," she explains, panting after a hard evening's workout, "I didn't have much self-confidence. I didn't feel I was worth anything. But here I worked through my fears. Master Kim knows how to push you and he knows when to let you figure it out on your own. Has martial arts helped me? It has changed my life."

Cool Web Sites to Visit

The Martial Arts Network
www.martial-arts-network.com

Martial Arts Resource Page
www.middlebury.edu~jswan/martial.arts/ma.html

Martial Arts World Search
www.martial-law.hypermart.net/search/

Hot Concepts!

Moonlighting

"Moonlighting," according to the *Random House Dictionary,* means "to work at an additional job after one's regular, full-time employment, as at night." Many of us have been there, that's for sure.

For some, moonlighting is an unfortunate necessity. Working two or more jobs is the only way to make ends meet. Neither job may be what you want; neither is considered a career. Both are just plain work.

However, many of us moonlight to gain a foothold in a new career, to transition from our "day job" to something better. Some of the careers in this book allow you to do that—work part-time in order to get started. Sports coach and voice actor come quickly to mind. There are also others that, at first, seem like ideal part-time endeavors, yet are not. Traditionally residential real estate and travel agent, for example, were seen as careers you could "dabble in." Be careful! From independent college counselor to zookeeper, the work is hard and, if you hope to make a career of it, requires a dedicated, full-time effort.

Moonlighting to get going, feel your way around, may work for some careers. In others, you are going to have to quit your day job and take the plunge. Good luck!

MOTION PICTURE CAMERA OPERATOR

Don't think all they do is look through the camera, point, and shoot. There's the art of composing, not to mention the ability to handle temperamental actors and directors. Both technical and people skills are a job requirement.

With four camera operators poised to get the shot, you'd think at least one would succeed. Yet, if Mike St. Hilaire, an operator with 30 years' experience, hadn't known to go "handheld" instead of using a tripod, a costly and dangerous stunt on the set of *Lethal Weapon 4* might never have made it to the screen.

Standing on a barge, with two crew members ready to pull him to safety should the projectile fail to fall short, Mike aims his Panaflex G2 camera skyward as a flaming 55-gallon oil drum falls toward him in a 100-foot high arc. "With one eye closed and the other in the camera's viewfinder, you lose depth of field," he says. "But my assistant kept yelling in my earphones, 'You're OK, you're OK.' The drum crashed into the water, three feet in front of me. I was the only one to frame the sequence."

Why Mike put that one "in the can," while other operators failed to do so, says as much about concentration as it does about experience.

"Yes, I knew enough to study the test shots, to anticipate the drum's trajectory as it arched out over the water," Mike continues. "But, more than that, a good camera operator concentrates, blocks out everything else. Today, with lenses faster, film faster, and depth of field shrinking, it's tougher than when I started."

A Crew Job

New technology and the collapse of the old studio system have impacted the career of the camera operator. Nonetheless, today, just as when Mike began work three decades ago, a union-negotiated contract places a traditional camera crew on every motion picture production. In a rigid hierarchy, the crew comprises the director of photography, camera operator, first assistant, second assistant, and, often, a film loader. Each has a specific job.

The director of photography, also known as the cinematographer, is actively in charge of photographing a motion picture. He supervises the entire technical crew. He reports to the director.

The camera operator answers to the director of photography. Tim Wade, business representative for International Photographers Local 600, and an experienced director of photography and camera operator, describes him as "the person behind the camera, the one that composes and frames each shot." It is a demanding job, requiring physical stamina, artistic talent, and political savvy.

Working directly with the camera operator is the first assistant. A technical person, his job is to be sure the camera is in perfect working order all the time.

The second assistant receives and keeps inventory on raw film stock, prepares the slate describing the scene, and marks the talents' (actors') feet during rehearsal.

Finally, there may be a film loader. He keeps reports of film checked out, handles all film reloadings, and helps store camera equipment. His is often the entry-level position.

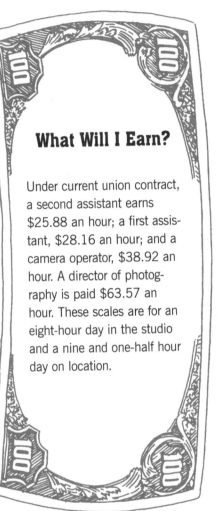

What Will I Earn?

Under current union contract, a second assistant earns $25.88 an hour; a first assistant, $28.16 an hour; and a camera operator, $38.92 an hour. A director of photography is paid $63.57 an hour. These scales are for an eight-hour day in the studio and a nine and one-half hour day on location.

Point and Shoot

Mike broke into the industry not as a film loader but as a second assistant at Universal Studios, in 1965. "It was marking feet and getting to know the system," he says. "From there, I went to Disney as a first assistant. My sole mission was to maintain the camera. It's a critical job."

How critical, Mike was reminded of during a recent production. "The first assistant brought his camera in from a day's outdoor shooting. He then set up for a series of night shots. Trouble is, he left the outdoor filter on. Two days of filming were ruined. They fired him."

If you are willing and able to go beyond the technical to the artistic, your next move is to camera operator. But it's a big step. "It is physically demanding," Tim explains. "You have to bend, twist, and move like an athlete. The older you get, the harder it is to do that. It's something to keep in mind."

Even more, you must become an artist. The camera operator works to compose the shot. "When I was ready to make the transition," Tim continues, "I spent time going to art galleries and museums, looking at how artists and still photographers framed their work."

"Everyone wants my job," Mike says. "It's the most visible, out-in-the-open position on the set. They think all I do is look through the camera, point, and shoot. But in addition to the art of composing, I have to know how to handle an actor who's not quite on his mark or a director of photography who's having a bad day. And I have my assistants to take care of. Heck, my job is 80 percent political."

The leap from first assistant to camera operator can be tricky, too, as Guido Frenzel, a young camera operator from Germany found out.

"To make the move, I dropped out of the business, so to speak," he confides. "I spent two years at the American Film Institute [AFI], as much to gain knowledge as to get away from being seen as a first assistant. Sometimes, if you're a good assistant, people want you to stay there. I had to get away and be forgotten as a first assistant. Then, when I returned, I was ready to start fresh as a camera operator."

Steady, Steady

As in most fields today, technology is changing the very nature of what is being done. One advance that has revolutionized the camera operator's work is, of course, the Steadicam® system, invented by Garrett Brown and developed and manufactured by Cinema Products

INFORMATION

For More Information

American Film Institute (AFI)
(213) 856-7628

What to Read

The Professional Cameraman's Handbook
by Verne Carlson
and Sylvia Carlson.
Focal Press, 1994.

Corp., under exclusive worldwide license. According to Eric Swanson, an expert on its use, "The Steadicam is a camera stabilization device that, in the hands of a skilled operator, combines the image steadiness of a dolly with the freedom of movement of a handheld shot.

"It works in three ways," he says. "One, it isolates the camera from all but the largest movements of the operator. Two, it spreads the mass of the camera to increase resistance to rotation. And three, it brings the center of gravity outside of the camera to where the operator can manipulate it directly."

So, what does this mean, what does it accomplish? "Most hand-held shots suffer from a distinct jerkiness," Eric says. "This is because the camera is subject to all of the movements of the operator—including the undesired shocks and bounces that accompany each footstep. In the human body, the muscles, joints, tendons, and ligaments absorb a large portion of these shocks; what the body does not absorb, the muscles of the eyes and the image processing of the brain corrects for, turning a bumpy ride into a smooth flight."

The Steadicam is designed and manufactured to provide, in the hands of a skilled operator, isolation of these movements. It is particularly suited to moving the camera in tight quarters, making shots over rough ground, where you wish to simulate vehicle motion, to name but a few uses. "The Steadicam operator can do a lot of shots without a dolly or dolly track," says Tim. "But it is not something you learn to use overnight; it's a skill camera operators need to acquire."

Of course, photography in general is going digital, a technological revolution affecting all of cinematography. Theaters are beginning to experiment with digital projection systems. The digital motion picture camera is here right now, of course. How long it will be before they are widely used is anyone's guess. "It will take some time," says Denis Sitar, owner of Modern Design Services in Los Angeles. "It is just too expensive right now. But we are going to get there sooner than later." Remember when digital

still cameras cost $1,000 to $2,000? Low-end units now sell for under $200. More for the camera operator to keep up with.

Your Images Onscreen

Other things have changed as well, such as long location shoots that require being away from home for months. "There were times when I was on location so long that when I returned my son was two inches taller," Mike confesses. "This is not a field where marriages last long."

Being away from home is tough, yet the long hours may be even harder—and often downright dangerous.

"When I started out, ten, eleven-hour days were common," Tim says. "But in the 1980s it went to twelve-hour days. Now, a fourteen-, even sixteen-hour day is a frequent occurrence. While the money's great, safety becomes an issue."

On March 6, 1997, second assistant Brent Hershaman, 35 and the father of two, worked a 19-hour day. On his way home from work he lost control of his car and was killed. George Spiro Dibie, president of International Photographers Guild Local 600 IATSE, asks: "Who is to blame for Brent Hershaman's death? The producer? The union? Elected officials? It's hard to say."

"In addition to time away and the long hours, the biggest downside to this career is not knowing when and where you'll work next," Mike says. "But when you are employed, the pay and benefits, at least under union contract, are terrific."

The salary is only part of the high.

"Being a camera operator has been an exciting journey," Guido says. "I've been to Latin America, Asia, and Europe a number of times. I have traveled the world."

Then there's the satisfaction of seeing your work onscreen. "Nothing's quite like going into a movie theater and staring at 'your image' up there," says Tim.

"I love the competition, it makes me try harder," Mike concludes. "I like to prove to the young kids coming up behind me I'm as good as anyone." Then, as with the camera he operates, Mike points his finger in focus. "The flaming oil drum shot proved that!"

Cool Web Sites to Visit

Cinematography.com- Professional Motion Picture Camera People & Resources
www.cinematography.com/ inded.asp

The Motion Picture Camera Goes to War
www.lcweb2.loc.gov/ammem/ sawhtml/sawsp1.html

Student Pages
www.herricks.org/spindex.htm

NETWORK ADMINISTRATOR

Are computer network administrators in demand? The Bureau of Labor Statistics claims that database administrators, computer support specialists, and computer scientists are an elite group that constitute three fast-growing occupations for the 1998–2008–period.

Charles Hollins, Los Angeles County Network Control Center administrator, loves football. That would explain why, on a Saturday afternoon, in fall, 1997, he is relaxing at home, beer in hand, watching the USC/Oregon game.

Yet, just as USC snaps the ball on their own 10-yard line, the phone rings. "Our network is down," the voice at Children's Services, a client of the control center, says. "We need help, fast."

A short pass to USC's tight end and the sprint is on, avoiding tacklers, weaving in and out. Charles is has to tear himself away from the runner's progress on the screen, but the network guru's brain is already in another place, troubleshooting the problem at work. "By the time USC scored a 90-yard touchdown, I had arrived at the solution," he says, with a momentary lapse in modesty. "It was clearly a subnet mask configuration issue."

Extra point accomplished, Charles heads for his office in Downey, 12 miles away. There, it takes him but two minutes to bring the children's center back online. "All such network administration solutions should be so easy!" he laughs.

Top Demand

Unfortunately, most network crashes and other malfunctions are not. That's why it takes a knowledgeable and experienced individual to cope with the myriad problems a network conjures up every day.

Here is an ad seeking a network administrator to work for an imaging management company in the northern suburbs of Dallas, Texas (flunkies need not apply!):

> *We are seeking a Network Administrator to join our dynamic IS&T team. Responsibilities include maintaining a 200-node LAN, maintaining NT, Web and Mail servers, 4 Novell servers, and managing our help desk function, which provides user support for networking and software issues.*
>
> *Potential candidates should have 4–5 years network administration experience, 2–3 years Novell network experience, and 1–2 years of Windows NT experience. Candidates must have experience with hardware and software installation, support, configuration, and maintenance, and should have a working knowledge of hubs, bridges, and routers, and security management. This position requires strong communication and interaction skills.*
>
> *Salary range: $80,000 to $90,000, with an excellent benefits package.*

Generally, a network administrator is responsible for a single group of communications networks within an organization. This includes all hardware, such as file servers, workstations, printers, faxes, telephone PBXs, and other office equipment hooked to the local area network (LAN). One must also maintain Internet servers and e-mail messaging systems.

How much are such network administrators in demand? According to the Bureau of Labor Statistics, database administrators, computer support specialists, and computer scientists are an elite group that constitute the three fastest-growing occupations for the years 1998–2008. As Melissa Grace Henderson, a technical recruiter with Ciber, a consulting firm in Hoboken, New Jersey, puts it: "It is, today, the toughest and most rewarding career in the whole world. It is a great thing to be an engineer right now."

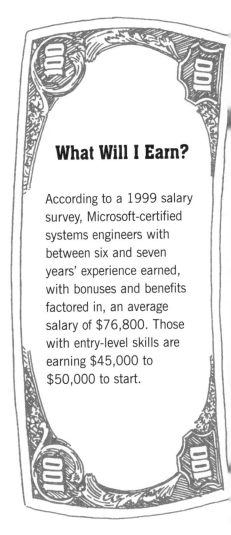

What Will I Earn?

According to a 1999 salary survey, Microsoft-certified systems engineers with between six and seven years' experience earned, with bonuses and benefits factored in, an average salary of $76,800. Those with entry-level skills are earning $45,000 to $50,000 to start.

More Jobs than Students

Those coming out of college and entering the field certainly know they're in hot demand! "It's tough recruiting recent college graduates," confesses Melissa. "Network engineers graduating from technical schools and engineering programs know they have options galore. They're not concerned about their economic future. They've never seen a war or experienced an economic downturn. They haven't struggled. Let's face it, right now there are far more jobs than students."

Charles Hollins, however, is from a different generation. A graduate of Los Angeles Trade Technical College, back in 1965, he has seen ups and downs, good and bad times in the world of technology. "My life has been a story of meeting people's technology needs and riding the crest, then jumping onto another wave," Charles says. "For me, in the '60s it was two-way radio, the '70s, avionics, and in the '80s microwave and fiber optics. Now, of course, it's networking and the Internet. Tomorrow, who knows!"

Through it all, Charles has grown and matured along with the technology he deals with. He has earned his bachelor's and master's degrees, as well as a slew of network-specific certifications, the Cisco-certified network associate (CCNA) and Cisco-certified design associate (CCDA) among them. "You can't stop, look, and smell the roses," he says. "You must keep going, learning all the time."

Today, as the chief network administrator for a county that covers over 400 square miles, Charles's job has five aspects:

1. *Network management.* Formerly called fault management. "If it goes bad, you have to fix it," he says.
2. *Security management.* "It's keeping the bad guys out, letting the good guys in."
3. *Configuration management.* "That's what the subnet problem at the children's center was all about."
4. *Accounting management.* "Someone has to pay the piper. We have to charge for our services."

5. *Performance management.* "Can we improve on what we have? If we're getting 20 mpg, can we get 22 mpg? The more performance management we do, network optimization, the less time we must spend on fault management."

Once again, being able to handle all aspects of network administration is a challenge, one requiring a well-educated, trained, and experienced individual. No wonder such folks are in high demand.

Certified to Do the Job

To make it as a network administrator, qualified to earn a six-figure income, do you have to hold a degree in engineering or computer science? Lisle Hirschhorn, a network administrator at Ezralow, a property management company in Calabasas, California, has neither. Responsible for keeping their Novell NetWare 3.12 and Windows 2000 networks up and running, helping users with countless problems, installing new software and hardware, troubleshooting the system, and deciding what to purchase, Lisle is a busy, valued employee. Yet, as she says, "I fell into the job. I was an office manager with computer skills picked up along the way. Before I knew it, I was running the network."

Well, not so fast. Though Lisle lacks a technical degree, she has something many consider as valuable, or even more so—certification. She is a Microsoft-certified professional (MCP) and a Microsoft-certified systems engineer (MCSE), both highly coveted indicators of network expertise. "They signify real-world know-how," she says. "You can't acquire these certifications without having been on the job for some time."

Many organizations offer network certifications. However, as of this writing, two certifying programs stand out, those offered by Microsoft Corporation and Cisco Systems, Inc. Whole sections of your local bookstore are devoted to the subject of certification. Determining which certifications to pursue, gathering the materials, attending seminars, and, of course, passing the exams, some of

INFORMATION

For More Information

Certification magazine
www.certmag.com

Institute for Certification
of Computer Professionals
2200 East Devon Avenue
Suite 268
Des Plaines, IL 60018

What to Read

All About Administering NIS+
by Rick Ramsey.
Sun Microsystems Press, 2000.

which can last two days, require research. Help in determining the correct approach is as close as the Internet. Search on both "Microsoft" and "CISCO" plus "training" and a plethora of information will flood your computer screen.

"To be a success as a network administrator, you must be certified, period," says Melissa. "All our clients are looking for that. The Microsoft-certified systems engineer is key. If you are also Cisco-certified, you are a diamond in the rough." Melissa recommends getting on the certification path as soon as you graduate. "If you wait too long after that, life gets in the way. You'll be too busy with other things."

George Hukassian, a network engineer at TelePacific, has two Cisco certifications: Cisco-certified network associate and Cisco-certified internetwork expert (CCIE). "The CCIE," he says, "requires lots of experience. You have to know what you're doing, know the shortcuts, to pass the two-day exam, three-quarters of which is hands-on. Luckily, here at work I had access to the equipment; I was able to learn a great deal on the job."

Without certification are you going nowhere, will you never get a networking job? Not at all. "We are not so narrow-minded as to think that if you don't have the certification you don't know your stuff," says Brian Castro, of Edge Technology, a network consulting company. "Some of our clients insist upon it, and in that case there's no choice. But for others, it is less important."

"Yes, in some cases it is significant," adds Joanna Sobran, of IT Consulting in Hinsdale, Illinois. "For example, we had a client looking for someone with expertise in setting up checkpoint firewalls. They insisted on certification."

"Certification gets you in the door," says Charles. "But it's your knowledge and ability to analytically solve problems that is crucial. Certification is not the end-all. Just as in school, there are folks who don't test well, don't ace the exams. Many of the people can still do the job."

People Skills Count, Too

Besides, the certification exams only test for technical expertise, just one aspect of what it takes to succeed in this career. "We look for three things," says Brian. "One, we want technical skills, you have to know your stuff. Two, people skills are critical. It is important that our people can go into a client's operation and blend right in. Whether it's suit and tie or cut-off jeans, you can't disrupt the environment. You have to be a chameleon. And three, being a consulting firm, we want individuals with an entrepreneurial outlook. We are a small company, will they grow with us?"

"Your technical skills are very important," agrees Melissa. "But getting along with others is vital. It is an intangible no one tells you about when you're out looking for work. Techs that can't work with anyone are in trouble."

"If you don't know how to approach people, you can get everyone mad," says Robert Welch, a sales engineer at Cisco. "It's a problem in this field."

Lisle agrees: "People skills are what's lacking in our occupation. Most computer folks want to sit in front of a computer all day. That won't cut it. I have to deal with everyone from the receptionist to the CEO."

Seeking Balance

Of course, as with any job, network administration has its share, maybe more, of frustrations, people-generated or otherwise.

"It can be like brain surgery," says George. "You get to the point where you apply all your knowledge and experience to a problem but no solution materializes. Even when you look in the Cisco books the answers aren't there."

For Charles, frustration comes in realizing that so few people—his clients—have any idea what his department does. "We are one of the best-kept secrets within the county," he laments. "Some don't even know we exist. I suppose, in a sense, that's a good thing. It probably means we're doing our job."

"There will always be those who are not carrying their weight," adds Melissa. "As a result, you put in the long, tiring hours, all to keep that network running."

"You must have a personal support structure in order to survive, to avoid the inevitable burnout," cautions Robert. "Those who are overachievers, driven to succeed, will have a tendency to sacrifice their personal lives. You need that personal life, if for no other reason than to provide balance."

Technical Turn-on

But there is, of course, as Charles says, "an uptick, too. It is a challenging, exciting environment, where autonomy is high. No problem today is like any yesterday. It's a technical turn-on."

"A lot of our candidates love the challenge," says Melissa. "Especially in a consulting environment, they get out to different companies, work with new systems. They're able to work for us full-time, yet wind up in different industries. It gives them more exposure, widens their experience."

For Robert, satisfaction is building something that works, systems people are excited about and can depend on. "It is terrific when you see the lights go on. You get immediate gratification."

"When I go home at night," concludes Lisle, "I know for the most part that I have helped people do their job. The network is so pervasive today, it's hard to find a company that isn't totally dependent on it. If the network is down, no one is working. Keeping it up is critical. I like to think that I'm a part of what it takes to make that happen."

Cool Web Sites to Visit

Benefits and Productivity Gains Realized Through IT Certification
www.ibm.com/education/certify/news/peridc.htm

Sun Book Catalog
www.sun.com/books/catalog

PARAMEDIC

Knee scrapes, flu symptoms, traffic accidents, stabbings, heart attacks—paramedics are trained to handle whatever comes along. When a 911 call is taken, paramedics respond to provide pre-hospital emergency care.

Even with 18 years' experience as a Los Angeles City Fire Department paramedic, Captain Stephen Johnson stood awestruck at the disaster unfolding before him. A three-story apartment building in a predominantly Latino district of Los Angeles was totally engulfed in smoke and flames.

"People were leaping from windows, climbing down fire escape ladders, and lowering themselves with sheets tied to balcony railings," he says. "At one point, I found myself cradling an infant brought out in full cardiac arrest, pupils fixed and dilated, asystole on the EKG [electrocardiogram]."

Of 29 individuals treated at the scene in that early May 1993 calamity, 18 had to be hospitalized. Tragically, nine people lost their lives, six of them children.

Nevertheless, the 100 firefighters and 16 ambulances dispatched to the scene were able to save many, among them an eight-months-pregnant woman who went into labor as paramedics administered cardiopulmonary resuscitation. Stephen observes: "When you lose a child, as in this case, it's a traumatic experience. As paramedics we have our routine, mundane days. This, most certainly, was not one of them. Emotionally, it was the worst."

All in an Emergency

Paramedics are trained to handle whatever comes their way. Be it knee scrapes, flu symptoms, traffic accidents, stabbings, and heart attacks, when a 911 call is taken, paramedics respond to provide pre-hospital emergency care.

Alan Cowen, former Deputy Fire Chief, Los Angeles City Fire Department, describes a first response setting: "Paramedics control bleeding, open airways for breathing, treat for shock, immobilize fractures, bandage, and manage emotionally disturbed patients. In addition, they can be called upon to provide advanced life-support, such as defibrillating a patient, administering solutions, both orally and intravenously, and interpreting EKGs." What paramedics don't do is intervene surgically. Short of that, the timely medical aid paramedics do provide can, and often does, save lives.

In addition to the obvious training all emergency medical technicians (EMTs) receive in medical procedures, they must be compassionate and emotionally stable. "You are dealing with people at their most vulnerable," says Allen. "Courage, physical dexterity, and good driving skills are critical. While most people couldn't handle an unforeseen disaster, EMTs make crises their everyday stock in trade. They must calmly and quickly administer expert health care."

Lieutenant Paul Maniscalco of the L.A. fire department remembers his efforts to free a woman trapped under a subway train, less than a foot away from the third rail, which carries a half-million volts. "I can't describe the feeling of rescuing that woman, of delivering a baby, or of having a heart attack victim who was near death three days ago sit up in a hospital bed and shake my hand," he says. "These are everyday occurrences for an EMT."

No Routine Emergency

Paramedic Frank Gilbert Jr. of the Portage Fire Department in Porter County, Indiana, embodied all the positive characteristics of a paramedic, and more, according to every one who knew him. "From a personal standpoint, he was one of the nicest guys you'd meet," says Mike Bucy, secretary with Firefighters Local 3151. "He'd do anything for anybody."

"Whenever he could he went out of his way, which seemed to be almost always, to help someone or be active in his church or community," adds Chief of Emergency Medical Service (EMS) John Bojda. "Those who knew him would say that's 'typical Frank.'"

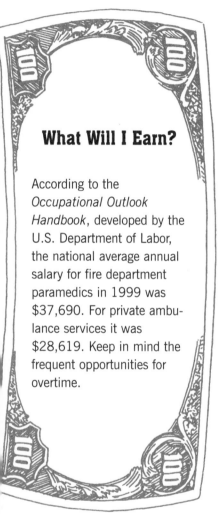

What Will I Earn?

According to the *Occupational Outlook Handbook*, developed by the U.S. Department of Labor, the national average annual salary for fire department paramedics in 1999 was $37,690. For private ambulance services it was $28,619. Keep in mind the frequent opportunities for overtime.

But what should have been a routine emergency medical run, one of thousands for Frank, 38, turned into a tragic accident on Saturday, October 26, 1996. He was tending to a patient in the back of the ambulance when the driver had to take evasive action to avoid hitting a Valparaiso Street Department truck. The ambulance, which had been running with its lights and sirens on, swerved off the roadway, crashed through a business fence, hit several utility poles, and hit a tree.

"Both the ambulance driver and the patient were treated and released," says John. "Paramedic Frank Gilbert was not as fortunate. He was thrown around the back of the ambulance and fractured two vertebrae, leaving him paralyzed and unable to breath without the aid of a ventilator. He also suffered numerous other injuries.

"Frank spent the next six months in Chicago's Northwestern Memorial Hospital rehabilitation unit. He was discharged on May 1, 1997. He arrived home to a parade held in his honor. On May 3, he was admitted to Porter Memorial Hospital where he remained in intensive care until he passed away on May 29, 1997."

"It's a dangerous profession," says Allen. "Most people think that just because you're riding in an emergency vehicle with the lights flashing and sirens blaring, you're safe, immune. That is not the case."

Classroom Training First

Kalyca Green, 20, and Scott Menard, 21, are determined to become paramedics, come what may. Enrolled in a four-unit, six-hour-a-week, three-month EMT course at Los Angeles Valley College, their focused, disciplined, and alert bearing bodes well for their completing the class, taking the state certification examination, and passing.

"My sister took the exam, and she's now certified," says Kalyca. "I want to be, too. Except for a medical assisting class I took, I've had no medical training, yet I know I can do this. Yes, there's lots of stuff to memorize. And they pack so much into so little time. Still, I know everything they're teaching us is critical."

"What we are learning will help us no matter what we do," volunteers Matt. "Personal safety, telltale signs of a heart attack, what to do in an emergency situation, it can't hurt anyone to know this stuff."

INFORMATION

For More Information

National Association of
Emergency Medical Technicians
102 West Leake Street
Clinton, MS 39056
(601) 924-7744

What to Read

Paramedic Emergency Care Exam Review
by Richard A. Cherry.
Prentice-Hall, 1997.

Paramedic: On the Front Lines of Medicine
by Peter Canning.
Ivy Books, 1998.

True, but the class Kalyca and Matt are taking is more than first-aid instruction. "They are learning about being an EMT," says Pat Brown, their instructor. "They must know what to do when they arrive on a scene. They must be able to stabilize the situation until more experienced, higher-level, medical help can arrive."

"It's pretty exciting to think that in three months I can be certified and be out in the field," says Kalyca. "To actually serve on an ambulance."

Well, not quite. To become a paramedic with the Los Angeles City Fire Department, you must first become a firefighter. Though that's not the case everywhere in the country, it is a trend that is growing. The competition is fierce.

Of the literally thousands who, in Chief Cowen's words, "circle City Hall each year for applications," only five hundred or so will, after an extensive written exam, physical agility test, medical screening, psychological review, preliminary background check, and interview, be given an "academy date." Even then, only 35 to 40 of the 500 applicants will actually begin the arduous 16 weeks of preparation they hope will lead to rookie firefighter status.

As part of that four-month paramilitary firefighter training, you'll spend approximately 130 hours becoming an emergency medical technician Level 1D, assuming you do not already have the state certification. Thus every Los Angeles firefighter can, at the least, extricate people pinned in vehicles, do advanced first aid, administer oxygen, and perform cardiopulmonary resuscitation.

Upon graduation from the academy, you're rotated through three fire stations in the first year. At each, you are exposed in turn to engine, truck, and ambulance duties.

Two years after becoming a firefighter, you may apply to attend an advanced paramedic school. If chosen, you're in for a grueling five- to six-month commitment. Two months will be in the classroom, two months at a hospital, and one and a half months in the field—a total of 1,000 hours in an intense, competitive, environment. The reward? If you pass, you're a state licensed firefighter paramedic (EMT3). Also, you get a 17 percent pay raise.

Although the L.A. City Fire Department has close to 600 paramedics (over 80 are women), becoming a paramedic does not require you join a fire department. "A number of private ambulance services hire civilian, single-function paramedics," Alan explains. You'll need to attend the same paramedic schools firefighters do, of course, and obtain your state license.

The Paramedic Life

Is running the paramedic training gauntlet and subjecting yourself to the Darwinian selection process worth it? Stephen, now district commander, thinks so. "The environment is exciting. When you arrive on scene, you're confronted with a puzzle you have to put back together. Someone is injured, how do we fix this, how do we help them? It may be minor in our eyes, but to them it's an emergency. We help, they're happy, it's a great feeling.

"The time off is good, too," Stephen adds. "With four days off between three, twenty-four-hour constant platoon-duty shifts, I have time to water ski, hike, do the active sports thing."

What about burn-out? With all the stress, surely mental fatigue must be a factor? "It is," Stephen explains. "But now that paramedics are also firefighters, there are places to go within the organization. You can become a dispatcher, inspector, do fire prevention, or be promoted up through the ranks, for example. A lot of options."

Alan Cowen took advantage of that last option. Starting as a paramedic in 1967, he has worked his way to the very top, holding all ranks in the EMS hierarchy. "I don't consider this a job—being a firefighter, a paramedic," he states. "It is a way of life. It's people going out and helping someone they've never met, someone they don't know, someone they'll probably never see again. And they will lay down their life for that person—without thinking. Why? Because they are trained to do so. They are there to render care, to ease suffering. It is a noble, grand profession."

Cool Web Sites to Visit

Emergency Medical Technicians
www.angelfire.com/ok/marvin1226

Journal of Emergency Medical Services
www.dotcom.com/jems/jms/jem0299.html

Women in Emergency Medicine
www.members.tripod.com/~narp

PERSONAL TRAINER

Personality, that's the key to succeeding as a personal trainer. Trainers must have the ability to communicate with their clients. A great body is not enough.

It began, in the mid-1980s, with the likes of Madonna, Costner, Cruise, and Cher. Used to being pampered and indulged on a personal level when they ate, bathed, dressed, and traveled, as the workout craze exploded, no way were celebrities going to spend time in sweaty, smelly gyms, rubbing up against common folk. Besides, the plethora of weights and stretch machines was so confusing. How was one to know what to buy, where to begin? If movie stars and the like were going to work out, they would need the assistance of an expert, a person who could guide and inspire them, one-on-one, in an upscale fitness center or, better yet, in the privacy of their home or on location. To get the bodies they, and their public, demanded, the Hollywood elite would need to hire: personal trainers!

Jeff Perlow was there during those hectic and exciting years. "They were cool times, when a few trainers were actually earning $300 to $500 an hour training stars in their Beverly Hills digs," he says. "Even I was making $35 to $70 an hour working the San Fernando Valley south of Ventura Boulevard."

Today, things have settled down, both for the profession and for Jeff. Sitting in his own club, Premier Fitness Center, in Tarzana, California, the well-built, energetic entrepreneur elaborates: "We handle over three hundred appointments a week. Sure, some clients are 'power players,' both in the biz and out. But for the most part it's just people who want to get and stay in shape, and who need the guidance of a professional to help them do so."

Personal Trainer—Doing it Right

Certified personal trainers, of which there are an estimated 190,000, in all categories, nationwide, are there to do just that, provide group and one-on-one motivating, safe, and effective exercise. What does this mean? According to the American Council on Exercise (ACE), a personal trainer "knows about basic exercise sciences, including exercise physiology, anatomy, and applied kinesiology, as well as basic nutrition, fitness assessment, exercise programming, and instructional and spotting techniques." In other words, he or she understands the human body and how to get it in shape.

But knowledge is not enough. The key to succeeding as a personal trainer is, well . . . personality. "Trainers must have the ability to communicate with their clients, express empathy," says Richard Cotton, ACE vice president for publications. "Many trainers are in their twenties, their clients are in their forties, and beyond. You can't come off as an immature kid who just loves to work out."

Aerobics Instructors: Pumping Air

Aerobic (meaning "with air") exercise, which conditions the body to process more oxygen with less effort by raising and sustaining the rate of heartbeats per minute, is considered central to any fitness program. Such instructors are part of the physical fitness team. Linda Granata, executive assistant at IDEA, The Association for Fitness Professionals, in San Diego, California, reports that the new, more inclusive term for these instructors is *group fitness professional.* "It's more than just aerobics, it is kickboxing, stepping, cycling, even Latin dancing. Anything that pumps air."

If certification by the Aerobics and Fitness Association of America (AFAA) is any indication of how much the field is growing, then practitioners are breathing easy for sure. Since 1983 this organization has certified over 145,000 fitness professionals from 73 countries. The AFAA certifies aerobics instructors, personal trainers, step instructors, weight training instructors, and kickboxing instructors.

Qualified aerobics instructors work for health clubs, exercise studios, corporations, and for individuals as personal trainers. "It is a

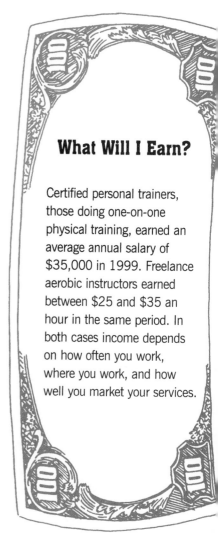

What Will I Earn?

Certified personal trainers, those doing one-on-one physical training, earned an average annual salary of $35,000 in 1999. Freelance aerobic instructors earned between $25 and $35 an hour in the same period. In both cases income depends on how often you work, where you work, and how well you market your services.

fast-growing field," says Linda, "particularly for those suited to seeking out or creating their own opportunities."

Certification—Don't Stretch Without It

Does demand for instructors mean anyone with an Arnold Schwarzenegger or Jane Fonda body to show off can be a personal trainer or aerobics instructor? Not, says Richard, if you want to be a serious professional, one who "sees personal training as an occupation rather than an avocation."

To become that professional, you need, more than anything, certification. Such certification is obtainable from a number of organizations, AFAA being one, and ACE, which is the largest nonprofit certifying agency. It requires you to pass a three-and-a-half-hour, 175-question, multiple-choice test on everything from program implementation to professional responsibility in order to become certified to instruct group exercises (aerobics) or one-on-one (personal training), and to consult on lifestyle and weight management issues. The organization receives over 130,000 inquiries about certification and exercise per year.

The American College of Sports Medicine (ACSM) administers health/fitness instructor exams at 45 sites throughout the United States. "Our exams are both written and practical," Ann Partlow, director of certification, says. "Passing our exam tells clients the trainer has met specific levels of knowledge and proficiency."

The ACSM offers three certification levels in its "Health and Fitness Track," designed primarily for leaders of preventive health programs, which are aimed at apparently healthy individuals in corporate, commercial, and community settings, or people with controlled diseases.

In the ACSM exercise leader certification, you are involved in "on-the-floor" exercise leadership. The successful candidate must demonstrate hands-on techniques for teaching safe, effective, and fundamentally sound methods of exercise.

With the ACSM health/fitness instructor certification, you are qualified to conduct individual and group exercise programs, fitness testing, and health education for apparently healthy individuals.

And for the ACSM health/fitness director certification, you will need to demonstrate administrative leadership skills for health and fitness programs primarily for healthy individuals.

Choosing Which Way to Go

ACSM, AFAA, IDEA, ACE—this alphabet soup of training and certifying organizations can get mighty confusing. Which ones do you join, which ones offer education but not certification, and which ones certification only?

Kathie Davis, executive director of IDEA, a noncertifying organization, tells us what consumers search for in a qualified personal trainer: "Anyone can say he or she is a personal trainer, but not anyone can perform the important functions of a personal trainer. With dozens of certifications available in the United States today, and with each certification organization having different standards and methods for testing a candidate's knowledge, consumers can easily be confused. It is critical that they know what to look for when choosing the personal trainer who's right for them."

From this, it is clear that the would-be trainer has some research and study of his or her own to do in selecting which way to go.

The field today, though, does seem to be telling us that being certified, regardless of from what reputable organization, will serve you well. It also may have a lot to do with whether you work or not. "All my trainers must have liability insurance," Jeff says. "They can't get that without certification or a college degree in an exercise-related major. While nine out of ten of my trainers have such degrees, all twenty-two are also certified."

Super Trainer

The IDEA lists 11 questions it recommends consumers ask in helping to assess a trainer's credentials and level of expertise.

INFORMATION

For More Information

American College of Sports Medicine (ACSM)
P.O. Box 1440
Indianapolis, IN 46206-1440
(317) 637-9200

American Council on Exercise (ACE)
5820 Oberlin Drive, Suite 102
San Diego, CA 92121-3787
(619) 535-8227

IDEA: The Association for Fitness Professionals
6190 Cornerstone Court East
Suite 204
San Diego, CA 92121-3773
(858) 535-8979
www.idealfit.com

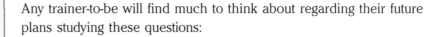

What to Read

The Personal Trainer Business Handbook
by Ed Gaut.
Pierpoint-Martin, 1994.

Personal Trainer Manual, 2nd Edition
by Richard T. Cotton.
American Council on Exercise, 1996.

Any trainer-to-be will find much to think about regarding their future plans studying these questions:

1. What is your exercise and educational background? Are you certified by a nationally recognized organization?
2. Are you a member of a professional association with a commitment to continuing education? Do you adhere to a code of ethics and professional standards?
3. Are you certified in cardiopulmonary resuscitation (CPR) and first aid?
4. Do you require a health screening or release from my doctor?
5. Can you give me references from other clients and industry professionals familiar with your knowledge and abilities?
6. Will you keep track of my workouts, chart my progress and update my medical history periodically?
7. Do you provide clear-cut policies on cancellations, billing, etc., in writing?
8. What is your rate per session? Do you offer any discounts or package deals?
9. Will you help me focus on reasonable goals, not unattainable results?
10. Do you have a network of professionals such as physicians, dieticians, physical therapists, and other fitness/health professionals?
11. What is your communications style with your clients?

Kathie Davis adds one more thing people look for in a trainer: "Careful consideration should also be given to the personality of a potential trainer. Make sure your trainer's approach—energetic versus relaxed, aggressive versus low-key—fits your personal style. Gender is also an important consideration, since some people like working with a trainer of the same sex, while others prefer one of the opposite sex."

Taking Care of Business

OK, you're in great shape, you've studied for the exams, and you're now certified. How do you make a living as a personal trainer?

There are two essential steps. You start by working for a club as an employee. At this juncture you'll handle 10 to 12 clients a day, earning $8 to $12 per hour. That works out to about $20,000 a year.

But soon you'll want to become an independent contractor. Here you must get, and keep, your own clients, then pay the club for use of the facilities. Working in a client's home eliminates this charge. With luck, ability, and personality, you're now making $25,000 to $35,000 a year, though Jeff is quick to point out: "I have independent contractors earning $100,000 a year, driving Lexuses and Porsches. It all has to do with personality and marketing."

Richard agrees, adding: "When you reach that level, you're not just doing one-on-one training. It's tedious to train professional clients eight hours a day, starting at sunrise, breaking at midday, then working into the night. Now you also want to be training the trainer, providing continuing education programs, even writing articles and books. That's success!"

True. Yet being a trainer isn't just about money. "Not every personal trainer is going to be working with the Costners, Cruises and Chers, earning the megabucks," Jeff concludes. "I'm also training nurses and teachers. It's great to see how exercise has made a tremendous difference in their lives."

Cool Web Sites to Visit

Aerobics and Fitness
Association of America
www.aerobics.com

American Fitness
Professionals & Associates
www.afpafitness.com

The Fitness Zone
www.fitnesszone.com

PHOTOGRAPHER

Most professional photographers specialize in product, portrait, or media photography. A few do work in specialties that might surprise you. There's definitely more to it than weddings and bar mitzvahs.

It looks good enough to drink—almost. Problem is, the chocolate milk shake has begun to settle in its vintage soda fountain glass. After all, the concoction's been sitting atop a meticulously creased tablecloth for three hours. It has taken that long for Kathryn Russell just to get the lighting right and to make the necessary adjustments to her various pieces of equipment.

Now, with her $3,400 large format camera secured on an even more expensive monopod (single-legged camera support), Kathryn, a professional food photographer, is ready to replace the stand-in milk shake with a fresh, mouth-watering treat. "I'll mix the new beverage myself," she says, pointing over her shoulder to the kitchen cabinets, stoves, and refrigerators lining an entire wall of her 1,200-square-foot studio in Hollywood, California. "Then, I'll snap a dozen photographs in the hope of getting one incredible picture. That photo will go in the next issue of *Single Image*, a trade catalog for advertisers and photographer reps. That one-page layout, costing $2,500, will be seen by art directors around the country."

Kathryn, whose clients include Nestlé's, Target, Disney, and Ralph's Markets, still must keep her portfolio current. "Even after a dozen years in the profession, I have to constantly show my work, prove my pictures are better than the next person's."

What makes them superior? "Style," Kathryn declares. "Style comes from how you use light, color, composition, design. For me, it's creating lots of warm, diffused light in my food images. And, you know the old saying: 'If you want to shoot for McDonald's, you've got to show hamburger.' I'm hoping the milk shake photograph will reveal my unique food-photo style."

Beyond Weddings

Professional photographers, about 139,000 nationwide, use cameras to capture the mood that sells products, provides entertainment, highlights news stories, or brings back memories. The range of what they shoot and how they shoot it is extensive.

While most professional photographers specialize in product, portrait, or media photography, there are some fascinating specialty fields. For example, industrial photographers take photographs for others to analyze engineering projects or as records of equipment development or deployment, such as the placement of an offshore oil rig. In hospitals, photographers document surgeries and other medical procedures. James Lewis, photography instructor at Los Angeles Trade Technical College, says, "There's definitely more to it than weddings and bar mitzvahs."

Regardless of what they shoot, today's photographers are working less in-house and more as independent contractors (free-lancers). After graduating from Art Center College of Design in 1984, Kathryn assisted Teri Sandison at her studio in Hollywood. "But within a year I was out on my own doing editorial photography for *Sunset* magazine," she says. "They'd say, 'Go down to San Diego, cover the Orchid Festival'! With that one client, I was paying the rent. It was a great start." Today, four out of 10 professional photographers are self-employed, a much higher proportion than the average for all occupations, according to the U.S. Department of Labor.

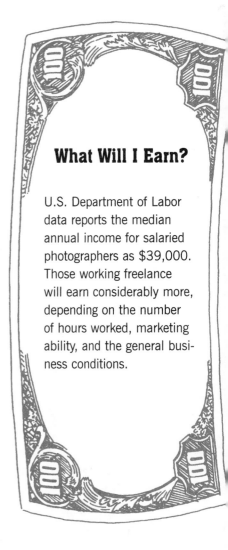

What Will I Earn?

U.S. Department of Labor data reports the median annual income for salaried photographers as $39,000. Those working freelance will earn considerably more, depending on the number of hours worked, marketing ability, and the general business conditions.

Heavy Metal Photographer

Jeanie Hill, like Kathryn, has freelanced for over a decade: "Three years ago I built a custom studio behind my garage. When I'm not on site, I'm holed up in there shooting photos."

For Jeanie, bread and butter work involves bright, shiny metal. "I have seven different wheel clients," she says. "American Racing, TSW, Epic, GNC, and Beckman, to name five. I've gotten well known for shooting metal racing rims. Clients bring high-intensity, polished wheels to my studio. I end up creating the glossy images they need for brochure and magazine layouts."

For freelancers, finding and keeping clients is crucial. "In this profession, acquiring clients who consistently bring you business is a major plus," says Jeanie. "Yet, it's a freelance game—you don't always know where business will come from. I can be busy for three months, then for a month have no work at all."

Being an entrepreneur demands well-honed business skills. "It's probably easier to make a living as a moderately good photographer and a fantastic businessperson," James volunteers, "than it is to be the world's greatest photographer but an idiot at business."

Dorie Ford, national executive director for the Advertising Photographers of America (APA), agrees that those skills are important, but adds, "It takes more. Talent, vision, how you transform what you see into something tangible . . . that's what the business is all about."

Images in Zeros and Ones

As with other image-producing endeavors today, digital technology is transforming photography.

"The digital camera, which gives us the ability to store and manipulate a filmless image, is revolutionizing our profession," James says. "Though the capital investment is still high, eventually all professional photographers will go digital for at least some of their work."

"Clients love digital," Kathryn says. "They think because there is no film and color separation, they're saving money." Jeanie, however, isn't so sure they are. "A lot of digital houses are less than honest with their clients, saying there are no film costs, etcetera. But the client must still get everything scanned from disks. Equipment expenses are passed on to the customer."

Nonetheless, the new technology is here to stay. "Digital extends the opportunity for photographers," Dorie says. "It should be seen as another tool to both deliver and manipulate photographic images. All photography schools teach the new technology."

The future of photography as a profession may well depend on it. Mark Middlebrook of Silicon Imaging predicts there will be 35 percent fewer freelance photographers in the next two to five years as a result of digital technology. "Yet that doesn't necessarily mean there will be fewer photographs," he adds.

"Freelance photographic businesses will diminish unless photographers are prepared to adjust to the future trends in the commissioning and purchasing of images," says Martin Evening, writing in the *British Journal of Photography*. "Our industry is certainly facing a major shake-up as a consequence of digital technology, but one can foresee this creating new opportunities which will enable photographers to diversify and carve out new careers for themselves rather than become redundant."

That is certainly what longtime photographer Ron Murry at Image Active in Los Angeles, has done. Rather than see digital as a threat, he and his company have totally embraced the new medium. "It has revolutionized what we do, and not just because we have erased the cost of film," he says. "With digital, I can immediately see the results of my work. I know I have the shot. If not, I take it over until I do get it. In the end, I take less shots and the percentage of my 'keepers' goes way up."

Digital photography has also resulted in the merging of traditional roles, particularly with regard to the photographer vis-à-vis the graphic designer. "Everyone is now capable of using digital technology of some form or other and each is eager to defend their corner of the market," says Martin. "These days, no single business is able to maintain a monopoly on the type of service they provide, because a consequence of technology is that we all have the means to do someone else's job."

Ron has experienced this phenomenon firsthand. "My graphic designer friends are taking more photos using the new technology," he says. "They don't need me as much. Yet, I can now do more of what they do. With photo-manipulation software, such as Adobe Photoshop, the careers of illustrator and photographer are merging. I'm becoming a graphic designer."

INFORMATION

For More Information

Advertising Photographers
of America
27 West 20th Street, Suite 601
New York, NY 10011
(800) 272-6264
(212) 807-0399

Professional Photographers
of America, Inc.
57 Forsythe Street, Suite 1600
Atlanta, GA 30303
(800) 786-6277

What to Read

*Lighting Secrets for the
Professional Photographer*
by Alan Brown.
F & W Publications, 1990.

*Professional Techniques for
the Wedding Photographer*
by George Schaub.
Watson-Guptill Publications,
1985.

Stock Shock

If all this change wasn't enough, going digital has meant a huge increase in "stock" photography, both royalty and royalty-free. Stock is used when someone, say an art director or ad agency executive, contacts a stock photo agency and says, "We are looking for two girls playing on a playground, seven-to-ten years-old." The stock agency searches its files, finds an image, and sends it to the purchaser. Payment is split between the stock company and the photographer. Every time the photograph is purchased, the photographer gets a royalty.

With royalty-free CDs full of stock photos, it is a one-time deal for the photographer. While payment may be good, the photographer gives up all rights to his image. The client may use the image over and over again, as often as he or she likes.

With advances in digital technology and the use of the Internet, acquiring such stock images becomes even easier. Here's an Internet scenario to ponder:

An art director clicks on a Web site for stock agencies that make their pictures available online. The site immediately sends out an "agent" that searches each online stock company's catalog for the right image. Within seconds, appropriate thumbnails begin to appear on screen. The three most promising images are blown up. A final selection is made, and a high-resolution image is requested. The selected image is injected with an invisible watermark specifying copyright status, etcetera, and the file is sent over the Internet to the art director. He is billed accordingly. All in less than 20 minutes. It is happening right now.

While someone, presumably a professional photographer, photographed all the images appearing in stock company archives, there's been a negative affect on work for hire. "Take the example of my grocery store account," says Kathryn. "Every week a mailer would come out, I would be shooting broccoli, lettuce, tomatoes. It was my bread-and-butter, if you'll excuse the pun. But now someone supplies royalty-free CDs that the client can use over and over again. All of a sudden, that portion of my business is gone."

The Right Image

Whether working with film or the computer, being a professional photographer isn't synonymous with commercial photography. Ed Goldstein, of Goldstein Studio in Santa Monica, California, has done his commercial gig for 20 years, but today his forte is fine art photography. "I interpret different areas of the world and create a feeling for what I see," he explains. "Whether I'm in Spain, Thailand, or Mexico, I am looking at another culture, observing different people."

Can one make a living doing fine art photography? "Yes," Ed says, "it can be quite lucrative. But it took me thirty years to get here. You must have commitment and the ability to step out of societal boundaries."

In fine art or commercial photography, the operative word is the same—competitive. "Though there will always be photographers," Kathryn declares, "and more photographs are printed today than ever before, photographers' ranks aren't growing appreciably. Competition is fierce."

People flock to photography schools everywhere. "Places like Art Center College of Design in Pasadena and Brooks Institute of Photography in Santa Barbara graduate a class of twenty or so would-be photographers every fifteen weeks," says James. "It's a glamorous field, on the surface. In reality, it is darn hard work, physically and mentally."

But, what field isn't? As Kathryn says, "If you're good, you'll work. You must be technically skilled and know how to use your equipment well. In addition, it's necessary to be a problem solver and able to execute a good idea. Make your clients look terrific through the pictures you take. If you remember that simple point—you're going to work."

Cool Web Sites to Visit

Advertising Photographers of America
www.apanational.com

APPA-Commercial Photographer of the Year 1999-Merle Prosofsky
www.appa.ab.ca/comm4.htm

Food Styling, Writing and Photography Forum
www.webfoodpros.com/ wwwboard/style/index.html

Hot Concepts!

Online Job Search

Online job searching is here. According to the investment firm of Thomas Weisel Partners, the number of online job seekers was expected to rise from 1.5 million in 1999 to as many as 10 million in 2003. And it isn't just computer types who are using the services of online job finders such as Monster.com and HotJobs.com. According to Bernard Hodes, president of CareerMosaic, "Though computer and engineering jobs are still widely sought online, the Web is increasingly going mainstream."

With online job search sites, you can both search for a job and be sought after. But before clicking your way through job-hunting cyberspace, Erin Arvedlund, a staff reporter for TheStreet.com, extends this cautionary note: "Over 90 percent of resumes and applications submitted online never get an acknowledgment or response. Also, job seekers outnumber positions by a margin of five to one."

So keeping that in mind, here is a listing from Hunt-Scanlon Advisors of the online job search firms most frequently used by company recruiters:

- Monster.com   59 percent
- CareerMosaic   37 percent
- Headhunter.net   26 percent
- America's Job Bank 26 percent
- JOBTRAK   24 percent

The important thing is, according to Erin, not to "limit yourself to online job sites to find that perfect job. Traditional methods should not be forsaken."

PRIVATE COACH

Joe Friel spent so much time writing out individual triathlon schedules for his customers that he sold his running equipment store and began private coaching full-time. The 1990s could well have been the first decade of the private coach.

Hot Career

31

"A sprinter is born, a distance man, made," so goes the mantra in the running world. Many track and field coaches consider it gospel. Not coach David Buchanan, whose physique, at 51, concedes little to Arnold Schwarzenegger. "Sure, I don't claim I can turn a slowpoke into a Carl Lewis," he says. "But speed can be taught. I will never tell a kid, 'I guarantee you'll run 4.3 in 40 yards.' But I do promise him he'll run faster than ever before, and, most importantly, more efficiently."

Brian Adams, now 20, is an example of whom coach David speaks. As a sophomore, playing junior varsity football at Chaminade High School in Canoga Park, California, Brian needed to increase his speed in order to reach full potential. "His dad called me out of the blue," says David. "'Can you work with my boy, speed him up?' he asked me. It was my first assignment as a private coach and I jumped at the opportunity."

Three times a week, for over a month, David worked with Brian at a local park. "His problem was the one many runners have," says David. "They don't use their arms at all, or, if they do, they use them incorrectly. Arms should not rotate across the chest when you run. They should be at your side."

With each workout, Brian dropped his arms further. And as he did, his running times fell, too. "He was running 5.3 in 40 yards when we started," David says. "A month later, he hit 4.8 seconds, a school record. The kid was on his way to a successful season. And I was on my way to a career as a private sports coach."

Not Just Tennis and Golf

Private coaches, tutors, instructors, whatever they're known as, provide individual instruction, for a fee, on every aspect of a sport, just like the neighborhood piano teacher does for music lessons. Eric Sondheimer, *Los Angeles Times* sports staff writer, has said that the 1990s may have been the first decade of the private coach. "Parents now pay money for so-called experts to teach their children how to hit, throw, pass, run, kick, dribble, you name it. An amazing growth is taking place."

The *Los Angeles Times* reported that in 1999 Southern California parents spent an unbelievable $1 billion to give their children "the edge" in sports.

Reggie Smith, former L.A. Dodger, charges a fortune as a batting coach. He attracts clients from as far away as Japan to his hitting clinics.

When Jim Parkay, who pitched for the Chicago White Sox, came out to California, he told a few friends he would be giving lessons at a local park. So many folks showed up, they had to take a number.

When Joe Friel opened a running equipment store in Fort Collins, Colorado, customers began asking him how they should train for the triathlon. Before long, he was spending so much time writing out individual schedules, for a fee, that he sold the store and began private coaching full-time. The author of five books, including *The Triathlete's Training Bible*, Joe now coaches only 12 athletes a year, has three associates who do likewise, and is making a good living as a private coach.

Simon Essl is marketing manager for Carmichael Training Systems (CTS), a full-service coaching company based in Colorado. "Having our star pupil, Lance Armstrong, win the Tour De France, hasn't hurt our reputation," he says. "Yet, our program isn't just for people like Lance. We try to bring high-quality coaching to the masses."

That's a similar goal for two former Olympic coaches, Lois Daigneault and Nick Backer. Founders of Peak Performance Swim Camp based in Florida, they travel all over the world to help swimmers of all ages and abilities swim better. "After five years in business," Lois says, "we are finally seeing the fruits of our labor. We are making money."

Being paid to coach individuals is for many a new and unusual concept. But why not? "Many ex-college players, their careers over, are making money as club coaches," says Eric.

But shouldn't these folks want to do it gratis, especially with youngsters, out of dedication, the kindness of their heart? "I discourage people from doing it for free," says Sam Callen, applied sports science manager at the USA Cycling Federation. "It waters down the value of their service. People are willing to pay for tennis and golf lessons, why not for instruction in other sports?"

Looking for That Edge

Chad Smith, a 15-year-old who plays football and runs track at Crespi Carmelite High School in Encino, California is here at Los Angeles Valley College, working with Dave one hour a day, four days a week—Monday and Wednesday with weights, Tuesday and Thursday with running.

"I want an edge," the buffed and toned player says. "I just don't get enough individual attention from my high school coach. I'm not sure why."

Chad's father, Frank, who accompanies him to every workout, and is shelling out $200 a week to see his son develop, interjects: "I am from the old school, when coaches coached," he says. "Today, they are either wannabes or has-beens. The coach doesn't know how to punt, run, or jump. Either that, or he doesn't have the time."

Dave is less judgmental. "I say to their coach, 'Hey, I have the time, you don't. You are more concerned with the overall game, the grand strategy. I'll take care of the details.' Still, often my athletes won't tell their school coach they have a private coach. It could cause problems."

"Parents look for one of two things," says Eric. "Some want a babysitter, of sorts, someone to watch over the kid for a few hours,

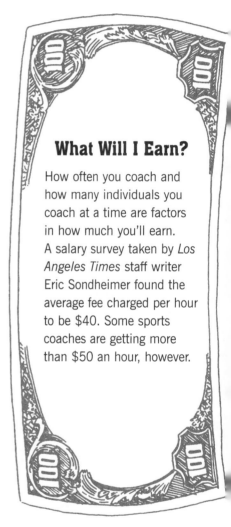

What Will I Earn?

How often you coach and how many individuals you coach at a time are factors in how much you'll earn. A salary survey taken by *Los Angeles Times* staff writer Eric Sondheimer found the average fee charged per hour to be $40. Some sports coaches are getting more than $50 an hour, however.

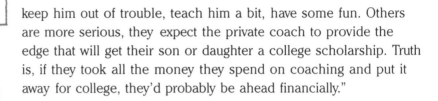

INFORMATION

For More Information

National Clearinghouse for
Youth Sports Information
(NCYSI)
(800) 638-KIDS

keep him out of trouble, teach him a bit, have some fun. Others are more serious, they expect the private coach to provide the edge that will get their son or daughter a college scholarship. Truth is, if they took all the money they spend on coaching and put it away for college, they'd probably be ahead financially."

Private Coach, Private School

Central casting would be hard-pressed to find a better Don Drysdale look-alike than Tim Costic. At 28, and decked out in his baseball uniform, he looks, well, like the baseball player he is. After four years with the Minnesota Twins organization, Tim now works full-time at the West Coast Baseball School ("home of future prospects") in Agoura Hills, California. The school, employing nine former baseball players, operates year-round. "We have our high periods, January to June, and our slower times, around Christmas. But we're a going concern."

Charging $30 for a half hour and $49 for a full-hour, Tim and his colleagues have youngsters ages 10 to 18 lining up to swing the bat, pitch the ball, and, generally develop their skills. It's money well spent, he feels. "Heck, around here horseback riding cost $60 an hour. We're a better deal than that."

For Tim, being a private coach in a private school setting seems ideal. "I am doing something I love, coaching, in the game I love, baseball." he says. "What more can I ask? I'm making a living in baseball."

A Coach's Life for You?

Must you have played pro ball, coached in the Olympics, or won the Tour de France to become a successful private sports coach? "Not at all," says Sam, "though it certainly helps if the coach has participated in the sport."

Beyond that, however, there is the ability to communicate, to get your point across. "In a large group, you may have to individually communicate with each athlete, deal with them as individuals,"

says Sam. "A football coach, for instance, knows that with some players he can yell in their face and they'll respond positively. With that same approach, other players may quit on him."

The Australian Sports Commission lists a half dozen criteria for successful coaching:

1. Proficiency in the sport
2. Good interpersonal skills
3. Appreciation of the developmental needs of young athletes
4. Enthusiasm and a strong interest in the sport
5. A high level of physical fitness, discipline and dedication
6. Possibly, a previous career as an accomplished sports person, although this doesn't guarantee success as a coach.

"The important thing is people skills," advises Joe. "No matter what the knowledge, if you're arrogant or self-centered, you'll just turn everyone off."

"It's someone who can get along with kids and, just as important, their parents," say Eric. "Parents have to trust that you know what you're doing. I am not sure it matters if you're getting results."

"For some, it is how far can we go, how many meters, miles, we can swim," says Lois. "We believe it's a triangle: physical, mental, and technical. You have to look at an athlete and be able to determine where you think he or she should go. It is knowing the personality and where to direct it."

Richard Stratton, of the National Youth Sports Coaches Association (NYSCA), sums it up, at least when working with youngsters, this way: "It's what Rainer Martens, in his book *Successful Coaching,* says is the foundation of the Bill of Rights for Young Athletes, 'athletes first, winning second.' Or, 'the main thing is to keep the athlete the main thing.' This does not rule out winning as a goal. It merely suggests that it be a secondary goal in youth sports programs."

Achievement is certainly not to be ruled out, either. And since athletes are paying to be coached—as adults or as children whose parents pay—they expect results. Which leads us to the business end of what you do as a sports coach.

What to Read

Successful Coaching
by Rainer Martens.
Human Kinetics Publishers,
1996.

*The Triathlete's Training Bible:
A Complete Training Guide
for the Competitive Multisport
Athlete*
by Joe Friel.
Velo Press, 1998.

Not All Fun and Games

Whether you're operating as an individual, charging $20 to $50 an hour to coach in a school gym after hours or at a neighborhood park, or running your own school with a staff and permanent facilities, you'll have to tend to the business side. For some, that's just fine. For others, it's time away from the sport, what they truly love.

"We did not come from the business end," says Lois. "We were coaches working for a committee at a set salary. What a change! There is so much involved. We had to learn to stand back and say, 'Let's not get this part of us involved. This is the business end.' It's keeping in mind the final product, we have to go on deck and coach. The majority of our time is spent just getting there."

"You must have some business sense," cautions Sam. "When I first started out, I gave everyone in my group the whole training program for the marathon at one time. Well, they didn't have a whole lot of incentive to pay me that fee next month. I now parcel out my advice week-by-week."

"Basically, we act as a marketing tool for the coaches we hire," says Simon. "They are independent contractors, located around the country, and we feed new clients to them."

"I spend up to two hours a day just answering e-mail messages from athletes around the world," Joe says. "Yet, it wasn't always that way. You're essentially a freelance coach. Like a freelancer in any job, it's tough. You have to establish who you are, your credibility."

True. But once that happens, look out. "I am turning away business," David says. At first I sent out reams of flyers with little response. But then Brian came along. His breaking the school record was my greatest advertisement. Word-of-mouth has done the rest. We are both winners."

Cool Web Sites to Visit

The National Youth Sports Coaches Association
www.nays.org/nysca.html

Sports Coaching as a Career
www.ausport.gov.au/coapro.html

USA Cycling
www.usacycling.org/corp/?documents/history.html

PRIVATE INVESTIGATOR

*A .357 Magnum in your right hand, a bottle of
scotch in your left, and a beautiful blonde sitting on
your lap. . . . Forget that image! Being a PI is
more like being a reporter, where your basic infor-
mation-gathering technique is to ask who, what,
why, when, and where.*

Hot Career

32

The biological father, Carlos, no longer has the right under
California law to keep his three-year old daughter; two private
investigators have a court order to prove it.

Still, grabbing the child and placing her in a mother's waiting
arms isn't going to be easy. Advanced planning demands that a male
and female PI, the mother, and two cars (one to block the suspect
should he attempt pursuit) will be necessary to pull it off.

With a stakeout in progress, Carlos drives into the shopping center.
As he exits his car, child in tow, a "husband and wife" approach,
exchanging admiring glances. "What a gorgeous child," the woman
says, kneeling to stare into the little girl's hazel eyes. In a flash, the
child is lifted, swung around, and shoved into the outstretched arms of
her mother, who, on cue, has emerged from a nearby car.

"Don't be a jerk," barks private investigator Richard Mora to the
father. "Here is the court order. Legally, she belongs with her mother."

As mother, child, and the PIs drive off, Carlos's attempt to give
chase is thwarted, his exit blocked by a strategically placed car.

Reuniting a child with a rightful family member is tricky but
rewarding PI work. For the most part, though, it's, as Richard, a
licensed private investigator and owner/manager of Deano
Investigations, Inc. in Granada Hills, California, explains, "Gathering
information on people, places, and things for a fee."

More specifically, according to a Security and Investigative Services
Fact Sheet distributed by the State of California Department of
Consumer Affairs: "A private investigator is an individual who (1)
investigates crimes; (2) investigates the identity, business, occupation,

honesty, etcetera of a person; (3) investigates the location of lost or stolen property; (4) investigates the cause of fires, losses, accidents, damage or injury; or (5) secures evidence for use in court."

Where and how does a PI work?

Wayne Little, president of the West Coast Detective Academy in North Hollywood, California, says that "many do surveillance or undercover work. Undercover is great because you might work 90 days to a year in one place, such as inside a company. Yet others do a straight 9-to-5 thing in-house at an agency, handling locates and asset searches."

Who hires private investigators?

"Whether working for themselves or an agency," Wayne continues, "just about everyone: hotels, insurance companies, retail stores, hospitals, government offices, attorneys, collection agencies, and even amusement parks."

Gumshoes and the Internet

Until recently most private investigators were ex-cops. As Richard explains, "Police officers get off the force with a pension and PI work seems like a natural. But they don't always make good investigators. As ex-cops they may have been good interrogators, with the ability to trick someone into answering with strong cross-examination. As PIs, however, they must take a different approach, one that gets information out in a more beguiling, captivating manner."

Wayne agrees, but goes one step further. "Most ex-cops are police-minded but not business-minded," he says. "Law enforcement isn't necessarily the best experience for today's private investigator. Investigation now often means surfing the Net. From an office, the PI can research employee theft and set up electronic countermeasures to protect valuable company information. And you don't have to spend time schmoozing down at the courthouse."

But, as Richard is quick to point out, "you still have to be outside to pull a case together. A PI has to know the streets, be able to follow someone out of Dodger Stadium, if need be."

Take surveillance. It requires a certain knack, savvy. Richard illustrates: "A private investigator sitting in his car and feeling like a private

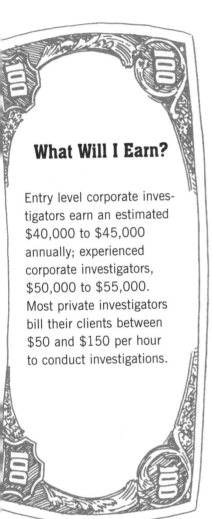

What Will I Earn?

Entry level corporate investigators earn an estimated $40,000 to $45,000 annually; experienced corporate investigators, $50,000 to $55,000. Most private investigators bill their clients between $50 and $150 per hour to conduct investigations.

investigator is wrong for the job. You have to sit in that car and belong to the neighborhood, to whatever pretext cover story you're supposed to be part of. If you have any other mindset, it won't work. Databank junkies, as we call them, are needed. But the gumshoe is key."

Licensed Know-It-Alls

The California Association of Licensed Investigators (CALI) is holding its annual convention in Reno, Nevada. Perusing the program, one is struck by the breadth of seminar subject matter. To be a PI, you really must be a know-it-all.

There's the seminar on Advanced AOE/COE Investigation. It focuses not only on identifying the factors of stress claims but more importantly on how to identify the indicators of a "faked" stress claim. This includes what type of questions to ask when conducting work-related stress injury claims and how to effectively interview the claimant, coworker, and others related in the claim.

Or there is the Tort and Negligence Liability seminar. "Do you know the prima facie for negligence?" Presenter Lisa Rosenthal asks. "Do you understand when a duty of care is owed? The answers to these questions are important in conducting an effective liability investigation either for the plaintiff or defense side of a case."

Of course, Crime Scene Analysis is a must seminar topic. "From bloodstains to footprints, crime scene analysis is an art in itself," says Gary Sims, seminar presenter and a criminalist working in the DNA lab of the California Department of Justice. His most notable case was the O. J. Simpson trial, at which he testified as an expert witness. Gary uses slides from the actual murder scene of that case to demonstrate how to analyze the crime scene for pertinent evidence.

For your own protection, there is Liability Protection, a seminar given by James Cawood, president of Factor One, Inc., and Protective Solutions, Inc. "In our ever-growing litigious society, the inevitable can happen to you," he warns. "What preventative steps can you take to avoid getting sued by your client or a third party?" James discusses how you can reduce the odds of someone taking you to court.

Being a PI, it's not all *The Rockford Files*. Oh that public image!

INFORMATION

For More Information

Contact your state's association of licensed investigators.

What to Read

Introduction to Private Investigation
by Joseph A. Travers.
Charles C. Thompson
Publishers, 1997.

Undercover Operations:
A Manual for the Private
Investigator
by Kingdon Peter Anderson.
Carol Publishing Group, 1990.

Prying for a Living

Whether on the Net or knocking on doors, the PI's persona is a mixed one.

"We love the clever, danger-defying, free-spirited PIs portrayed in novels and on television," says Carter Spohn of Spohn Investigations. "Yet, we know PIs are snoops, sneaks, even spies, and often that means looking at ourselves. It's not a profession that'll ever have a great image. We look into peoples' backgrounds, pry a lot."

Carter cites the Rebecca Schaeffer case as an example of what can go wrong. Rebecca Schaeffer was an actress who starred on the television series *My Sister Sam*.

"Many people blame a greedy PI for the actress's murder by a deranged stalker," he says. "A PI was hired by the stalker to get her address, and he did so through DMV records. The incident quickly became an 'access to public records' issue. As a result today—and I'm not saying it's not necessary—a private investigator has to be licensed and bonded to have that kind of access."

To be fair, prying and probing has its individual and societal benefits.

Sharon Hilke, executive director of the California Association of Licensed Investigators (CALI), says, "There is a legitimate need for information. Locating witnesses, investigating insurance fraud, finding abducted or stolen children, the list goes on and on. In the process, we've become one of the most regulated industries in the nation."

And for good reason. Richard gives an example: "Say you are in a restaurant following a suspect. You place a briefcase with a listening device say eight to ten feet away. Are you violating the law? Yes, you are. I am recording a conversation without the authority of the people involved. But what do I do with the information? If the man is arrested, the recording will be thrown out of court. But as a PI, I don't really care. I just want information, to get what I can on the guy. It is confidential between me and the client. But I admit it is a gray area."

PIs, once again, are not cops. Yet, while no PI carries a badge, many carry state licenses.

"If you only do work involving public information, you don't need a license," Richard explains. "But for surveillance, undercover work, and to open your own shop, you'll want to become a licensed PI." Doing so is not easy.

In California, for example, to qualify to take the two-hour exam, which covers laws and regulations, terminology, civil and criminal liability, evidence handling, undercover investigations, and surveillance, you must have three years (2,000 hours each year, totaling 6,000 hours) of compensated experience in investigative work; or a law or police science degree plus two years (4,000 hours) of experience; or an associate's degree in police science, criminal law, or justice plus two and a half years (5,000 hours) of experience.

It should be noted that having a license gives you no more rights or privileges than the average citizen, and no more liberty to intrude. Furthermore, if you want to pack a gun, which is not always necessary or even a good idea, you'll need to obtain a permit. That can be an arduous process, at least in most states.

Setting the Image Straight

Being a PI is not all work. "I had an interesting case involving an American and a Mexican national," Richard says. "I had to go down to Mexico, do a background search, work with both the U.S. and Mexican customs officials. But when it was over, I got to spend a few days in Cabo San Lucas, fishing and partying it up."

Ah, there's that movie image again, one Richard has to deal with, even at home.

"One day," Richard goes on, "my twelve-year-old daughter said: 'Dad, tomorrow my teacher will ask me what you do for a living. Explain it again.' I said, 'Honey, I am a private investigator. That means I have a .357 Magnum in my right hand, a bottle of scotch in the left, and a beautiful blonde, whose problems I'm solving, sitting on my lap. . . . Actually sweetheart, its just like being a reporter, where the basic information gathering technique is to ask who, what, why, when, and where. Keep that concept in mind and you'll know what we do.'

"Of course, when she got to class she remembered only the first part. If you're thinking about becoming a private investigator, keep the second part, with its more realistic image, in mind."

Cool Web Sites to Visit

Private Investigator Directory
www.rominberlegal/PiUSA.htm

Private Investigator Listing
http://home.hiwaay.net/~pvteye/geo.html

The Spy Shop
www.w2.com/docs2/z/spyshop.html

PUBLIC SPEAKER

*The field is extremely competitive. You'll need to
spend years honing your craft, marketing yourself.
It will take effort. The challenge is in building a
business, providing for a possibly very high
income.*

Though having similar last names, no one paying for their
services would ever confuse Tony Robbins with Ed
Robinson. Tony, the seasoned infomercial king, charges
$125,000 for an all-day seminar. Ed, on the other hand, is just tran-
sitioning into the professional speaking ranks. For tonight's one-
hour speech, to 50 ethnically diverse students seeking their GED
(general equivalency [high school] diploma), Ed will be paid considerably less.

Never mind. The 40-year-old, self-assured TV talk show host
from Compton, California, is fired up, ready to go. He has an
evening's work cut out for him here at the Pasadena College
Community Education Center in Pasadena, California. The students, many of whom must remain standing as they crowd into
a tiny classroom, have themselves paid nothing to hear Ed's
inspirational message. So unlike the typical audience for motivational speaking, business types who arrive eager, indeed
demanding, to be inspired, the students, ages 18 to 48, seem
bewildered, out of place.

"*Yes, I have college degrees,*" Ed begins, as he paces before
suspicious eyes and folded arms. "*My B.A. is in Blatant Adversity.
I have a B.S. in Battle Scars. I earned an M.A. in Much Agony
and an M.S. in Much Suffering. I even have an M.B.A., you know,
Many Bad Attitudes. Nonetheless, my Ph.D. is my proudest
achievement. I am, today, a Pretty Happy Dude.*"

Frowns turn to smiles, heads bob, arms unfold. With a great
opener, Ed has hooked his audience. It's going to be a good night.

Astronauts to Jokesters

Professional public speakers, those who earn a fee for speaking to corporations, associations, colleges, and the like, are talking it up everywhere. While no one knows how many speak for a living—part- or full-time—speakers' bureaus, the organizations that act as go-betweens for speakers and those looking to hire speakers, such as management companies, professional meeting planners, and production companies, report booming business. "We have four thousand speakers," Kate Anderson, senior vice president of Leading Authorities, Inc., perhaps the nation's largest speakers' bureau, says. "Right now, adventure speakers are hot, those that climb mountains, circle the globe in a balloon."

Indeed, Leading Authorities' 200-page, four-color guide includes just about everyone you've ever heard of, from astronaut Buzz Aldrin, to Scott Adams, creator of *Dilbert*. All those listed—masters of motivation, game theorists, sports strategists, humorists, and values disseminators—are making money for talking.

How much money? Those on Leading Authorities' A-list earn under $5,000 per speaking engagement, but make it to their G-list and you'll start at a cool $75,000 per. Sounds great, doesn't it? All that money just for, in some cases, an hour-long speech? Reality check. As Mark French, president of Leading Authorities, told the *Wall Street Journal* recently: "There are probably a couple hundred who are doing well. There are probably twenty who are doing exceptionally well."

Yes, it's a tough business, often requiring years of preparation, when you spend time not only honing your craft but marketing yourself and developing those all important back-of-the-room (BOR) products (tapes, books, course materials) to sell. "In the business of speaking," says Doug Malouf, perhaps Australia's best known professional speaker, "the elevator to success is permanently out of order. The only way up is via the staircase. Am I saying it is hard work? That it will take effort? Believe it!"

"Most speakers don't start out wanting to be professionals," says Terry Paulson, president of the National Speakers Association (NSA), and author of *50 Tips for Speaking Like a Pro*, "Usually, they simply begin doing it on a volunteer basis, talking to associations. Then all of a sudden they're asked to speak for a fee. They realize this is a profession. Yes, there are moneymaking opportunities. But the challenge is in building a business, providing a steady income."

What Will I Earn?

Fees are dependent not only on what you charge per speech, but how often you speak.

INFORMATION

For More Information

National Speakers Association
1500 South Priest Drive
Tempe, AZ 85281
(602) 968-2552
www.nsaspeaker.org

Toastmasters International, Inc.
23182 Arroyo Vista
Rancho Santa Margarita, CA
92688
1-800-9WE-SPEAK
www.toastmasters.org

Connection, Not Perfection

Ed Robinson is 15 minutes into his speech, then, *wham*—he utters the F-word

"*Fear, it's a killer, folks. Fear, that four-letter word, has done more to destroy aspirations, hopes, and dreams then anything else. I want you to see fear as an acronym. F is for focus; E for expectations; A, attitude; and R, responsibility. Let me show you what I mean. . . .*"

Watching Ed's audience, you sense they're in the presence of a pro, one who understands what it means to communicate, to connect.

But just what are the elements of effective public speaking? For answers, we need only turn to Jack Barnard, speaker, performer, group leader, and author of *We Get Our Cue from You.*

"Connection with the audience and the ability to be in the present moment are equally as important as content," he says. "If you have great content but are not connecting with the audience, they're already thinking about lunch. Remember, what that audience is hoping for is a magic moment. They want connection, not perfection."

Why is that so hard to achieve? "Too many speakers are talking about themselves; their whole approach is insular," Jack continues. "The audience doesn't feel it's about them. As a result, retention is nil."

Michael Jeffreys, author of *The 8 Success Secrets of the Motivational Superstars*, and a full-time professional speaker for groups as diverse as Head Start and Boeing, agrees. To break down speaker/audience barriers, he uses humor, probably the most important element in public speaking. "Your message must be entertaining as well as informational," he declares. "Above all, don't take yourself too seriously. Remember, the size of your funeral will always depend on the weather anyway."

Business-Speak

"*My mother was forty-five years old when she came home one day, gathered her nine kids around her, and said, 'I need to talk to you. You know, I never finished high school. I want to finish, I want to graduate, I want my GED.'*"

Thirty minutes into his talk, Ed has hit paydirt with a story from his own life. The audience is mesmerized. "The man can relate," one hears an older student whisper.

Yet, delivering a good speech, connecting to your audience, giving them something, as Jack says, "to cheer about, to cry for," is only part of what it will take to succeed as a professional—a person who speaks for a living. There is a business side—one you will need to cultivate as earnestly as you do your next presentation.

"The speaking industry is extremely competitive, but not impossibly so if you are willing to learn about how to market yourself," says Dottie Walters, founder of the International Group of Agents and Bureaus, owner of Walters International Speakers Bureau, and author of the best-selling "bible" in the field, *Speak and Grow Rich*. Here are questions Dottie says you should ask yourself:

- What are your areas of expertise?
- What else do you offer: seminars, panels, consulting, products?
- Do you have presentation kits prepared: demo tapes and a fee schedule with a menu of services?
- Do you have an office set up with dedicated fax line(s), a system to send your full packages out while you are on the road, and a way to return phone calls within 60 minutes of someone leaving you a message?

These are but a few questions you better have positive answers to, Dottie insists. "Consider yourself a speaker who is a manufacturer of programs and products," the talkative and vivacious dean of the subject continues. "Those products: audio tapes, videotapes, posters, books, workbooks, can often be 50 percent or more of your income.

"Only after you have developed such back-of-the room materials," Dottie states, "and you have done at least one hundred paid dates for fees of at least $2,000 per one-hour program, on topics that can be sold to association, corporate, or college markets, should you approach speakers bureaus. Consider the speakers bureau as your manufacturer's rep dealing with independent clients, associations, corporations, and the like."

What to Read

50 Tips For Speaking Like a Pro
by Terry Paulson.
Crisp Publications, 1999.

Public Speaking
by Steven Frank.
Adams Media Corporation, 1999.

Speak and Grow Rich
by Dottie Walters
and Lilly Walters.
Prentice Hall, 1997.

The Everything® Toasts Book
by Dale Irwin.
Adams Media Corporation, 2000.

One route to professional status is to obtain your Certified Speaking Professionals (CSP) designation, an honor that is earned, not awarded, by the National Speakers Association. Those who earn the certificate are educated, committed, and creative professionals who are considered masters in the industry. It is a coveted reward for hard work and speaking accomplishment. For further information, contact the NSA.

Take Me Home

But what if you want to speak professionally, yet you're just starting out, or you simply don't have the time or the knowledge to market yourself? Is there an alternative to the traditional speakers bureau—which will take 25 to 30 percent of your fee, assuming you can get them to take you at all?

"Yes," says Susan Levin, publisher/owner of *Speakers for Free and Fee, Consultants & Entertainment Directory* (*www.speakerservices.com*), a bimonthly publication distributed free. "We are a marketing tool for professional people to grow their business through speaking," she says. "I recognized that if a professional person could get out in front of an audience of seventy-five to one hundred people, it would be a great marketing tool; a terrific way to attract clients, develop mailing lists, and sell their seminars, workshops, and BOR products."

There's that BOR thing, again. Why, aside from income, is it so important?

"People want to take you home with them," Susan explains. "After a great speech, they'll be hungry for more. They will want to ingest you. BOR products give them the chance."

Ed, whose listing was found in Susan's publication, has yet to develop much in the way of BOR materials. Too bad. As he concludes with "*Life is hard by the yard, but essential by the inch*," tonight's audience clearly wants more, to embrace his message in an ongoing way.

The BOR products will surely come. Perhaps a book of family stories? "You know," Ed says, "my father, on his deathbed at age fifty-one, told me he was illiterate. My dad must have had a very frustrating life. I can't forget that conversation. I want to give something back. I may never 'Speak and Grow Rich,' as Dottie's good book says. But this I do know—every time I speak, I grow."

Cool Web Sites to Visit

NSA Professional Speakers magazine
www.businessconsultants.net

Professional Speakers, Keynote Speaker-Gary Wollin
www.garywollin.com/index.html

Speakers Platform
www.speaking.com/index.html

PUBLIC RELATIONS SPECIALIST/PUBLICIST

This is not a field for baby-faced amateurs.
In PR, you are almost like a bodyguard.
Sometimes you're there to take a bullet.

Hot Career

34

OKS! OOKS?—you've never heard of them? Well, that's about to change if Shari L. Goldstein, a public relations specialist, operating out of Syosset, New York, has her say. Shari plans to take OOKS, the little hardware hooks used to hang pictures in museums, major art galleries, and she hopes, soon, your home, on a national marketing campaign. All a result of PR inspiration.

"This fellow calls me and says, 'I make picture hanging hardware and I can't get any respect,'" the savvy, solo practitioner explains. "He needs to sell his product not to the press or the public, but to a major hardware store chain.

"So, I hire a guy who holds the Guinness world record as the fastest painter in the world," Shari continues, her excitement evident. "We set up an event in a local hardware store: balloons, coffee, donuts, raffles, giveaways, the works. And, of course, we videotape the whole thing, including the artist splashing out a painting every minute and a half. We're plastered with local radio and TV coverage.

"A week later, my client goes into his big pitch meeting with video clips and audio tapes. Wham!—the chain guys buy it, he gets shelf space—nationwide. That PR promo convinced store executives that my client was committed to getting people excited about his product. I love the creative side of public relations."

Sales Job

It's the creative side that attracts people to the profession. According to U.S. Labor Department statistics, over two hundred thousand work in the field—in-house, for a PR agency, or as a sole practitioner. Approximately twenty thousand are members of the Public Relations Society of America (PRSA). Sixty-five percent in the organization are women.

As a PR specialist or publicist, you are above all an advocate, be it for a business, government, university, hospital, or charity. You strive to build and maintain positive relationships with what are called "publics": consumers, employees, community groups, and those in the media.

"Public relations is more than media relations," says Sam Waltz, CEO and board chairman of PRSA. "Today, a public relations specialist must be able to work broadly across disciplines: PR, advertising, special events, management, and seminar presentations."

"PR is difficult to get your arms around," Dan Durazo, executive vice president of Durazo Communications in Los Angeles, says. "It is so diverse. If our clients need a certain skill set, we provide it. Other agency's clients may have totally different needs. Our clients, Anheuser-Busch, GTE, and Merrill Lynch—deal with the Hispanic market, media, and community. We live within that world for our clients."

Being a publicist is similar to working in PR, with an important difference. "PR is more corporate, business," says Shari. "As a publicist you handle individuals, say a sports figure or a movie star. You navigate them through the world of controlled publicity."

Though the work is broad, PR is still, at its heart, about relating to the public. "Essentially, this profession is a lot like sales," says the Women's Wire Web site. "You work for a person, product, or company that wants to get its message out. Your job is to convince journalists, most of whom have little interest in hearing from you, that they should cover your client, whether it's in a front-page news article or a momentary blip on a local TV show. It can also be your role to respond to journalists when they poke around asking unflattering questions about your clients."

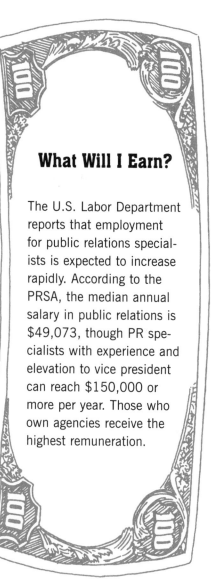

What Will I Earn?

The U.S. Labor Department reports that employment for public relations specialists is expected to increase rapidly. According to the PRSA, the median annual salary in public relations is $49,073, though PR specialists with experience and elevation to vice president can reach $150,000 or more per year. Those who own agencies receive the highest remuneration.

Damage Control

Joann Killeen, of Killeen Communications, Los Angeles, knows what it's like to put out the fires. In the spring of 1997, while working as an account supervisor for a PR firm whose major client was one of the world's largest software firms, all hell broke lose. A hacker broke into the corporation's Web site and crashed it. Not only were millions of consumers inconvenienced, the embarrassment was unbearable. "It was a challenging assignment because it impacted so many people," Joann says. "But we quickly sprang into action and were able to calm the users down. We let everyone know security was a top issue, that we took it seriously. We had a patch in place within twenty-four hours. The problem was solved with good, effective PR."

Burke Stinson, senior public relations director for AT&T, isn't so sure PR professionals still have what it takes to respond so effectively. "This is not a field for baby-faced amateurs," he insists. "In PR, you are almost like a bodyguard. Sometimes you're there to take a bullet. Many in the field are so insecure in their abilities to express themselves or relate to the media that they run for the shadows. Almost anyone can handle good news. It's how you deal with bad news in a professional, candid way that separates the superb from the mediocre in public relations."

Most public relations professionals come from a journalism background. That's understandable, because you have to know how to work with the press. "In the old days, say twenty years ago, it was hard to get into PR unless you had exposure in journalism," says Dan. "Now, you can get there straight from college. But if you don't understand the world from a journalist's viewpoint—deadlines, what makes a good story, how to sell that story—you're going to be at a disadvantage. You have to know the journalist's hot buttons."

"PR's inherent quality is knowing how news and events happen, how they flow, how they affect outcomes," Peter O'Malley, a public relations specialist based in Ottawa, Canada, says. "It is not so much the personal relationship with a reporter, but the mechanics of distributing information that you must understand. A systematic approach to the job determines outcomes."

INFORMATION

For More Information

International Association of Business Communicators (IABC)
One Hallidie Plaza
Suite 600
San Francisco, CA 94102
(415) 547-4700
fax (415) 544-4747
www.iabc.com

Public Relations Society of America (PRSA)
33 Irving Place
New York, NY 10003-2376
(212) 995-2230
fax (212) 995-0757
www.prsa.org

"You must possess an above-average ability to think clearly, write well, and analyze objectively," says Burke. "Those basics are being disregarded by many folks who fancy themselves as people persons; you know, integrators, facilitators, brainstormers. They seem to think reading, writing, and basic PR scholarship should be done by others."

"Above all, you must have personal credibility," says Laurie Gasper Owin, public policy manager for the Southern California Gas Company and president of the Los Angeles chapter of PRSA. "You are representing a client. Credibility is incredibly difficult to obtain and so easy to lose."

Credibility and, with it, self-confidence: "If you are going to represent yourself to the public, you must have great presence, maturity, the ability to carry yourself well," says Dan. "Self-confidence."

More Work Than Time

It took a lot of self-confidence for Brenda Sullivan, with no plans and no goals, to go out on her own and set up the solo proprietorship of Brenda L. Sullivan Communications in San Diego, California, in early 1999. That and plenty of experience. After graduation with a degree in journalism she spent seven years in Washington, D.C., with Ogilvy PR Worldwide, one of the world's largest advertising and PR firms. "When working for an agency, you are at your client's beck and call," the outgoing, 36-year-old explains.

"You have to keep a lot of things going at the same time.

From Ogilvy PR Worldwide, Brenda took up with a nonprofit, the National Safe Kids Campaign. "Yes, being the communications director of a nonprofit is different," she says, anticipating the question. "Nonetheless, you are still serving peoples' interests at some level."

After a stint with an Internet start-up that didn't work out for her, Brenda took the leap and went out on her own. "Everyone kept telling me that if I did, they would refer me business. I finally heard what they were saying and I have never looked back. Literally, from the day I started I've had more work than time. It's the best business decision I ever made."

With major clients such as Steve Morris Design, the Berman Institute, and Rokenbok Toy Company, Brenda is busy preparing press kits, writing brochures, and placing articles in trade journals. "Writing is the foundation of everything I do," she says.

Brenda's biggest challenge in transitioning from agency work to operating as a solo practitioner has been in realizing she is just one person. "I am used to directing multimillion-dollar programs out of D.C., with a ten-person staff. This is the first time in a decade I've had no secretary."

Variety at All Levels

If eventually you are to do what Brenda, Joann, and Shari have done, go out on your own, you need to start first at an in-house PR department—one that services a company's PR needs—or at an agency. "When working in-house, the company you work for is your client," says Dan. "You are part of a communications team. Your job is to communicate the company's message to all their publics, be they consumers, vendors, regulators, media, employees. A corporation is going to have many different publics to communicate with.

"On the agency side, however, you may have ten or twenty clients, each could have you dealing with one public or a certain program. At an agency you have to be able to switch gears quickly."

How do you get started? "With over two hundred colleges and about a hundred graduate schools now offering degree programs or special curriculum in public relations, usually in the journalism or communications department, education and training is available," says Dan. "And, yes, there is a role in our business for those just out of college. I started as an intern while still in school."

But then there's that maturity thing. What would a recent college graduate do?

What to Read

The CEO Playbook
by Ron Rhody.
Academy Publishing, 1999.

Cool Web Sites to Visit

Canadian Public Relations Society
www.cprs.ca/cprspriaise.html

Shari L. Goldstein Public Relations & Editorial Services
www.prpro.net/contact.html

Careers in Public Relations
www.prsa.org/resume2.html

"Entry-level people implement strategies and programs more experienced practitioners have developed," Dan explains. "Arms and legs are needed to get things done. If you are entry-level, you can be those arms and legs while learning the business and making a living. Those at the top, the strategists, have been at it for a while."

Still, variety can be found at all levels. Laurie has been in PR for over 20 years. Even early on at the gas company, her experiences were varied and exciting. "They ranged from dealing with fairly technical people, working on remediation of a hazardous waste site, helping to promote marketing programs, and developing third-party support programs for specific legislation," she says. "The wide range makes it fun."

Fun? Is PR fun? "There is the downside, of course," adds Laurie. "Often the hours are long. And, in media relations you are essentially on call twenty-four hours a day, seven-days-a-week."

What type of person makes a good public relations specialist? Are they people people? "Yes," says Dan, "you do have to like people, be a team player, be energetic, and have a good attitude. But it bothers me when I get a call and I hear, 'I'm a great people person, I love people.' Yes, well cannibals love people, too."

Unlike journalism, where your job is to report things as accurately and fairly as possible, in PR this is not your top priority. "My job is to get my client's message across," Dan says. "I won't do that in a deceptive or unethical way. But I am an advocate for my client."

"Ethics are extremely important," Laurie says. "My company has an ethics policy, and I let it guide me. But in the end it comes down to personal ethics. I must maintain my personal standards. Fortunately, at the gas company I can."

For Shari, her ethics firmly in place, public relations is a great profession: "I try to do it all. Some marketing, business counseling, speech writing, even business letters. I have found it a financially and intellectually rewarding career."

RADIO COMMERCIALS PRODUCER

With over eleven thousand radio stations across the country, those in the business of producing radio commercials at in-house facilities or independent production houses are busier than ever.

A s Sandy Biddle looks out her window, past a sleeping puppy lying on the windowsill, all she sees are grazing Holsteins for miles on end. Having moved to a two-acre rural Pennsylvania homestead in 1989, 20 miles from the nearest FedEx drop site, Sandy and her husband, Steve, wake to the sounds of farm animals grunting and the smell of fresh air. In fact, upon arriving from Florida to live and set up shop, the pair immediately renamed their radio commercials company Fresh Air Productions.

The name was soon changed again, however. "We wanted something to signify the ultimate in hope," says Sandy. "A symbol indicating all that is possible with radio. Having recently bought a tiny crystal pig, I hit upon a new name—Flying Pig Creative Services. In radio, we can do anything, even make pigs fly."

Being a mom-and-pop operation, based in a home studio, Flying Pig, and its capabilities would be easy to underestimate. Mistake! With 52 years of combined radio production experience, Sandy and Steve know their way through jingles, spot ads, and ear-catching sound effects. And with a studio second-to-none, crammed with the latest in digital audio production and transmission equipment, they're as good as being in downtown Philadelphia, or anywhere else. "We contract with Digital Generation Systems in San Francisco," Sandy says. "I download commercials to them, they then upload the thirty- and sixty-second spots to radio stations all over the world. Who needs FedEx!"

Streaming Commercials

With over eleven thousand radio stations across the country, those in the business of producing radio commercials at in-house facilities or independent production houses are busier than ever.

Working directly with clients or, more often, with ad agencies, creative audiophiles review agency-written scripts or create their own material, select and then direct voice actors in recording scripts, mix music and sound effects with voice recordings, consult with ad agencies throughout the production process, make copies of finished commercials, and manage recording studios.

"With the constant stream of commercials required, there's work galore," says Jerry Vigil, editor of *Radio and Production*, the magazine for radio's production personnel. "And don't forget, in addition to commercials, you have promos and station IDs. Then there's Internet advertising, plus all the non-broadcast material, from in-store promotions to airline announcements, to talking toys. If you enjoy playing with audio, the work you can do today, especially with digital technology, boggles the mind."

John Brooks, of ProComm Studio Services, agrees: "We do voice-overs for educational and training videos, CD-ROMs, telephone messaging, anywhere a commercial voice is needed."

Typically, the radio commercial creator is a three-in-one talent: recording engineer, producer, and director.

"The engineer is the technical guy, the person doing the mixing, the one messing with the signal-to-noise ratio," says Bob Jump of Studio Center, a 12-studio independent production house in Norfolk, Virginia. "The producer puts everything together; that is, the commercial he's already created in his head. And the director's job is to get the right read from the voice-over talent. At large facilities there may be a different person doing each job. But in most cases, it's what I call a 'combo' position. One individual does it all."

Commercials for radio are commissioned by one of three entities.

"There are the direct advertisers, like your local car dealer or furniture store," says Sandy. "They'll ask us to design and produce an ad to move out their overstocked SUVs or oak filing cabinets. Then you have the ad agencies, which will present us with a completed script or ask us to take on a project from scratch. We are also seeing a growing third

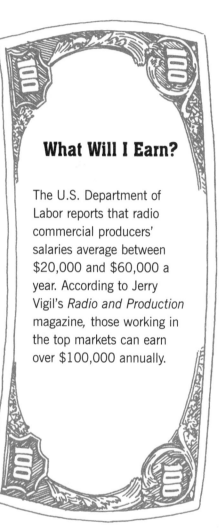

What Will I Earn?

The U.S. Department of Labor reports that radio commercial producers' salaries average between $20,000 and $60,000 a year. According to Jerry Vigil's *Radio and Production* magazine, those working in the top markets can earn over $100,000 annually.

market, the radio stations themselves. With deregulation, many stations have reduced their staffs. There aren't as many warm bodies doing writing and production. We fill the gap."

Filling that gap is easier than ever, given Internet technology. "Through our web site, you can listen to sample voices, schedule the job, receive an estimate, and have the finished audio delivered to dozens of radio stations," says John. "As an ad agent, you can go on vacation and do a complete recording session over your laptop while lounging at the beach."

Getting Listeners' Attention

"The fantastic thing about radio as an advertising or entertainment media is that you're working with a person's imagination," says Brent Walker, founder and president of Soundscapes, a radio production company in Little Rock, Arkansas. "If you give someone an image to carry with them, it's their image, it will stay with them."

Brent knows what he's talking about; his company puts out close to nine thousand radio commercial spots a year.

"A terrific commercial draws listeners in and leaves them with a picture long after the sixty-second spot is over," Brent explains. "A good engineer knows how to put sound effects together so realistically that people believe it's actually happening to them. We have 'jumped out of airplanes' using washer-dryer combinations to create the sound effects. Try doing that with TV!"

What kind of people make good radio commercial production artists? "Producers, in any media, are the ones with strong organizational skills," says Dan Ciernia of CAI, an independent house in Gilbert, Arizona. "They are detail oriented and good researchers; they dig deeper than the first answer they get."

"Most come from a radio background of some kind," says Bob. "They start at the local radio station down the block, doing whatever is necessary to get in the door. Some, it turns out, have a natural aptitude, a feel for what it takes to bring all the sounds together. Others have been doing it for years, yet still haven't a clue as to its full potential."

"Many studios will simply lay sound effects into a script, just like the script tells them to," says Brent. "Nothing ever pulls together. But if

INFORMATION

For More Information

National Association of
Broadcasters
1771 N Street N.W.
Washington, DC 20036

Radio Advertising Bureau
304 Park Avenue South
New York, NY 10010
(212) 681-7200

Radio and Production magazine
www.rapmag.com

done well, it's like adding the right pinch of salt. Salt draws all the flavors together. Disparate elements must be weaved in with mixing and production to make it real for listeners."

The Seven Essentials

Spotworks, an independent providing low-cost production to advertisers in medium to small markets, as well as radio stations looking for a "fresh perspective, a new voice," has an information-filled Web site. They're eager to share what they consider the seven essentials of an effective radio commercial:

1. *Identify your core message.* The main thing is to keep the main thing "the main thing"! The more sales messages you have, the less effective your commercial is. You must resist the temptation of throwing in other stuff just because you have 30 seconds.
2. *Develop a strong hook.* The hook is the headline for the spot . . . the "ad for the ad." If the first 5 seconds of the commercial does not compel the listener to want to hear more, you need a stronger hook!
3. *Touch emotions.* Find out what the emotional state of your target audience is, and tap in to it.
4. *Paint a picture—tell a story.* Radio is a visual medium. Telling a story is painting a picture in the listeners' minds using emotional experiences they can relate to.
5. *Sell the results of the product.* The listener has a problem. You have a solution. Demonstrate the product. Michelin doesn't sell tires—it sells safety for your baby. Crest doesn't sell toothpaste—it sells cavity-free kids.
6. *Make a specific offer with urgency.* We are talking "limited quantities" or "a deadline to buy before the sale is over."
7. *Ask for specific action.* Always, always, always—without exception—tell the listener what you want them to do. A call for action generates the need to respond.

Spotworks goes on to list a few common pitfalls: too much information, too many details, too many prices, more than one idea or theme. A radio commercial above all must be different, unique, have the ability to attract and hold the listener. Of course, top-notch production and a good delivery—a great "read"—are essential. But creativity is key to making it all work.

Breaking In

Creativity is in Sandy's blood. "Two days after I was born, my parents got their first TV," she declares. "I was a TV kid. I couldn't wait for the commercials to come on, to sing along with Speedy Alka-Seltzer or the little penguin. Turns out Steve was into it, too. He started building microphones out of Tinkertoys before his voice changed, and it turned out he was a lovely baritone."

Sooner than later, Sandy was writing ad copy for radio and television. "I love to know what pushes people's buttons," she confesses. "I like to play with words in a clever, funny way to get people's attention. That's the ultimate challenge with a radio commercial. Heck, people don't want to hear it. They want more music, the DJ's next joke, the weather, anything but the ad."

Today, Sandy and Steve do most of the recorded voices themselves; that is, they are their own voice talent. "But we're fortunate," says Sandy. "With Penn State University just over the mountain, there's plenty of talent to draw on: theater majors, broadcast majors. When we need another voice, we hire it."

Brent's path into radio production was a bit different. "I suffered through playing horrible music on the air," he says. "I wanted to go downstairs and produce commercials for four hours. For me, being a disc jockey was just a ticket into commercials."

Another route in is as a recording engineer. "When you get tired of working with rock and roll bands until four in the morning, you may be ready to switch," advises Brent. "Believe me, that can be a bummer."

You could move into commercials from the ad agency side, too. "There's creative talent over there," Brent declares. "That's definitely another way to break in."

What to Read

The Advertising Handbook for Small Business by Dell Dennison. Self-Counsel Press, 1995.

Long Days, But Fun Days

Once you're in, working as a production assistant at a radio station or independent commercials house, your long day begins.

"Folks think a sixty-second commercial takes sixty seconds to produce," says Sandy. "Make that sixty minutes, if you're lucky. Getting the right words, adding music, producing and mixing in the sound effects—all takes time. And with the client often breathing down your neck—well, you get the idea."

"With all the home gear around: fancy camcorders, audio equalizers, computers, and even relatively inexpensive mixing consoles, folks don't often appreciate what goes into a professional recording session," says Dan. "But to get the quality you need for radio broadcast, you must move to a higher level."

"People think this a glamorous field," says Brent. "They're always asking me, 'So, when are you going to move up to TV?' It's fun, but there's nothing glamorous about it. It is hard work."

"For the longest time, the production department in radio wasn't given its due," Jerry says. "Ten, twenty years ago it was rare even to find a production director. The midday guy got off the air and did some production. Same with the night fellow. The result—inconsistency. With the demand for a better product, a given individual took over production."

Today, much has changed, mostly for the better.

"If you can get into it and make a living, it's wonderful," says Jerry. "Sure, there is a downside, when you're up against a deadline, for instance. But if you find a place that has respect for what you do—great! The rewards are daily. You get to hear your work as you do it. Remember, you're not live on-air, you can keep honing the material until it is exactly what you want. For the most part, you're in a relaxed, fun atmosphere."

Fun is the word Sandy keeps using, too. "There is this old radio producer who, on tape, drained Lake Erie, made a sucking sound, then filled it with whipped cream and topped it off with a cherry from a helicopter. Where else but in radio can you do that? As I said before, with radio, anything is possible!"

Cool Web Sites to Visit

How to Work With ProComm
www.procommss.com/howto.html

About *Radio and Production* magazine
www.rapmag.com/aboutrap.html

Spotworks
www.spotworks.ab.ac

Hot Concepts!

Trade Shows and Conventions

In 1999, 123 million people—85 percent of all working adults—attended industry trade shows and conventions.

From small, esoteric mini-conferences to Las Vegas extravaganzas, at these shows you can find hundreds of places to see the latest advances in your field, exchange ideas, attend seminars and workshops, and sell yourself. You can get a year's education in a single day.

Most trade shows and conventions are divided into two major components: the main exhibitor's section and the technical, that is, breakout, sessions. Entrance into the former is often free; however, attendance at the technical sessions, which can include seminars and workshops, is usually anything but.

We'll concentrate on the freebie, exploring the exhibit area. Here you can take the "shotgun" or the "searchlight" approach. If you shotgun it, you visit as many exhibits as possible, bag all the literature you can, and usually wind up with sore feet. With the searchlight method, you're more focused, visiting displays of particular interest.

So, how do you find such shows and conventions?

Here are suggestions:

1. Look in the business section of your local newspaper.
2. Peruse trade and association journals.
3. Contact your local convention center.
4. Look for postings on college campuses.
5. Contact your local Chamber of Commerce.
6. Get on the Internet and use the search engines to find sites in the fields you're interested in.

RECORDING ENGINEER

Today, it's all done on the computer. You take music from a tape recorder, download it into the computer library, and manipulate the resulting bit patterns digitally: fading, panning, and stretching the sounds.

Though small by Hollywood standards, the 12 by 18 foot studio in Burbank, California, is crammed with the latest in audio and video recording gear.

In the control room, a 32-input/8-output, automated Mackie mixing console—with its patch bay, meter bridge, multicolored LED barographs, and I/O module strips of preamps, equalizers, slide pots, auxiliary sends, and fader controls, is arrayed like the flight deck of the *Starship Enterprise.*

Immediately to the console's right, an effects rack, filled with reverb and echo creation circuits, waits, almost begging to be put into play.

Multitrack tape recorders are positioned to the left and back of the console, next to two stereo machines used for mix-downs. Huge monitor speakers, placed eight feet apart, hang on a wall above the console. A Macintosh computer, two TV monitors, and an A/D board stand within easy swivel distance of the seated recording engineer. Straight ahead, a large, tinted window isolates the control room from the sound-tight, acoustically tuned recording room where musicians set up to jam with each other using their instruments.

Today, however, no musicians are in evidence. Michael Julian, the recording engineer, has all the music he needs on DAT (Digital Audio Tape). His job is to overdub the recorded music for the cartoon characters scampering about on the TV monitors.

"Right now, I'm only dealing with the music," Mike says. "Later, dialogue and sound effects will be dubbed in."

How is it all put together?

"Everything is done with the computer, in this case in a Macintosh environment using a program called Pro Tools," Mike says. "The software allows me to take music from a tape recorder, download it into the computer library, and manipulate the resulting bit patterns digitally: fading, panning, and stretching the sounds. Presto! Music-to-video, new millennium style."

Mix, Remix, and Match

Putting sound to video is just one talent in the recording engineer's repertoire. Whether he or she is called a recording engineer, sound engineer, music editor, or sound mixer—it's all the same—live or in the studio, their job is to put sound to tape or hard disc. As Blair Jackson, executive editor of *Mix* magazine, describes it succinctly, "Recording engineers facilitate the recording of sound."

Specifically, as a recording engineer you record sound during a live show, a documentary production, a symphony concert, CD recording session, or filming. Making it work isn't easy. The recording engineer must possess broad knowledge in many fields, including acoustics and the behavior of various sound sources.

According to Francois Patenaude, author of *Studio Production Handbook*: "Sound engineers must be familiar with the various recording and playback media they use, from microphones to analog and digital processors, recorders, and editors; and with the impact of listening and playback conditions on product quality." Furthermore, "their job is not simply to record or recreate a variety of sounds using electronic devices; rather they must capture all the beauty of sound, with the dynamics, warmth, color, and nuances desired by the performer or announcer."

Mike has succeeded in this demanding occupation because he possesses the technical, artistic, and people skills required. The latter, often overlooked, are critical. "Recording engineers must understand they are providing a service," he explains. "Though the engineer sees himself as chief of his domain, this can be a problem. The producer may say, 'I want the sky to open up this

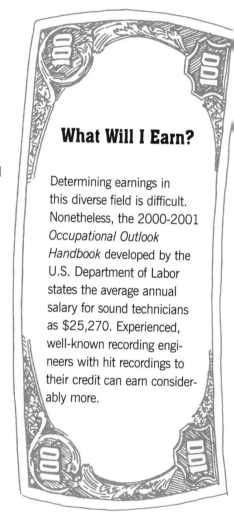

What Will I Earn?

Determining earnings in this diverse field is difficult. Nonetheless, the 2000-2001 *Occupational Outlook Handbook* developed by the U.S. Department of Labor states the average annual salary for sound technicians as $25,270. Experienced, well-known recording engineers with hit recordings to their credit can earn considerably more.

INFORMATION

For More Information

Recording Musicians Association
817 Vine Street, Suite 209
Hollywood, CA 90038-3779
(213) 462-4762

UCLA Extension: Entertainment
Studies & Performing Arts
(310) 825-9064

way, put the drummer in the middle.' How does the recording engineer give the producer what he wants, while moving the drummer to where he belongs?

"I am often asked, 'What type of person makes a good recording engineer,'" Mike continues. "They expect me to respond with electrician, engineer, electronics technician. How about beautician or bartender? Why? Because if you go to a beautician you want your hair to be just so. The beautician must satisfy you and their craft. You must walk out feeling you got what you wanted. But the beautician has to feel satisfied, too. It's the same with a recording engineer. It takes diplomacy."

Blair agrees: "Ego suppression, that's the trick," he insists. "When an artist's ego conflicts with the engineer's, the engineer must give in if he wants to work."

But technical and artistic skills are crucial, too. "Good hearing and attention to detail are uppermost," Blair says. "You have to know if the sound is off, even by 3 milliseconds. You must understand your equipment, its strengths, weaknesses, and when it's not operating at 100 percent."

Where do you get such knowledge? Recording engineering schools, two-year community colleges, and even four-year universities abound to provide training and education. Furthermore, assuming you're ready to make the commitment, you can create your own home MIDI (Musical Instrument Digital Interface) studio. "Using a $2,000 MIDI sequencer, a songwriter can compose, arrange, demo, and even record his or her own music in a den or garage," Julian says. Lee Curreri, songwriter, producer, arranger, and keyboardist whose credits include works by Natalie Cole and Phil Perry, concurs: "The MIDI sequencer is integral to the production of much of today's popular music as well as commercials and soundtracks for film and television."

Creating a home studio, hanging with recording engineers, minicourses, or a full-blown certificate or degree program are all ways to garner the knowledge and skills to succeed in this competitive field.

The Cottage Recording Industry

Can you actually build a home studio? And if so, can you do professional recording in it?

The answer to both questions is yes, at least according to Bob Dennis, editor of *Recording Engineers' Quarterly*. "The home recording of today is much like the professional recording of decades ago," he says. "While I worked for Motown, we cranked out over twenty gold records in the mid-1960s. The interesting thing is that the studio was not that far off the 'cottage' recording studio of today."

So just what is this cottage recording industry? Again, Bob has an answer: "It is a system of recording a musical production where much of the recording is done in a well-equipped home studio and a larger, better-equipped studio is only used for recording or mixing functions that are beyond the capabilities of the home studio.

"The cottage recording studio began appearing in the 1970s when major record producers and recording artists began to install home studios to try out or start a production without the cost or pressure of a professional recording studio. "Originally this was a rich man's activity with the 'cheap' 24-track recorders costing $30,000 and decent recording consoles costing $50,000. Today, however, an 8-track, 20-bit master recorder can be had for less than $2,000 and a full-function all-digital console can be purchased for as little as $4,000. Thus the cottage recording industry is booming."

Mike says that, "today, a guy can put together a recording studio in his bedroom, come up with ideas for audio material, ads for radio or TV, for example, and put it together. Then he shoots a scene with a camera, puts the music in it, and goes to a local retail outlet and says, 'You want to buy it?' The opportunities are unlimited."

The leap from your own recording studio to your own independent record label is not impossible to make. Robert Trujillo did it, forming his own independent record label, Project Tru. "We cater to Orange County [California] bands, providing rehearsal studio space and recording facilities," he says. "Business is going gangbusters.

"Independents don't have the overhead the majors do. I don't have to sell 250,000 units to make money. There have been bands

What to Read

Audio Made Easy (Or, How to Be a Sound Engineer Without Really Trying) by Ira White.
Hal Leonard Pub., 1997.

Practical Techniques for the Recording Engineer by Sherman B. Keens.
Multimedia Communication & Training, 1989.

dumped by the majors when they didn't hit a half-million copies. With us, a punk band can cut a whole CD in a day or two, with almost zero production costs, relatively speaking."

For Robert, being behind the scenes keeps him in the business. "I love to play music, I'll always be in a band of some kind. But with the recording studio, hopefully someday, I'll be part of someone's dream, making it as a star."

Party with the Band?

If you love music, being a recording engineer will give you unique opportunities to enjoy it. But as in any profession, there is a downside. "You'll work weird hours," Blair notes. "With some studios operating twenty-four hours a day to pay the bills, midnight recording sessions are becoming common."

If you're on the road, doing live shows, that can be a special kind of hell. "Small towns, hurried setups and tear-downs, bad acoustics, bus travel, dingy lodgings—it's grueling," Blair continues. "Road work is not a life-time career."

But the biggest danger you face may come when the show's over. "Partying with the band, that can be your downfall," Blair cautions. "The music industry is littered with those who couldn't handle its excesses—drugs, alcohol, sex."

That, however, is not Mike's problem. He's doing just fine providing audio for the hottest morning television cartoons. "I'm the interface between what the producer wants and all these knobs and lights," he says as he reaches to adjust a fader circuit. "I may not be the star of the show, but I play a tremendously satisfying part."

Cool Web Sites to Visit

Beatles-RockTalk Chat
with Richard Lush
*www.onnet.com/webworld/
rocktalk.htm*

Hansen, Biarne
www.cybernet.dk/users/qnedk/

Pro Audio.net
www.soundwave.com

RESIDENTIAL REAL ESTATE AGENT

Whether they are scheduling appointments, showing clients properties to rent or buy, mediating differences between buyers and sellers, assisting clients in applying for loans, or keeping records and filing copies of all transactions, real estate agents work hard for their money, as the song says, but there can be a lot of it.

Hot Career

37

The referral was a good one—after all, homes in Agoura, an upscale suburb 30 miles north of downtown Los Angeles, start at around $500,000, with more than a few selling for up to ten times that amount. Still, Barbara Singer, a sales agent at RE/MAX On the Boulevard, in Studio City, 20 miles to the south, would be working as an out-of-area agent; she would have to do her homework to get the listing.

"I drove the area for several days, then checked dozens of comparable properties," the stylish, 40-something sales associate says. "I felt what I presented to the seller was realistic, uninflated. A competing agent promised them the roof. Still, I got the listing at $629,000."

The eight-year-old, 3,000-square-foot property hit the market at 1:00 P.M. on a Monday. By 3:00 P.M., thanks to the latest in computer technology, brokers were lining up to see the Spanish-style house. An hour later one called back with the magic words, "My client wants to make an offer." By 10:00 P.M. the sellers had their buyer. All in a day's work!

Actually, it took until Wednesday, after counteroffers flew back and forth, before a SOLD sign was hammered into the front lawn. The sellers got $607,000 for their home, and Barbara was looking forward to a nice commission. But hold on—what looks to be another "California Dreamin'" real estate deal—list at sunrise, sell by sundown—won't be over until it's over.

"You have to go through escrow," Barbara reminds us. "For the next thirty days I worked my tail off with loan approval, inspections, disclosures, appraisals, CC&Rs [conditions, covenants, and restrictions], you name it. What started out as a sale from heaven turned out to be an escrow from hell. I wasn't sure of a deal until Day Thirty. I earned my commission with that one, every penny."

Seller's Market

The opportunity for real estate agents across the country to earn that "penny," and then some, has never been better. The National Association of Realtors (NAR) reports that 5.2 million homes changed hands in 1999, the fourth straight record year. Nearly a million—986,000—new single-family homes sold in the same period. A report titled "The State of the Nation's Housing 1999" by the Joint Center for Housing Studies at Harvard states: "The number of U.S. households is projected to increase by approximately 1.1 million each year throughout the next decade, with 'echo boomers'— those born to baby boomers—accounting for more than 10 percent of the nation's owner households and 40 percent of its renter households by 2010." For those involved in the sale, purchase, and leasing of this real estate, the future would seem bright indeed.

Whether such state licensed sales associates—or real estate agents—are scheduling appointments, showing clients properties to rent or buy, mediating differences between buyers and sellers, helping clients fill out applications and other paperwork, assisting clients in applying for loans, keeping records and filing copies of all transactions, preparing rental advertising, and answering phone inquiries, they are working hard.

"It's an exhausting business," Denise Bitkower of DBL Realty in Beverly Hills, California, declares. "First, you're looking for a client. Once you have one, you must find them a house. You then have to sell it to them—and their parents, in-laws, and all their friends. You have to negotiate the deal, do all the inspections, and then renegotiate the deal. And that's just the beginning. There is escrow, where you often get what's called 'escrow face' by concentrating so hard

What Will I Earn?

Most residential real estate agents work on a commission, usually 5 to 6 percent, which is split with the company you work for. Income depends on location and amount of sales.

to hold the deal together you seem to be doing it with your face! By the time a commission check arrives, you wonder if it's all worth it. If you're truly service oriented, you can work your butt off."

The New Breed

Barbara did just that with her Agoura listing. Take the issue of disclosure obligations, what the seller must disclose to the buyer. In California, as in most states, there are natural hazard disclosure zones: earthquakes, wildland fires, and flood hazards. There are lead hazards, Megan's Law (notifying the public about registered sex offenders), and the Mello-Roos Community Facilities Act. Smoke detectors must be in place and water heaters braced. And we mustn't forget disclosure of a death, federal flood disaster insurance, HUD/FHA home inspections, and military ordinance locations. The list seems endless.

"Since the buyers, a young couple in their late twenties, loved the house, they bought it in an 'as is' condition," Barbara says. "That means while the seller was still compelled to disclose any problems, he was not required to do any repair. But being a nice guy, the seller agreed to fix one or two things, gratis. Well, mistake. That opened the floodgates to endless requests from the buyer for favors. We fell into heavy negotiation again."

Selling real estate today is for the hearty. "Salespeople are more independent-minded, savvy, entrepreneurial now," says Elyse Umlauf-Garneau, in *Today's Realtor*. Downsizing in corporate America is bringing a new breed of business-minded recruits to the industry. And immigrants touching U.S. soil for the first time are anxious to grab a piece of the American dream—often by tapping in to an ever-growing pool of fellow immigrants eager to own property."

There are other trends, too, making today's realtor different from the one your parents knew. The average age is 48, but Sherry Matina, executive vice president of Wm. Rigg Inc., Fort Worth, Texas, tells Elyse, "I have noticed a dramatic rise in the number of young people entering the business directly out of college. I'm

INFORMATION

For More Information

National Association of REALTORS®
430 N. Michigan Avenue
Chicago, IL 60611-4087
(312) 329-8458
www.nar.realtor.com

seeing a whole generation that thinks they're going to be able to do it better than we did."

Denise remembers her auspicious start, back during the 1984 Olympics. "I spent six months hunting up those Olympic leases, you know, the sardine barons willing to spend $50,000 to live in the Hollywood Hills for two weeks. It was a complete bust, the party no one ever came to. Of course, interest rates averaging 20 percent didn't help our business, either. Still, I stuck with it, persevered, and today I'm with a top-notch office, working hard, making it happen every day."

It is that can-do attitude that Jay Belson, owner-broker of RE/MAX On the Boulevard, one of the most successful offices in the worldwide franchise, looks for in his agents, too. "When I bring someone on," the exuberant, 42-year-old Jay explains, "I look for an attitude that says, 'I have faith in me.' Such a person will do well in any field, be it building a building or running a restaurant. They do what it takes to learn any business—and they succeed. That attitude, plus technical savvy, will make them successful in today's real estate."

Doing It on the Net

Ah yes, technology. You're at IPIX (*www.ipix.com*) taking in their 360-degree photographic virtual house tour. You scroll around a room in a complete circle from doorway to doorway, from floor to ceiling. It's like viewing a scene on the inside walls of a globe, and when your mouse jumps, you get dizzy. The company uses a tripod-mounted camera equipped with a fish-eye lens to take the photos. Software melds the photos and corrects curved wall distortion. For $99 the company will come out to the house you want to sell, take the necessary photographs, and set you up on the Web. Clients can view your home without ever leaving theirs. Welcome to the twenty-first century real estate agent.

"I am not sure where all this technology is going," Stacey Moncrieff, editor of *Realtor* magazine, says. "But more and more steps related to the transaction are going online. A buyer can get a password and see if the appraisal has been done, the loan approved. It gives him a sense of control."

Will that control diminish the agent's role? It is the question many in the profession are pondering. "Rather than taking our job away from us," says Michael Clancey, in the August/September 1999 issue of *California Real Estate* magazine, "the Web provides so much information that the average agent has gone from acting as a gatekeeper who gets consumers in the door to acting as a filter to help the consumer figure out what the information is."

Don Hobbs, CEO of Hobbs Herder Advertising, in Newport Beach, California, echoes that theme: "Given the complexity of a deal today, an agent is needed now more than ever," he insists. "Yes, 70 percent of all transactions are initiated by a client online. It is the first thing people do. But then they come to us."

"There will be fewer agents," says Dick Barnes, real estate editor at the *Los Angeles Times*, "with the Internet chiefly responsible for purging the industry of marginal producers. Business will be a blend of high-tech and high-touch with service, not information, the key contribution of agents."

Jay is tuned in to both those needs. "You can load your desk with the latest DSL lines, software, et cetera, but by itself it won't make you money," he says. "You need great salesmanship, good business sense, and a commitment to being productive with the technology. But no doubt about it, five years from now there won't be a functioning real estate agent who isn't using computer-based technology."

No Room for Part-Time

Like Rodney Dangerfield, many real estate agents feel they get little of that precious commodity, respect. "They, the public, are simply unaware of the knowledge and education we have," says Barbara. "We know our business. Yet, they think all we are out for is the commission. Well, our commission is our livelihood. We get paid for doing a job, like anyone else."

What to Read

How to List and Sell Real Estate in the 21st Century by Danielle Kennedy and Warren Jamison. Simon & Schuster, 1998.

Real Estate License Examinations: Salesperson and Broker by Joseph H. Martin and Eve Steinberg. Prentice Hall Books, 1993.

Cool Web Sites to Visit

Tom Murphy Realty-Careers in Real Estate
www.sold1.com/info/career.htm/

Realtor magazine
www.realtormag.com

What Is a Buyer's Agent?
www.realty3.com/tips/buyers.htm

"The client thinks all we do is drive them around to look at houses," Bruce Holmes, president of Century 21 Venture, Ltd., in Augusta, Maine, says. "That's just the tip of the iceberg. More than good salespeople, we now look for agents with an excellent business sense. A bright smile and a glad hand, yes. But given all the legalities involved, we need intelligent people with the ability to communicate."

All that takes a full-time commitment. "Real estate used to be something you did on the weekends or evenings," says Don. "You know, it was the teacher looking for summer work, the firefighter doing it on his or her day off. Given the commitment and investment you must make, there is no room for part-timers anymore."

"For years we operated just above a car salesman," comments Jay. "Now, with the education required to get a license, and keep it via continuing education, our image is changing. The public is seeing a different, sharper agent. It's not the Beverly Hills housewife with long fingernails as portrayed in the media."

Denise works in Beverly Hills, and yes, she likes visiting beautiful houses in nice neighborhoods. She also likes the freedom being a real estate agent affords. "When I am finished caravaning, I can do a little shopping, take care of personal business. I am not locked in the office looking at walls all day."

Denise has paid her dues to get where she is at. Even now, she's no "agent to the stars." "Those deals are few and far between," she claims.

So what keeps her going, in a business where she can never be sure of her next dollar? "It's like playing cards," Denise says. "You never know what the next hand will bring, what you might trip over. An agent in our office just did both sides of a deal, listing and selling, on an $8 million home. She'll get close to 6 percent of that. In our business the earning potential is unlimited. There is nothing holding you down but you."

RESPIRATORY CARE PRACTITIONER

In respiratory care, there's an emphasis on the equipment. Respiratory care practitioners have an interest in the technical areas of health care.

Biomedical equipment crams the intensive care unit. A cardiac monitor beeps to the beating of an infant's heart. Intravenous and feed pumps drip life-giving fluids. Above a pink cotton blanket, a ventilator supplies humidified oxygen through the patient's trachea. Only Lisa's tiny head and neck protrude, her coal-black eyes staring in wonder.

Seven months old and not yet seven pounds, Lisa suffers from spinal muscular atrophy, otherwise know as Werdnig-Hoffman disease. Her spirits are high this evening, for her eyes eagerly follow Jerry Hammersley, a respiratory therapist, as he lowers the respirator's oxygen level from 50 to 35 percent. She blows saliva bubbles, her mouth broadening into an innocent smile.

"I'm afraid it's fatal," Jerry reveals. "Lisa will live to age three, at most. All we can do is make her comfortable. But that doesn't mean she'll remain in the hospital. We're training Lisa's mother and father to do all this at home. Hopefully, in a couple of weeks, that's where she'll be."

Breathing Easier

Jerry is one of 50 respiratory care practitioners working at Northridge Hospital in Northridge, California. He is in charge, in fact, as the education/quality improvement coordinator for Respiratory Care. Tonight, however, Jerry is working staff, which means he'll be with patients like Lisa for a 12-hour shift.

"This is not a normal situation," he explains, adjusting the ventilator and checking the trachea tube again. "Sure, we see sick kids all the time, but most go on to other therapy or directly home. Lisa will need a ventilator all her life."

About nine out of ten respiratory care practitioners (RCPs), of which there are 125,000 nationwide, work in hospital departments of respiratory care, anesthesiology, or pulmonary medicine. The remaining jobs are in durable medical equipment rental companies, home health agencies, and nursing homes. Regardless of where they work, RCPs evaluate, treat, and care for patients with breathing disorders.

According to the American Respiratory Care Foundation (ARCF), the patients are people with chronic lung problems (such as asthma, bronchitis, and emphysema) but also include heart attack and accident victims; premature infants; and people with cystic fibrosis, lung cancer, or AIDS.

The job can get messy. As Gregory Cousin, also an RCP at Northridge Hospital, says, "When a therapist performs chest physiotherapy, mucus is removed from the lungs. The therapist must place patients in positions to help drain mucus, thump and vibrate their rib cages, and instruct them to cough. Patient care does mean patient contact."

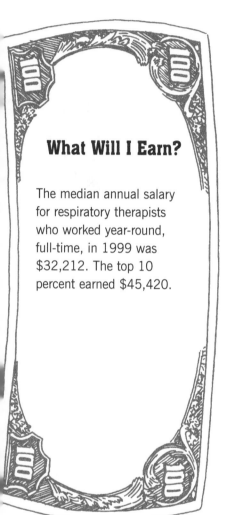

What Will I Earn?

The median annual salary for respiratory therapists who worked year-round, full-time, in 1999 was $32,212. The top 10 percent earned $45,420.

Providing the Breath of Life

As Jerry exits Lisa's room and enters Betty's, he travels from one patient extreme to another. "Have you been taking deep breaths from the ventilator?" he asks. Betty, 85 years old and immobilized with a broken hip, nods. "In two days she'll be out of here, on to the orthopedic floor, and then home," Jerry says. "My job is to prod Betty into taking plenty of deep breaths. We want to prevent the number one hospital complication following surgery—pneumonia."

Leaving Betty's room, Jerry anticipates a question. "How did I get into this profession? Two things did it," he says. "My mother was a nurse, she provided the initial exposure. But the real impetus came in a flash, so to speak. I am a Christian. One day, at Bible study, there was a call forward to people who wanted to know God's plan for them. I was told I was destined to help the sick. That was twenty-two years ago. I've been here ever since completing my training."

For Jerry, respiratory therapy is a great fit. An empathetic person, he's part of a broader profession, health care, which is filled with "nice people with caring hearts." Furthermore, Jerry is a tinkerer, a troubleshooter. "If something goes wrong with a ventilator, I can usually fix it," he volunteers sheepishly. In fact, Jerry is more than a repair person, he's an inventor. Having patented the Stronghold, a device that prevents accidental disconnecting of ventilator circuits from the trachea, he's seen his own creation save lives.

The emphasis on equipment in the respiratory care profession is important to remember. Frank Sinsheimer, professor of respiratory therapy at Los Angeles Valley College says, "In respiratory care you work with a lot of equipment that nurses don't. Respiratory care practitioners are probably more interested in the technical areas of health care."

That may be changing. David J. Pierson writes in *Respiratory Care*, the monthly journal of the American Association for Respiratory Care (AARC), "There needs to be a shift from an equipment focus to an education- and care-coordinating focus. The respiratory care practitioner needs to become an educator, a consultant, and a coordinator of care, and less a person installing or operating a medical device."

In health care, change is everywhere. For respiratory care professionals that may mean protecting your job from lurking predators. Michael Gibbons, associate editor at *Advance*, the nation's respiratory care biweekly newspaper, explains, "Today, respiratory departments have many wolves circling them: downsizing, turf takeovers, mergers, capitation, managed care, and the uncertain future of Medicare."

Jerry concurs. "Some hospitals have tried to integrate respiratory care and nursing to save money. It's hard to do. Most respiratory care practitioners spend two years studying the cardiopulmonary system. Nurses, because they have broader responsibilities, spend maybe three weeks."

INFORMATION

For More Information

American Association for
Respiratory Care
11230 Ables Lane
Dallas, TX 75229
(214) 243-2272

American Respiratory Care
Foundation
8310 Nieman Road
Lenexa, KS 66214

The lack of respect among health care professionals and lack of knowledge by the general public concerns respiratory therapists, and particularly the American Association for Respiratory Care. Expanding on their 1999 "Breathe Easy: Respiratory Therapists Are on the Job" theme, the organization says: "The need for public education about respiratory health and why RTs need to be an integral part of any respiratory patient's care plan is at an all-time high today. The consumer's lack of understanding as to why RTs are so important contributes to the lack of urgency policymakers feel about competency and reimbursement—we must all make a collective effort to connect with the public on every possible level to help rectify this situation."

Job Outlook: Excellent

The job outlook for RCPs remains bright. The U.S. Department of Labor reports: "Employment of respiratory therapists is expected to increase much faster than the average of all occupations through the year 2005."

Frank goes one step further. "At Valley College many of our students start work the day after graduation, at $26,000 a year or more."

Take this classified ad in a Fargo, North Dakota newspaper:

> *MeritCare Health Systems Children's Hospital in Fargo, ND has 2 full-time openings for a Respiratory Therapist to staff its level III ICN, Pediatric ICU and general floors. Duties in Children's Hospital include ABG analysis, general therapy, ventilation with conventional, HFJ and HFO, attendance at high-risk deliveries, and neonatal transport. Pediatric ICU coverage as well as pediatric general floor coverage. We offer 12-hour shifts, rotating or straight nights, approximately every other weekend.*
>
> *This position requires RRT eligibility, NRP certification, which can be obtained after appointment,*

and North Dakota Licensure. Please send resume, references, and letter of application to . . .

Or, how about working as a home-care respiratory care coordinator or contingent respiratory therapist? Here's a listing out of Grayling, Michigan:

> *Both positions are responsible for initial in-home respiratory equipment setup and instruction. Coordinator responsibilities include coordinating day-to-day respiratory services, in-home visits, and setting priorities in collecting data and developing a plan of treatment with minimal on-call responsibilities. The successful candidate for the Coordinator position will be a Registered Respiratory Therapist with 1–2 years durable medical equipment experience a plus. The successful candidates for Contingent Therapist will be Registered Respiratory Therapist or Certified Respiratory Therapy Technician and will assist with after hours and weekend duties. For more information, contact . . .*

And when you're ready for a supervisory position, here's what you could consider from the Northern Colorado Healthy-Western Plains Health Network Hospital:

> *Registered respiratory therapist night shift supervisor working three 12-hour night shifts per week, the dynamic and experienced individual we are looking for will have the opportunity to utilize pressure control ventilation, prone positioning, vent weaning protocols, hellox, intubation and bronchoscopy with a health care system that has invested in top equipment and technology. Our busy Respiratory Department professionals also enjoy a diverse caseload including intensive care, Level II nursery, burn, ED, trauma, acute/long-term ventilator care and*

What to Read

Advanced Practitioner Respiratory Care Review by Gary Persing. W B Saunders Co., 1994.

pediatrics. Candidate must be an RRT with 3 years of supervisory experience, excellent assessment and critical-thinking skills, and a solid knowledge of the accepted practices and respiratory procedures and diagnostic tests including TDPs. Contact . . .

Cool Web Sites to Visit

American Association for Respiratory Care
www.aarc.org

National Board for Respiratory Care
www.nbrc.org

Respiratory Care Practitioner Course Listing
www.lsc.mnscu.edu/ programs/rcreq.htm

Trained and Licensed

To work as a respiratory care practitioner, you need to be educated, trained, and most important, licensed. With a two-year associate degree from an accredited community college program, you can sit for the registered respiratory therapist (RRT) examination. With a one-year degree from an accredited private institution, you're eligible, in many states, to take the certified respiratory therapy technician (CRTT) test. Thus, a respiratory therapist has two years of training; a respiratory technician, one year.

What do such education programs consist of? The Web site of the Mid-State Technical College, Marshfield, Wisconsin campus is instructive: "Our two-year associate program covers the therapeutic use of medical gases and administration apparatus, environmental control systems, humidifiers, aerosols, medications, ventilatory support, broncho-pulmonary drainage, pulmonary rehabilitation, cardiopulmonary resuscitation, and airway management. Both classroom instruction and clinical experience are included in the program format. The clinical portion of the program is held at various cooperating hospitals. Through clinical sessions, students learn to apply their classroom knowledge to actual contact with hospital patients and equipment."

Respiratory care practitioner is not a career for everyone. But if you'd like to do direct patient care and treatment and work in a challenging health field, it's well worth exploring.

Two weeks have passed since we first saw Jerry caring for Lisa. "There's good news," he tells us. "Lisa is going home today. She'll be in the care of loving parents for the holidays."

SCREENWRITER

Who's the biggest film producer in the world? Not Hollywood. It's the United States government. Commercial, industrial, instructional, and informational filmmaking all need screenwriters. It's a chance to be creative and make good money—while you wait for your big break.

Hot Career

39

Richard Walter, professor and chairman of UCLA's renowned film and television writing program, likes to tell his "everyone's a screenwriter" story.

"Settling into a taxi at the airport, on my return from a screenwriting seminar back East, I asked my driver, in as casual a tone as I could muster, 'So how's the script coming along?'

"He turned and looked me full in the face, his eyes as wide as basketballs. He gasped, 'How did you know?'"

For Richard, the question was a no-brainer. Everyone, at least in Southern California, is writing the great American screenplay.

But what are the odds that toiling scribes will ever sell their creations, let alone see them produced and distributed?

"A much more responsible financial plan would be to play the lottery," Richard says with a chuckle. "Actually, from a career standpoint, trying to get into this field isn't so crazy. Entertainment is now the biggest business in California. The major studios are taking in what they did during the golden age. More!

"Five over-the-air networks are now doing long form. Then there are the cable companies. USA Cable made twenty-six movies last year, more than Disney. HBO, Turner, Showtime, and Lifetime are in the same game. Business is thriving. And it all rides on the script. It all begins with the writer."

But is the writer, especially the emerging writer, able to flourish, or at least succeed, along with the business? "Yes, and particularly the beginner," Richard says. "In some ways, you're better off with no experience. You haven't been attached to development deals that didn't develop, to movies that croaked at the box office. As a new writer, you're a blank slate. You've never failed, never disappointed, never frustrated. Hollywood is a place where you start at the top, then work your way down."

Fade In

In Hollywood there are two kinds of writers: established and emerging. If you're among the emerging, you begin not with the written word, but with an idea.

"Some writers prefer to go through this step as quickly as possible and get to the paper," says Lawrence DiTillio, former scripts columnist for *Writer's Digest*. "I don't. If I can maintain passion for a concept for at least a few days, then the idea is strong enough to take me through the weeks I'll need to spend writing the script."

The script Lawrence writes, and the one you will, too, is the infamous "spec" script. From the word *speculation*, it's a complete screenplay you've sweated over, perhaps for years, without payment. You can only hope that someone, someday, will option or buy it.

You will need four or five, maybe a half-dozen such scripts behind you before taking the next step—pitching a screenplay. An art in itself, the "pitch" is an oral presentation to studio executives. If they like what they hear, they'll often ask for a detailed treatment, usually 10 to 12 pages (about 10 minutes per page).

Once your script is sold, the hard part begins. You will watch your baby, your dream, dissolve into the rewrite process.

"Movies are made by committee," Sally Merlin, East Coast editor of *Scr(i)pt* magazine, tells me. "The writer has to know this is not literature. In every other kind of writing, words are the most important thing. Here, it is crafting. This is a collaborative media. The writer brings one part of the blueprint to the film. He or she has to get excited about that, as opposed to wanting every word to stay in place."

Beyond Hollywood

Rewriting is, of course, done by someone—the screenwriter. It is coveted work that pays well and, in a critical sense, defines the screenwriter's working life.

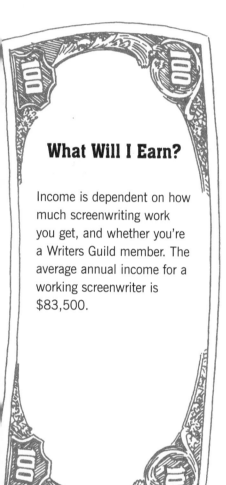

What Will I Earn?

Income is dependent on how much screenwriting work you get, and whether you're a Writers Guild member. The average annual income for a working screenwriter is $83,500.

"Everyone rewrites everyone," is Hollywood's golden rule.

"There are only three conditions under which we'll rewrite each other," says John Hill in the January 1999 issue of *Scr(i)pt*. "If we're given the slightest opportunity, if we're offered money, or if we're offered the implied hint of glory—our name on the screen."

"Of the money," Richard says, "most people think it's in film. But television is the arena where writers are treated and paid most generously. If a top screenplay price is, say, $4 million, consider that for creating and writing the TV series *Family Ties*, Gary David Goldberg earned more than forty million dollars."

Yet, those big bucks can be blinding.

According to the *Los Angeles Times*, "Only half the 8,000 members of the Los Angeles-based Writers Guild of America West, get writing assignments annually, and just one hundred and fifty movie writers earn $700,000 or more a year. The median annual pay for all screenwriters is $83,500."

Whether you find such numbers sobering or exciting, Hollywood need not be your only outlet as a screenwriter.

"Do you know who's the biggest film producer of all?" Richard asks rhetorically. "The United States government. I have done films for the army, the air force, the energy department, as well as corporations and tourist boards. Together, Hollywood is dwarfed by commercial, industrial, instructional, and informational filmmaking."

Should one pursue such work? "Absolutely," Richard says. "It's a chance to be creative and make good money. Sure, like all films, most stink. But some are actually quite good. You'll get excellent practice and sharpen your skills. Besides, it'll leave you time to do your own project, your spec script."

A Way to Win

Getting that spec script pitched to a major studio is an awesome challenge. Just getting a studio to invite you to pitch on a regular basis puts you in an exclusive league. After your family, friends, and coworkers pronounce your script brilliant, containing texture and dialogue even Robert Towne would envy, how do you get it to the people who count? According to most everyone in the "biz," you enter your work in contests, or competitions.

INFORMATION

For More Information

American Screenwriters Association
www.asascreenwriters.com

What to Read

The Screenwriter's Bible:
A Complete Guide to Writing,
Formatting, and Selling
Your Script
by David Trottier.
Silman-James Press, 1998.

The Whole Picture: Strategies
for Screenwriting Success in
the New Hollywood
by Richard Walter.
Penguin Books USA, 1997.

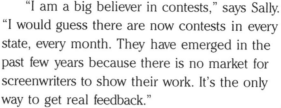

"I am a big believer in contests," says Sally. "I would guess there are now contests in every state, every month. They have emerged in the past few years because there is no market for screenwriters to show their work. It's the only way to get real feedback."

Aslihan Coker, director of the Hudson Valley Film Festival, agrees: "Our contest is for emerging and established screenwriters. But in addition to the prizes we offer, our top winners have their screenplays staged, right here at the festival. Writers that only heard dialogue in their head, now hear it for real, read by recognized actors."

Nancy Meyer, of the American Cinema Foundation, describes her organization's contest as theme-based. "'From many to one' is our slogan. The foundation receives two hundred-plus scripts to evaluate. First place gets $10,000, second and third place, $5,000 each. In addition, agents read all winning scripts."

Agents read all winning scripts? That's good for contest winners, but what if you're not so lucky, and luck does play a part? Should you, could you, get an agent?

John Scott Lewinski, writing in *Scr(i)pt*, has an interesting take on agents: "A strange relationship develops between writer and representative because it is one of the only employment situations in which the employee (the agent) decides if the employer (the writer) is worthy of the employee's work. As a writer, an agent hires you so they can work for you!"

OK, but *will* they hire you? "Agents are interested only when you're earning something they can take ten percent of," says Sally. "They are not likely to look at new material unless it is coming out of the contests or from a referral."

Richard sees it this way: "It's not hard to get an agent to consider new material. What's hard is to have good material."

Leslie Kallen, a nationally known literary agent in Sherman Oaks, California, says of her colleagues, "Some are, some aren't looking for new clients. Everyone wants to replenish his or her client base, keep

material flowing. Some agents deal with well-established writers. But even established writers have cold periods."

"What a new writer should do," she advises, "is write an outstanding script that can be used as a calling card. Then write a great query letter citing others who like your script. I'm looking for a terrific story well told. In the end, a great script finds the right buyer."

Assuming, of course, it has the right seller. You can, you *must*, do your part, agent or no agent, to sell your product and yourself.

"After you finish the project, you don't sell the project, you sell yourself," says Jason Payne, public affairs coordinator for the Writers Guild of America. "It all comes down to how you work in this town, who you are, your integrity. You can be the best writer in the world, but that's going to get you only so far if you're hard to work with."

Fade Out

But how to keep working, writing, with the odds of success so daunting?

"Above all, you must focus on being a writer and nothing else," says Sally. "Take any writing job, even if it's doing data entry from midnight to four in the morning. It will provide you with the time to write your screenplay."

If it's harder now to succeed as a screenwriter, all the more reason to make the investment—in time. "If you were going to be a doctor, you wouldn't hesitate putting in eight years," Sally likes to say. "Why should it be any different for a screenwriter?"

"Our typical student is a single mother, about 35, working at an ad agency writing copy for some department store chain," says Richard. "She's lived some life, she's had some experiences worth writing about other than the funniest thing that happened in the dormitory."

Yet, how can such a student ever find time to write?

"If you go to sleep a half hour later every night and wake up a half hour earlier each morning," Richard suggests, "you'll liberate close to nine, forty-hour weeks over the next year. With nine weeks in front of you to write, think what you can accomplish!"

Cool Web Sites to Visit

Internet Screenwriters Network
www.screenwriters.com/hr /writing/screennet.html

The Screenwriter's Master Chart
www.members.aol.com/mary /js/scrnrite.htm

Screenwriter's Store— Everything for Screenwriters and Filmmakers
www.members.aol.com/ linkwriter/prostore.html

SIGN LANGUAGE INTERPRETER

Hands swaying, face animated, they look like actors on a stage. But it's hard work being a sign language interpreter. Try holding your arms up and moving your hands at 200 words per minute for a solid hour.

For Richard Dickinson, interpreter for the hearing impaired, Los Angeles Valley College, it wasn't his usual sign language signing assignment—far from it.

"Normally I operate quite independently," the 32-year-old Richard says as he sits in a crowded office at the campus's Disabled Student Services Center.

"If I'm in a lecture hall, signing for an instructor, no supervisor is breathing down my neck. Working with a deaf student, accompanying him or her to class, I'm free to move about. And in a small group session, interpreting with American Sign Language [ASL] in sign-to-voice and voice-to-sign, I advance the communication process."

This day, however, Richard is being told by walkie-talkie-clutching, gun-toting, dark-suited types exactly what to do: when to enter, where to stand, who to talk to and who not to talk to.

Typically, a sign language interpreter wants to spend at least a few minutes with a guest speaker beforehand: getting to know his style, nuances, speech patterns. But not today.

"Even though I stood but five feet away from the president, conveying, along with my colleague, Kate Beiley, his words and feelings for over an hour in ASL, it wasn't until later, as part of his entourage to the airport, that we exchanged a few words. Signing for President Clinton during his Valley College visit on May 18, 1993, was, to be sure, a special moment in my interpreting career."

An Artistic Bent

Not all sign language interpreters get to "speak" for the president, of course. Yet, wherever they are needed, to translate spoken English to a visual/manual language and vice versa, they perform a vital task. With two million deaf people in the United States, plus passage of the Americans with Disabilities Act (ADA) in 1990, sign language interpreters are required now more than ever.

Employed full- or part-time, salaried or freelance, interpreters work, according to the National Information Center on Deafness (NICD), "in educational, medical, legal, recreational, mental health, religious, personal, financial, and vocational settings, wherever hearing, deaf, hard of hearing and deaf-blind communicators need the link of an interpreter to facilitate the flow of ideas and information in a communications environment that is barrier-free."

Sign language interpreting is a complex task As Suzette Schuster, interpreter/coordinator for Lifesigns, Inc., an interpreter referral service in Southern California, says, "Interpreting requires an individual to have a fluent command of both languages as well as excellent recall and short-term memory. He or she must translate from one language to another while simultaneously listening and storing new information and recalling what's being said.

"It's about skill level and awareness of the deaf culture. You must understand it is a language with a specific culture. You can't learn sign language interpreting from a book. A good interpreter is able to assess a client's ability in general language level. The interpreter must know where the deaf client grew up, where he or she went to school, his or her educational level. All of that comes into play when you are interpreting."

Developed from a tradition of volunteerism into a profession with high standards, national certification, a code of ethics, and professional organizations, it can take years of training and experience to qualify as a professional sign language interpreter.

"It's an artistic, flowing language," Suzette explains. "People who pick up sign language fast and have an artistic bent usually do well. Also, growing up with deaf parents can help."

What Will I Earn?

Depending on employer, experience, certification, type of interpreting (legal, medical, etc.), hours worked, and location, you can earn from $25,000 to $60,000 per year. For freelance work, $20 to $50 per hour.

INFORMATION

For More Information

National Association of the Deaf (NAD)
(301) 587-1788

National Center on Deafness (NCOD)
(818) 885-4973

Registry of Interpreters for the Deaf (RID)
(301) 608-0050

CODA Kids

Being a CODA (child of deaf adults), certainly was a factor for Richard in his career choice. "I was signing at eight months, before I was walking," says. "Sign language was my first and primary language."

"Being a CODA, immersed in the deaf culture and language, however, doesn't guarantee you'll make a good interpreter, or even a capable signer," says Caroline Preston, coordinator of interpreting services, National Center on Deafness (NCOD), California State University-Northridge, and herself a CODA. "People who are attracted to this profession are, for the most part, those who love languages and, yes, have some connection with the deaf."

Suzette agrees, adding, "Beyond skill level, awareness of the deaf culture and language is important. You can't get a book and learn it. Cultural factors are important."

Skill level, nonetheless, is key.

"I can peg a good student by the way he or she learns to sign," says Caroline. "You show them once, they do it exactly the way it was taught. There's no mixing of left and right. Their visual and motor skills are superb. Such individuals have the proper facial grammar, they understand the use of space. Good interpreters are spatial, visual people."

Richard knew he was that kind of person early on. When he graduated from Van Nuys High School's Performing Arts Academy in 1984, he headed straight for an interpreting program at Abraham Friedman Occupational Center in Los Angeles. "After earning my fifteen-hundred-hour certificate, I was out and on my own, ready for hire."

People Over Technology

Jennifer Olson, PEPNet Resource Center specialist and employment coordinator at NCOD, and Ivan Strean, a 28-year-old sign language interpreter, are in Jennifer's office talking about how technology is affecting the role of interpreters.

Jennifer, who is deaf, assures that while computers, e-mail pagers, TTY machines, and video aids are great, interpreters will always be in demand.

"I'm a lawyer by profession," she says. "When in law practice, I wanted a sign language interpreter in court signing for me. Even with real-time technology, it just makes things go smoother with an interpreter there."

Later, Ivan explains what's going on during a session.

"When I hear a message, I break it down, get the exact meaning, then change it into a sign language. Working the other way, I watch the deaf person sign, get the concept, put it into English order, all the while matching the register of the person. It's not something that comes naturally. You have to learn how. Just because you're bilingual doesn't mean you're an interpreter."

Every Day Different

As a sign language interpreter, you will often work for a referral service, an agency that coordinates, dispatches, and assigns sign language interpreters for clients, be they individuals, private companies, or public service agencies.

"At Special Task Interpreters for the Deaf, Inc. (STID), we specialize in health care and mental health," Alicia Speare, founder, explains. "And to raise the level of confidentiality for our deaf patients, we provide the same interpreter for all scheduled appointments and procedures.

"Every day is different. Some think we got into this because we feel sorry for the deaf. That's not it. Being an interpreter opens up so many doors, puts us in so many places. One day I may have little to do. The next day I'm into a major trauma situation. Some days it's just going to a doctor's appointment. After twenty-one years I still love it."

You wouldn't think Amanda Goldsmith, a sign language interpreter with the Department of Rehabilitation, would see much variety in her work. Think again:

"I took a group to a jazz concert the other day. That's right, deaf people at a jazz concert. They loved the interaction, the happening, and, literally, the vibrations. It's a wonderful culture."

Looks So Easy

As in any profession, there is a downside. "We make it look so easy," Caroline declares. "Hands swaying, face animated, we look like actors on a stage. But it's hard work. Try holding your arms up and moving your hands at two hundred words per minute for a solid hour. Physical injuries: tendinitis, back and neck pain, carpal tunnel syndrome, they're for real."

"Burnout is also a factor," cautions Suzette.

"You can't be you. You become the deaf and hearing person in an interpreting situation. You lose yourself. I remember one case that was so emotionally intense for me, that upon returning to my car I broke down crying."

Still, few sign language interpreters regret their career choice.

Most have studied sign language for years. Many have completed any one of a hundred interpreter training programs throughout the country. A growing number are certified, either by the Registry of Interpreters for the Deaf, Inc. (RID) or the National Association of the Deaf (NAD), or both.

Gaining certification is crucial for those wanting an ongoing career, status within the profession, and financial rewards. "With certification you can work anywhere in the world," Caroline says. "I could find a job in Europe on my certifications alone."

"Certification is something every interpreter should aspire to," Nancy Rarus, assistant executive director for NAD, says. "Many states now have their own certification."

There's also the thorny issue of ethics. How active, in an interpreting setting, should the interpreter be? Should she or he just "tell in like it is,"—repeat only what is spoken by the deaf client and speaking person? Or should they be more pro-active?

What to Read

So You Want to Be an Interpreter? by Janice H. Humphrey. H & H Publishing Company, 1995.

"I am a strong advocate of the idea where the interpreter should step out of his more accepted role and help the client," says Nancy. "If I go to a doctor's office without an interpreter, and then my friends later ask me questions I never thought to ask the doctor, that's a problem. But if I had an interpreter in the office with me, if he was knowledgeable enough about medicine to help me formulate questions, well, you can see the advantage. I don't believe that is against an interpreter's code of ethics. Yet, it is so seeped into the interpreter's mind not to do that, you wind up with a catch-22. Remember, the code of ethics says a deaf person's needs come first."

It's a late but still sunny afternoon. The stadium stands are filled, and graduates, robed in black, flowing gowns, smile and chat amiably. Valley College's 50th anniversary commencement is proceeding nicely, with everyone in a festive, celebratory mood.

Richard has been signing for half an hour as the keynote speaker, State Senator Richard Alarcon (D-Sylmar) mounts the podium and approaches the lectern. Both Richards stand about five feet apart.

It's not the President, this time. Yet our exuberant sign language interpreter is signing as though it was.

Cool Web Sites to Visit

Becoming a Sign Language Interpreter-NICD
www.gallaudet.edu/~nicd/357.html

Interpreter Preparation Programs-U.S. and Canada
www.rid.org/itp2.html

Welcome to Deaf Resources
www.deafresources.com

Hot Concepts!

Salary Negotiations

Negotiating a salary and benefits package can be tricky; if done wrong you may lose the job offer all together. Recruiters and career coaches say it is best to have your negotiating strategy and goals firmly in place before you interview. Once you do, follow these rules, as presented in a *U.S. News & World Report* cover story.

• Be timely. Wait until you have a firm job offer in hand.
• Be enthusiastic but firm. After you show appropriate excitement, say that you must go home and think about it overnight.
• Be reasonable. Check with coworkers and industry associations for a realistic salary range. You want to be in the ballpark, but not out in left field.
• Be consistent. Don't keep upping the ante. That's just plain insulting.
• Be a one- or two-rounder. Go back and forth twice, but no more. It can't become an endless cycle.
• Be flexible. If a salary increase just isn't going to happen, try for bonus and incentive plans.
• Be gracious. After all, you're going to have to live with these folks if you get the job.

Remember, by taking a good look at your salary needs, understanding the market, and approaching salary and benefits negotiations that are mutually beneficial to both you and your employer, your chances for success are greatly increased.

SPECIAL EFFECTS EXPERT

Today, special effects aren't just for Hollywood. Trade shows, amusement parks, live theater companies, special events providers, even retail establishments, are hiring special effects experts to make things happen that can't.

PreVis, preview visualization, is a technique so new, only a handful of effects houses are known to be doing it. Keyframe Digital Productions, in Ontario, Canada, is the leader, and Daren Cranfrod, an affable, 31-year-old founding partner, explains what's involved:

"The studio sends us a script, along with a few storyboards. Their art department e-mails us specs for the set. We then build that set in a three-dimensional computer world, using a powerful program called 3D Studio Max. We place cameras exactly as they would be used in the film, say five feet off the ground, center stage. Then we create characters to represent the actors and we animate them, thus pacing the movie shot-for-shot."

Why do all this? What's in it for the studio?

"Money—they save a bundle," says Daren. "Instead of building the actual scene, at, say, $200,000, just to realize, whoops, we need to move a wall, I can do it all on a computer, at 'considerably' less. The studio then 'plays' with it: tilts the camera up, adjusts the lighting, et cetera. Set builders see through the camera I created to determine what to construct. Blueprints are one thing, a stage all lit up is quite another.

"Essentially, at Keyframe, we build major sequences for the movies. A director looks at the results and says, 'Yes, that's what I want.' Or, he can go to the studio suits and say, 'Here's my plan, what do you think?'"

Laser-based radar (LIDAR) is another term you probably haven't heard of yet. Nonetheless, you've seen its results, especially if you saw *End of Days*, with Arnold Schwarzenegger. The climactic battle scene, with Arnold combating Satan, in what is St. Vincent's Church in Los Angeles, owes its creation in no small part to what DigitalEffects, a division of Panavision, was able to do with their LIDAR system. Frank Durto, of Panavision, elaborates:

"We used LIDAR to scan the church's interior, capturing its 3-D geometry. Basically a 3-D camera, LIDAR captures five to six hundred points per foot. The resulting 'point plot' accurately samples the interior, with as much detail as is necessary to capture all the subtle geometry in the scene. Large areas were modeled quickly, even while the film crew worked. We provided a model as a reference for the smoke and fire that wrapped around columns. The results were a seamless integration of live action and computer-generated image [CGI] sequences."

Sculptors to Compositors

PreVis and laser-based radar exemplify the latest behind-the-scenes special effects. Their precursor is the 1977 classic, *Star Wars*, considered by many to be the most influential special effects film ever, largely for its use of motion-controlled cameras to create complex space battle scenes, composited from dozens of individual elements.

When we, the audience, view movies, the special effects we see are ones we know about, maybe. Broadly speaking, there are "special effects" and "visual effects." Some industry mavens make a clear distinction between the two, others do not.

"I tend to separate them," says Frank. "Visual effects deal with image trickery, things that will happen in 'camera effect.' Images are created using compositing software. Special effects, on the other hand, are things that happen on the set, you know, buildings blowing up. Two different groups are involved in each area."

Fletcher Chenn, who answers frequently asked questions concerning special effects on the Visual Effects HQ news group Web site *(www.fxfaq.com)*, is not so sure, writing that he believes the "generic, all encompassing term used by the movie-going public is 'special effects.'"

Special effects, visual effects, whatever, together constitute a broad field. Included are pyrotechnics, animatronics/robotics, animation, creature effects/suit creation, digital models and model scanning, liquid effects, wind effects, and lighting effects. Of course, there's also prosthetics/makeup effects, puppeteering, sculpting, stop motion/clay animation, VFX compositing, and rotoscope artistry, to name but a few more.

This fascinating and ever-changing industry employs artists, modelers, molders, lighters, animators, software developers, VFX camera operators, makeup artists, plus electronics specialists. From traditional sculptors to compositing applications programmers, there's a career to be had in special effects. And you don't have to work in, or for, Hollywood to make it happen!

Chrome-Covered Terminator Indoskulls

John Neil is a traditional sculptor from Kansas. He came west to make movie monsters and, despite ups and downs, is, at 31, fulfilling his dream. The cofounder of Prop and Custom Incorporated is at work in his suburban Agoura Hills studio, about 20 miles north of downtown Hollywood. Scanning his surroundings, eyes halt on what appears to be a giant computer keyboard. John elaborates:

"Those eight-inch square keys were done for a Kodak commercial. The thumbtacks are baseball size, the computer mouse is two feet long and a foot wide, and the pencil stands taller than the average person. We had to make everything you'd find atop a messy person's desk. Using foam rubber, it took one hundred and twenty hours, crammed into eight days. Getting two hours sleep a night was no fun."

Evidence of John's other projects abound: A high-tech latex machine gun for *Universal Soldier 2*, a Doctor Evil console used in *Austin Powers 2*, a baby dino head from *The Lost World*, and one

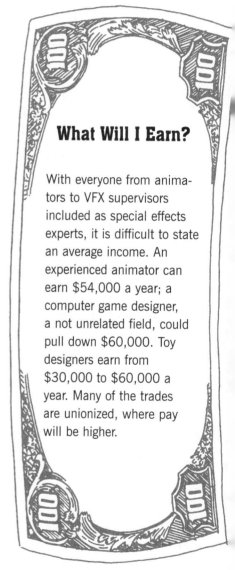

What Will I Earn?

With everyone from animators to VFX supervisors included as special effects experts, it is difficult to state an average income. An experienced animator can earn $54,000 a year; a computer game designer, a not unrelated field, could pull down $60,000. Toy designers earn from $30,000 to $60,000 a year. Many of the trades are unionized, where pay will be higher.

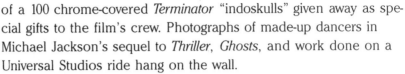

For More Information

Visual Effects Resource Center
www.visualfx.com

of a 100 chrome-covered *Terminator* "indoskulls" given away as special gifts to the film's crew. Photographs of made-up dancers in Michael Jackson's sequel to *Thriller*, *Ghosts*, and work done on a Universal Studios ride hang on the wall.

How did a fellow from Kansas get started in this field? "I got a job sculpting Christmas ornaments for Hallmark while studying visual communications at the University of Kansas," John explains. "I learned my trade from the guy who sculpted the first GI Joes. But I didn't want to do bunny rabbits and teddy bears all my life, so out to California I went. It was pretty much living out of my car until I worked on *Interview with the Vampire*, my first movie, where I made molds for Stan Wenston Studios in Van Nuys. Two years later a coworker and I struck out on our own, forming Prop and Custom Incorporated."

Beyond Hollywood

"We have snow, bubble, wind, haze, and misting machines," says Matt Carry, sales manager for Pre-Millennium Effects, a special effects manufacturer in Lynnwood, Washington. "Our new Ring Rocket Machine puffs out a twenty-inch smoke ring that'll travel over a hundred feet. Night clubs, science centers, and museums are addicted to it."

Companies like Pre-Millennium Effects scattered throughout the country, indeed, the world, produce special effects not only for film and TV but for some surprising industries and endeavors. "With the economy booming, tourism is up," says Matt. "We sell our products to trade shows, amusement parks, live theater companies, and even retail establishments. At Nordstrom's here in Seattle, our Little Blizzard Machine rains down snowflakes that evaporate on contact. Milling customers love it so much, they film the descent with video cameras."

Special effects are being done everywhere for every manner of activity. "We're seeing it popping up all over," says Kevin Martin, staff writer for *Cinefex*, the journal of cinematic illusions. "In India, Southeast Asia, Eastern Europe—anyplace there is electricity."

One such place is Cinema Secrets' manufacturing plant, location—a secret. It's two weeks after Halloween, and Maurice Stein, founder of the company and one of the 'original six' that did makeup for *Planet of the Apes*, tours his facility. Latex body parts and appliances are everywhere. Ears, chins, lips, frontal bones, wigs, masks, and full-body outfits are stacked floor to ceiling as they are ejected from molds, then hand-painted. "The movie industry doesn't absorb all this stuff," Maurice says. "We operate year round just to get ready for next Halloween. Special effects, I assure you, go way beyond Hollywood."

Computer Clay

But Hollywood, to be sure, is still a special effects mecca. To get those effects, the way out ones that dazzle us in theaters, experts must use ever more sophisticated computer programs, we need to go digital. Or do they?

"The computer has opened doors for effects in many ways," says John Merritt, of Merritt Productions, Inc., in North Hollywood, California. "It helps everyone do more. From where I stand, and I'm a traditional model maker, computers embellish what I do physically. Yet directors tend to shy away from complete computer generation. It just doesn't look realistic."

Matt agrees, adding, "Computer generated special effects can go only so far. Audiences are now more familiar with it, they can tell the fake from the real. Movies still use the actual stuff because it looks genuine."

"A few years back," Kevin says, "it seemed to be going all digital. Some companies just added digital to their name to be cool. Yet the model companies constructing physical miniatures are today doing more work than ever. Even if stuff gets modified in the computer, it's so much easier to start with something physical and enhance it rather than going to the computer from scratch. Besides, it is the physical items you want to show when promoting the film."

"When digital effects hit, perhaps five years ago," says Maurice, whose age and experience give him perspective, "everyone called me crying, 'I'm out of business.' Even though every six months the programs

What to Read

Encyclopedia of Movie Special Effects
by Patricia D. Netzley.
Oryx Press, 2000.

Industrial Light and Magic: The Art of Special Effects
by Thomas G. Smith.
Del Ray, 1991.

get twice as good, they still don't seem to be taking the place of what we do. A computer can replicate identical characters one hundred and fifty times. But only if the characters are in one shot, in a big room. If they are coming from left and right, dropping from the ceiling, popping from the floor, all at the same time, the computer can't do that—yet."

John Neil isn't worried about the digital revolution, but he isn't taking any chances either. "I saw software at a trade show last month," he says. "It allows you to sculpt in 'clay,' using a computer-enhanced tool. Holding the stylus, you can actually feel the resistance of the material. I need to get that program."

Making Things Happen That Can't

So, how do you break into what everyone agrees is a competitive though rewarding field?

"There are numerous ways," says Matt. "Companies like ours are all over. The customer service route was my entrance into the field. No question, though, a cinema or theater background would help. While school will carry you only so far, those are good majors to do."

"Everything I've read," says Kevin, "indicates that computer artist is a top growth market, job-wise. I recommend learning the latest software. Take classes wherever you can."

"I started by gluing model kits together," says John Merritt. "I then networked and freelanced around town for ten years. Wherever I went, I always had my work to show. Having a great portfolio is crucial. If someone came to me I would want to see their models, props, artwork, even if only in photographs. Then, if I hired them, they would start working doing simple tasks—sanding, being a set of hands for someone else. Eventually, they would come to understand how the system works, build their own prototypes, and move up. That's the best way, work from the ground up."

"You have to pay attention to detail," John Neil concludes. "Then practice, practice, practice. Our job is to make something happen that can't happen. That's the challenge that gets me up in the morning. And when I have a low day, I think of all the people who wish they were here, doing what I do for a living."

Cool Web Sites to Visit

NOVA Online/Special Effects: Anything Can Happen
www.pbs.org/WGBH/NOVA/specialfx/sfxhome.html

Rhythm and Hues Studios
www.rhythm.com

Special Effects
www.back-stage.com/effects/intro.htm

SPECIAL EVENTS PROFESSIONAL

With the Bicentennial and the 1984 Olympics, the special events industry came into its own. Today, worldwide, the industry generates $148 billion and employs approximately 30,000 professional planners and directors.

I t was an extraordinary event for entertainment-obsessed Los Angeles. A year in the planning and a full week just to set it up, the annual two-day Festival of Books at UCLA found seventy-five thousand book lovers soaking up two hundred author lectures and book signings, visiting over three hundred publisher and bookstore booths, and wallowing in the ambiance of the printed word. Eat your heart out, New York!

A happening such as the Festival of Books doesn't just happen, however. Ask Lisa Petty, senior event manager for UCLA Special Events and Protocol. As point person for the festival, a UCLA/*Los Angeles Times* joint project, she planned and coordinated the entire undertaking. "I didn't do it alone," Lisa concedes. "A dozen committees were formed, numerous contracts signed, reams printed, signs designed and made, transportation arranged, and a gala Friday night reception held for authors—hundreds took part. But I suppose as senior event manager for on-campus clients, I had a hand in making it happen."

Beyond Party Planning

Lisa exemplifies the new professional who plans and coordinates special events for a myriad of clients in venues from junkyards to ballrooms. Known as special events managers, planners, or directors, they are a long way from the party planners of old. "Actually, party planners will always be there for the smaller events," Liese

Gardner, editor/associate publisher of *Special Events* magazine, reports. "The industry is so much more now."

Beth Sewell, director of membership and chapter operations for ISES, the two thousand-member International Special Events Society, agrees: "Special event planners, producers and coordinators; meeting planners; wedding consultants and party planners; facility venue managers; fund-raisers; producers and managers of parades, festivals, circuses, carnivals, sporting events, and concerts; and convention and exposition service managers are all involved in this growing, exciting industry."

"Event planners have always existed, but the special events industry took off with the Bicentennial and 1984 Olympics," Liese explains. Today, according to Tim Lundy, ISES international president, "We're seeing a worldwide industry generating $148 billion and employing approximately thirty thousand professional planners and directors."

Pulling It Off

Black pipe and drapes cover the walls of the cavernous ballroom and hide its off-white plaster. A three-story backdrop shields an entry portal. The pillared balcony extends from center stage, with live green plants draping the entire expanse. Risers place dining tables at varying heights, each floral centerpiece pin-spotted from a light beam from above. Over three hundred Hilton sales executives and guests from around the country are here to enjoy a sumptuous meal in their own Anaheim Hilton. Awed by the surroundings though the participants are, it's when the Evita Entertainment Group's lead singer bellows out "Don't Cry for Me Argentina" that the room erupts into unrestrained applause. "At that moment," says David A. Granger, event director for Theme Warehouse, Inc., of Paramount, California, "I knew we had a success. All the weeks planning and days preparing were going to pay off."

David wasn't always so confident. "Eight years ago," the exuberant 31-year-old says, "I didn't know this industry existed. I was doing the

What Will I Earn?

Generally, special event managers earn what middle-level managers in any company earn. If you are in business for yourself, earnings can be substantial, as can the risks.

typical retail store management thing when a friend asked if I'd help out with his freelance floral work. Within a year I was working for *the* John Daly, one of the country's leading special events gurus. For the next six years I carried water, cut flowers, and schlepped, schlepped, schlepped. But in that entire time I absorbed everything. When I left John's employ I'd become production manager."

For the last two years, David has worked for Theme Warehouse. "When they offered me the position, I wondered, was I ready?" he confides. "But Lisa Tucker-Moreno, president, and Mark McCabe, general manager, offered me a chance to spread my wings and fly, to start using right-brain matter. Now I'm in on every event from concept to tear-down, to recap."

Great Event Basics

Gayle Jasso, author of *Special Events from A to Z*, has a pretty good idea what makes for a great event. "There are twelve phases to a special event," she says. From presentation to evaluation, every event should incorporate the following aspects:

1. *Presentation:* The proposed special event is researched and presented to the most appropriate, highest-level organization decision-maker for consideration. The goal is to receive approval for the organization to participate in or produce the event.
2. *Evaluation:* Appropriate personnel evaluate the special event and decide whether it is to the organization's benefit to participate in the event.
3. *Approval:* Approval is given for the organization to participate in or produce the event.
4. *Assignment of event coordinators:* Decisions are made as to which of the organization's departments will coordinate and oversee the event, who the overall event coordinator will be (staff member, outside consultant, or volunteer), and who will provide assistance to that individual (staff members, outside consultant, or volunteers).

INFORMATION

For More Information

International Special Events Society (ISES)
9202 N. Meridian Street
Suite 200
Indianapolis, IN 46260
(317) 571-5601
fax (317) 571-5603

ISES offers training seminars and certification as a special events planner (CSEP).

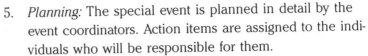

What to Read

Special Events From A to Z
by Gayle Jasso.
Corwin Press, 1996.

5. *Planning:* The special event is planned in detail by the event coordinators. Action items are assigned to the individuals who will be responsible for them.

6. *Preparation:* Preparations are made for each and every detail relative to the special event.

7. *Setup:* At prescribed times, all physical requirements, such as audiovisual equipment, seating arrangements, signs, table settings, centerpieces, awards, place cards, and handouts, are set in place prior to the beginning of each phase of the special event.

8. *"D-Day":* The special event occurs.

9. *Tear-down:* As soon as possible after the conclusion of the special event, all items that were set up and used for the event are torn down and returned to their proper places.

10. *Follow-up:* As soon as possible after the conclusion of the special event, all action and follow-up items that require attention are completed, such as thank-you notes and answers to questions.

11. *Debriefing:* The key special event coordinators, be they staff, outside consultants, or volunteers, meet together to determine the degree of success or, if applicable, failure of every major aspect of the special event.

12. *Evaluation:* Based on the debriefing session, the key special event coordinators evaluate the special event. The evaluation includes the results of the event and how it accomplished its objectives. The evaluation is a formal, written statement that is shared with appropriate senior organization personnel and kept as a resource for future event coordinators of the same or similar special events.

And you though those events just happened!

In addition, creating a positive ambiance is key to pulling off a great special event. Gayle has a few suggestions here, too. She says you'll want to have:

- An event site that is located in an interesting and well-known city with diverse people and interests
- Tasteful, well-appointed facility
- A clever event theme
- An appealing event color scheme
- Artistically designed printed materials
- Quality printed materials
- Delicious and varied food served in an appealing manner, including a menu that can accommodate the special dietary requirements of all participants
- An appropriate dress code
- Creative and clever decorations and centerpieces
- Thematic promotional items
- Unique gifts and door prizes
- Original awards and recognition items
- Suitable music
- Outstanding entertainment
- State-of-the-art audiovisual equipment
- Expert technicians
- Appropriate sound levels for the audience
- Pleasant, responsive, and attentive event coordinators
- Exceptional, prompt, helpful, and personable service
- Clearly posted, nicely printed signs informing participants where and when event activities are occurring
- Easy-to-read and attractive name badges, affixed in a manner that does not damage clothing and that can be easily removed
- Interesting, unusual, and exciting extracurricular activities
- Accessible, convenient transportation around the buildings or area of the event site
- Comfortable temperatures in all meeting and hotel rooms
- Prompt and sincere thank-you notes, responses to questions, and responses to special requests

Anyone forget anything? No one said this would be easy.

Making the Grade

OK, but who makes a good events professional? Who could do all this?

"A person who can keep many balls in the air at one time," Gayle says. A person who insists on doing one thing before going on to another isn't likely to succeed in this field."

Liese agrees and adds, "It's also people who make their own rules and are creative in finding solutions to a clients needs. Above all, a special events person must be detail oriented and keep excellent records."

Experience and knowing the not-so-obvious "little things" certainly helps, too. Lisa gives an interesting example: "We recently held an event for a foreign head of state. The consulate sent out seven hundred invitations for what they hoped would be a standing-room-only speech. Problem was, the venue had four hundred and twenty seats. Not enough? No, too many! You send out seven hundred invitations, you're lucky if half show. We convinced his handlers to use a smaller room."

Is this a high-stress job?

"Yes," says Gayle. "It helps to be a low-key person. But most in this field are high strung. They always have to be 'on.' It takes tremendous energy just to be so together."

"A half-day for me is an eight-hour day," David says. "Free weekends? Forget it! And throughout, you must never let the client see you shake. You can lose your mind *after* the event, on your way home."

In addition to stress, the issue of recognition, or lack of it, often comes up. "You will never be pulled out at an event to be congratulated for all your hard work," Beth says. And Lisa adds. "My client gets all the recognition. I'm not on the program, I am not the producer or the host."

"But there are highs in this field," David concludes. "When you watch the guests walk in, people you don't even know, and they stand in awe of the once-in-a-lifetime event you have created for them, it's terrific. And when your client gets tears in his or her eyes because the room looks so fabulous, well, there is no high quite like it."

Cool Web Sites to Visit

International Special Events Society
www.njises.org

Special Events Directory
www.specialeventsite.com

Wedding and Special Events by Sylvia Golden
www.eventsbysylviagolden.com

STOCKBROKER

To prosper today, many stockbrokers are moving beyond full service to "complete service." They are becoming money managers, financial advisers, asset gatherers.

It's 1982, the Lakers defeat the Philadelphia 76ers, four games to two, for the NBA title, *E.T. the Extra-Terrestrial* is a box office smash, and kids everywhere are chasing a moon-faced Pac-Man around on their television screens. Furthermore, the stock market, having just experienced its first 100 million–share day, is heading toward the magic 1,000 mark on the New York Stock Exchange.

It is also the year that Peter Begley's dad, hoping to steer his 12-year-old son into more wholesome and edifying video game pursuits, buys him Nintendo's newest adventure: The Wall Street Kid. "It got me started," Peter says. "The game covered everything you now see on the business channel. I would trade against another player to gain the best portfolio. Even back in junior high, I knew what I would someday be doing for real."

Today, as the stock market oscillates above 10,000, and billion-share days are common, Peter is a licensed stockbroker, providing private client services with a well-known banking and securities firm in Beverly Hills, California. But there's a difference now—"It's no longer a game," he says. "Working with a client's assets, money to put their kids through college and to provide themselves with a secure retirement, is serious business. It is a humbling experience."

Investing America

In 1998, U.S. households held an estimated 34.9 percent of their financial assets (that is, all investments excluding hard assets such as real estate) in stocks. That, according to the Federal Reserve Board, is the highest level on record. Over 2.9 million U.S. households had investable assets of $1 million-plus. Those who held general stock funds in the 1990s earned a 15.4 percent return on their investment. Individuals with tech stock funds were nearly twice as well off, gaining a 28.9 percent return. Clearly, whether in blue chip stocks, growth stocks, income stocks, cyclical stocks, or preferred stocks, not to mention mutual funds, as the new millennium dawned, investing in the stock market was the good-sense choice for millions of Americans.

Professionals providing the investment services needed by the majority of those "investing Americans," known as securities sales representatives, or more commonly stockbrokers, numbered 638,084 in April 2000, according to the National Association of Securities Dealers (NASD). Such broker-dealers provide investment services to clients and study financial reports, stock market activity, and general economic conditions. They solicit prospective clients, buy and sell stocks, bonds, and mutual funds, and offer information and advice to clients on investment opportunities. Due to a growing economy and vast technological changes in the way their business is done, the role of stockbroker is undergoing a sea change. Securities dealers who rely solely on the trade to make a living, may be encountering their own personal "bear market."

Full-Service Providers

Though he has been on the job less than six months, Paul McKenna of Edward Jones, is no newcomer to the world of work, having spent years in the cut-throat music business. As a new stockbroker, Paul is one of approximately 6,000 securities dealers in an equal number of Edward Jones' offices across the country. "We are one-person offices," he explains. "As such, I believe our full service is a little more personalized, the client knows who they'll see when they walk in—me."

Such full-service brokers are the mainstay of the brokerage business. They seek clients by cold-calling, meeting people face-to-face at charity events, soccer games, and PTA meetings, and by contacting local businesses. They find individuals and institutions that have money to invest and provide them with a full range of services: advice, trading, and, in many cases, plenty of hand-holding. Given the influx of new investors and the availability of online technology, however, many feel such brokers are dinosaurs, heading for extinction. With discount brokerage and 11 million-plus Americans doing their own investing online, the future is elsewhere, they say.

Mark Ingebretsen, who writes regularly for *Online Investor*, a magazine inclined to encourage new investment methodologies, isn't yet ready to write the full-service broker's obituary. "Such a broker is not dead," he says. "What we're seeing is a mixture, some individuals will do the bulk of their investing themselves, yet go to a full-service broker for specific services and advice: handling tough trades, buying options and convertible bonds—out-of-the-ordinary stuff."

Howard Kaplan, 59, recently retired as a controller for a large oil industry supply company, still requires such services. "I'm mostly into bonds now," he says. "Yet, I still need the full-service treatment. I just don't want to spend time online, doing all the work myself. I'd rather play golf. However, when I need advice, I want to talk to a real broker, one I have a relationship with."

"Most of my clients are elderly," says Ted Smith, of Transamerica, "and they are not equipped to do this on their own. Lack of knowledge, drive, whatever, keeps them coming to me. On the other end, many young professionals are too busy with their own careers to be heavy into investing themselves. Sure, I have lost some of them to online, even day trading. But most people need help along the way. After all, we don't, as a rule, do our own dentistry."

Nonetheless, Dan Hurley, a registered representative at a large discount brokerage firm in downtown Los Angeles, is busier than ever servicing 254 clients from his bank of phones and computer terminals. "Unlike some discount brokerages, at least when a person calls here they get the same broker," he says. "Still, I basically do the trades, little more. I make a commission on each transaction—period. The more stocks that trade hands, the more I earn."

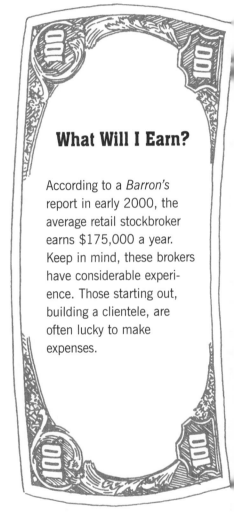

What Will I Earn?

According to a *Barron's* report in early 2000, the average retail stockbroker earns $175,000 a year. Keep in mind, these brokers have considerable experience. Those starting out, building a clientele, are often lucky to make expenses.

For More Information

The National Association of
Securities Dealers
1735 K Street N.W.
Washington, DC 20006
(800) 225-7720
www.nasdr.com

Securities Industry Association
120 Broadway, 35th Floor
New York, NY 10271

Going Where the Money Is

To survive, indeed prosper, today, many stockbrokers are moving to an even higher level, beyond full service, to "complete service." They are becoming money mangers, financial advisers, asset gatherers.

That's what Peter has done. After stints at a small firm doing niche financing aimed at specialized markets, and at a discount broker, he has moved to his present firm because, as he says, "This is where the money is." He's right about that. Peter works for the securities subsidiary of a large bank. "Anyone with over a million dollars who wants private banking services can come here," he says. "When they do, I walk down the hall, introduce myself, and, hopefully, start a relationship."

That relationship is performance-based, meaning the brokerage house earns 1 or 2 percent of the total assets managed. As those assets increase, so does the fee for service. "It puts me and my client on the same side of the table," says Peter. "He doesn't feel I'm just trying to sell him something to earn a commission."

"It's the direction things are going," agrees Ted. "We are going to see less commissions on trades and more financial planning, that sort of thing. Today's stockbroker better know about taxes, accounting functions, investment planing, various annuities, even insurance—the whole gamut."

Being a terrific salesperson doesn't hurt. "It takes a real salesman to get people to do that, to come over, say to Merrill Lynch, where we would manage their money," says Louis Sobel, a just retired 30-year veteran. "Having started out as an engineer, quite frankly I wasn't all that good at the selling part."

William Kraus, vice president of West America Securities Corp., in Westlake Village, California, sums it up well: "As commissions have narrowed, the emphasis is on asset gathering, where we charge a percent of the account. But to make that work, you must establish a deep, long-term relationship with your client based on competency and trust. You need to know his kids' names, his plans for them, and his overall objectives, even if he doesn't state them. Again, trust is what it's about."

Gaining that trust, getting a client to open up, share his or her complete financial picture, is one of the biggest challenges a stockbroker faces. "It is a very personal thing," confides Peter. "Yet, I must have the whole financial picture in order to do my job correctly. I am up front with a client. I tell him, 'It's like with your doctor, you can't hold anything back.'"

The Age Issue

At 31, Tony Mastandrea, a broker at one of the nation's largest securities firms, may seem a bit young to be managing other people's money. Even with a degree in finance and six years of solid brokerage experience at Prudential Securities, he does, from time to time, come up against age discrimination in reverse. "It is a challenge," he says, "even at my age there are people who consider me fairly young. There are times I wish for a few streaks of gray hair."

There is little chance for that in the near future, however. As a consequence, Tony has to rely on other ways to gain respect. "I simply tell clients that I'll try harder for them," he explains. "I also play on my youth with regard to technology. Clients tend to assume a younger guy may be more in tune not only with the technology to do the job, but with technology stocks in general."

He may be right. Howard makes an interesting observation: "I never really got into technology stocks because my broker was an older guy, not much into that sector. Perhaps it would have been better to work with a younger person, one more savvy in the ways of Microsoft, Cisco, or Yahoo!"

"It's a struggle," says Peter, referring to the age issue. "That's why I often partner up with older brokers, those graying or balding. Besides, we are all learning. Working with a more experienced broker on asset management is a win-win situation, for me and my clients."

William agrees. "A team approach is the way to go," he advises. "It can no longer be a single broker doing everything himself. A team is much more efficient."

What to Read

The Fast Track: The Insider's Guide to Winning Jobs in Management Consulting, Investment Banking, and Securities Trading by Miriam Naficy. Broadway Books, 1997.

Job Seekers Guide to Wall Street Recruiters by Christopher W. Hunt and Scott A. Scanlon. John Wiley & Sons, 1998.

Trying harder, developing trust, getting to know clients and working on their long-term interests—for most stockbrokers, young and old, that's the objective. Unfortunately, there have been, and continue to be, problems: "Any time you have lots of money moving about, you have the potential for abuse," says William, who, among other things, handles compliance issues—or matters involving government regulation of the industry—for West America. "With strong upper management, you can minimize the problem. Trouble is, some brokers can move quickly from one firm to the next, always staying one step ahead of compliance officers. If you're looking for short-term remuneration, it can work for a while. In the long run, however, it'll catch up with you."

It is the job of the National Association of Securities Dealers, Regulation Branch (NASDR), to monitor, investigate, and deal with any broker complaints and irregularities. In the end, it often comes down to the concept of "suitability," as Ami Hyland, of NASDR, puts it. "Brokers are bound to determine what a customer's financial needs are, their goals, and then make stock selections, risky versus non-risky, based on that information."

"It's about taking time to know your broker," adds William. "You wouldn't want just any doctor doing your heart surgery. Same thing with a stockbroker who is advising you on your assets."

"Bad trading is bad business," offers Dan. "It will come back to bite you quickly. This business is based on referrals and reputations. I would never knowingly make a bad trade."

"We are not buying and selling quickly," says Paul. "We are a conservative organization, with our clients for the long haul."

"'Need not greed,' should be the motto for broker and client alike," observes William. "In the end, it's still buyer beware. If it sounds too good, it probably is. Even with full-service brokers, clients need to do their homework."

Humbling Career

Becoming a stockbroker is not easy, even though over 638,000 practicing brokers have managed to become licensed. Though you do not need a college degree, those without one will find securing their first position an extra challenge. The bottom line requirement, no matter where you work in the United States, is passing the Series 7 examination, a tough, 250-question multiple choice test that can require three to six months of study. Some states also demand the Series 63, a shorter 50-question test.

"I have both licenses," says Peter. "In addition, I have passed the Series 65 test for private money management. I also have my Life and Agent insurance certificate. If you're going to do the full-asset management thing, the more exams you pass the better."

Is all this study and hard work worth it, especially during the first few years?

"It can be stressful," cautions Gregory Myers, vice president of West America. "I recommend a serious program of physical activity to help alleviate the problem.

"Still, the financial compensation can be considerable. And then there are less tangible rewards. It is the most wonderful feeling to be able to manage other people's crucially important asset, their money. Whether you are twenty-nine or fifty-nine, to have their trust is terrific. I can't think of another career where a young professional can call on a powerful professional and get them to talk about something as personal as their finances. Often you are working with people in their late years. They are setting up a trust for you to manage—after they're gone. It is a family's future you're dealing with. All the high power aspects aside, it is indeed a humbling career."

Cool Web Sites to Visit

Broker Facts—A Guide for the Aspiring Stockbroker
www.members.aol.com/ brokerfact

National Association of Securities Dealers Investor Resources
www.nasdr.com/2500.htm

TECHNICAL WRITER

It's not just writing anymore. Today, you must understand graphic design, layout, and desktop publishing. Forget the image of dry, uninspiring text. Technical writers are the bridge between high-tech experts and lay readers.

A befuddled consumer (we'll call him Jim) is about to have what Epson America has dubbed an OOBE, "Out-of-Box Experience." Seated alone before a 3 by 5 foot desk, in a room not much larger, Jim has been instructed to open a cardboard box, take out the printer, and set it up. Though he knows they are there, he can't see the three pair of eyes focused on him from behind a one-way window. Two individuals from marketing research and a technical writer, Karen Bergen, five years with the company and current president of the Society for Technical Communication (STC), Los Angeles chapter, observe and take notes on Jim's every move.

"It's frustrating when you see people making the same mistakes," Karen says. "You want to cry out, 'Look on page 14 in the manual!' But when, a bit later, the consumer pages through the same manual, searching for a troubleshooting hint you know isn't there because you failed to include it, your irritation increases. Our job as technical writers is to prevent such occurrences. If consumers have problems, we haven't addressed their concerns. Usability tests, such as the one I've described, help us to do just that."

Beyond Word Processing

Technical writers, more broadly known as technical communicators, write about technical topics, anything to do with specialized areas of science and technology. Blake and Bly, in *The Elements of Technical Writing*, say that "technical writing differs from creative writing—intended to entertain—and advertising writing—intended to sell—in that its primary goal is the accurate transmission of technical information. It generally deals with an object, process, system, or abstract idea. The language of technical writing is typically utilitarian and stresses accuracy over style. The tone is objective and focuses on the technical content rather than the author's feelings on the subject.

If you think this means boring, think again. "We get quite a few screenwriters coming to STC meetings," Karen says. "They are surprised at how interesting and creative our work can be; how they can be imaginative in appealing to the reader."

Tom Magnus, a technical writer for 20 years, describes a typical week: "I'm working on a brochure, a five hundred page document on Framemaker, planning out a proposal for an online help project, and creating a client's Web page. Such variety keeps me excited."

"A misperception plaguing technical writers," comments Raymond Urgo, of Urgo & Associates, a company specializing in procedures consulting for organizations, "is that we're merely scribes. Someone has information, they throw it over the fence and say. 'Here, make a manual.' No! We're beyond the era of punctuation, grammar, and spelling. It's about structured writing techniques, organizing ideas, considering the cognitive abilities of the reader. These are more advanced ways of looking at technical writing. We are dealing with the broader concept of 'information design.'"

Dr. John Giesler, a technical communicator with Aerotek, a nationwide engineering consulting firm, agrees. "The days of having a writer, typist, and illustrator are long gone. Today, a technical writer is all three. You must understand that being a technical communicator is more than being a technical writer. You have to sign up for a life-long commitment to learning. That means learning new tools, software, constantly expanding your knowledge of the technical, and knowing information design."

There's that term "information design," again. What does it mean? "More than just writing," explains Karen Axelrod, an independent technical communicator concentrating on high-tech marketing and public relations. "Information design refers to the way you put information together. You must understand graphic design, layout, desktop publishing. Knowledge of your audience is critical. Technical writers are often the bridge between high-tech experts and lay readers."

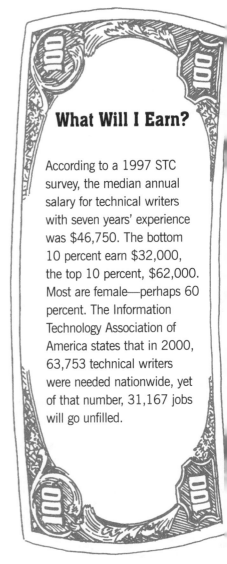

What Will I Earn?

According to a 1997 STC survey, the median annual salary for technical writers with seven years' experience was $46,750. The bottom 10 percent earn $32,000, the top 10 percent, $62,000. Most are female—perhaps 60 percent. The Information Technology Association of America states that in 2000, 63,753 technical writers were needed nationwide, yet of that number, 31,167 jobs will go unfilled.

INFORMATION

For More Information

Society for Technical
Communication
901 North Stuart Street
Suite 904
Arlington, VA 22203-1854
(703) 522-2075
fax (703) 522-2075
stc@tmn.com

Technical Standards Inc.
1165 Linda Vista Drive
Suite 113
San Marcos, CA 92069
(800) 889-7116
www.techstandards.com
An employment service
exclusively for technical writers.

The "Technical" in Technical Writing

Karen Bergen didn't start out as a technical writer. "I graduated from college in 1970 with a major in English. A few years later I began working as a production editor for Scholastic in New York."

After years in publishing, plus time out to raise a family, Karen moved west to California in 1986. "When I looked around there wasn't much in publishing," she continues. "What I did see was aerospace, software, and computer companies. If I were to write again, it would need to be in such industries. Technical writer was the obvious choice."

How did she acquire the "technical" in technical writer? "To succeed as a technical writer, two skills are required. One, *writing*, in the full 'information design' sense. Two, *technical knowledge*. To acquire the latter, if you didn't study it in college, requires a curiosity about the technology you're writing about. You must have an interest in the subject matter and know how to ask the right questions. It means probing, being resourceful and detail-minded."

Karen Axelrod concurs, and adds, "Subject matter expertise is important. Can you talk with engineers, software developers, technical experts? Your job is to convert information into something readable to a nontechnical audience."

"Not all technical types are as forthcoming with information as we'd like," Karen Bergen says. "In some environments, technical people feel we're not technical enough. Yet, getting their cooperation is crucial. Everything we do has to be confirmed."

John, who has managed groups of technical writers, puts it this way: "You'll work with technical people who are busy doing their job. They don't have time to share information. You must use your people skills to go in, get the information. After all, you can't just invent the stuff."

"The ability to learn is important," says Raymond. "You don't have to know the subject matter going in, but you must acquire the knowledge if you are to write about it. If you can organize ideas, size information, take into consideration the cognitive abilities of the reader, you will succeed as a technical writer."

STC to the Rescue

All professions have professional associations that will help the neophyte develop and succeed. For technical writers, the Society for Technical Communications is a must organization to join. Why? With 19,000 members and 144 chapters worldwide, it is the largest professional association serving the technical communication profession. If you are a writer or editor, graphic artist or technical illustrator, translator, manager or supervisor, educator or student, independent consultant or contractor, or photographer or multimedia specialist, STC can be of benefit.

In addition to its many programs and courses, STC sponsors the following international competitions:

- Technical Publication Competition
- Technical Art Competition
- Technical Video Competition
- Student Technical Writing Competition
- Online Communication Competition

The Job Description

What are documentation managers looking for in a technical writer? Here technical writers explain, in the March-April 1998 *Newsletter for Documentation Specialists*, published by Technical Standards, Inc., of San Marcos, California:

"The ideal technical writer is a good 'information organizer' capable of seeing the equipment or application they are writing about from several viewpoints and skill levels," says Drusilla Cursi, manager, Technical Publications Group, ASYMTEK.

"Some of the qualities I look for in a tech writer, beyond the generally accepted basic qualifications, are natural curiosity; highly developed analytical skills; ability to handle change; ability to learn from mistakes; and emphasis on content development, not 'pretty' format," adds Colleen Smith, information engineering team leader, NCR Corporation.

If you qualify, job prospects and salary compensation for technical writers are good. Speaking as president of STC, Karen Bergen says,

What to Read

Defining Technical Communications
by Dan Jones.
STC, 1996.

Technical Editing: Basic Theory and Practice
by Charles F. Kemnitz.
STC, 1994.

"Employment outlook is excellent. I am now seeing three or four new listings a week in Los Angeles."

The downside? "You'll always be a support function within a support function," says John. "You'll feel the brunt during layoffs, downsizing. And, remember, there is the work itself, which is very collaborative. You will rarely get your name on the cover of anything you write."

Perhaps the downsizing explains, in part, the proliferation of technical writing consultants. Four out of five technical writers are either freelancing or operate their own technical writing company.

For example, look at Tom. "Early on in this profession, I saw two paths I could take. One was into management. If I remained as a staff employee, it would be technical writer to senior technical writer, to management. Or, I could become a consultant. I felt management was too different a job, with its people problems, scheduling, et cetera. As a consultant I would be able to stay more on task, I would be more project-oriented. I would still be a technical writer."

But Tom soon found out it wasn't that simple. "Now I have the business end to work on, too," he says. "A lot of people have misperceptions, a rosy view of consulting. It is not all writing. Now I have to deal with a lot of things I don't want to deal with, like setting up my own IRA, buying office supplies, running a business.

Still, the rewards are there. "As a technical writer, you see a tangible product," Karen Bergen says. "If I can write something to aid the customer and save the company money by reducing technical support calls, great! And, if during product review the manual is cited as being well-written, easy to use—well, it feels terrific."

Cool Web Sites to Visit

ProEdit
www.proedit.com

Society for Technical Communications
www.stc-va.org

Writer's Resource Center
www.azstarnet.com/~poewar/ writer/writer.htm

TOY DESIGNER

Imagine getting a job assignment to design a really cool toy. You build the prototype. Then, you and your fellow workers play with it all day. Toy designers do just that sort of thing for a living. But it's not all fun and games, toy design is serious business.

Caleb and Christi Chung, a husband-and-wife toy design team, had just returned from their annual trek to Toy Fair, the largest toy trade show in the Western Hemisphere, held in New York City every February.

"Once again we were underwhelmed," Caleb, a former Hollywood special effects developer, says. "We determined, then and there, to stop working altogether, return home to Boise, and take the plunge, spend the next six months creating a product we knew our background and knowledge would allow us to perfect and exploit."

Toiling in their garage, the Chungs conjured up a being destined for life.

"I wanted to make it small and inexpensive," Caleb explains. "I started with a three-inch-high cone. We added a nose, a mouth, eyes, ears, and feet. We gave it a tilt and a bit of movement. And we crammed it full of gears and electronics, the latter developed by our new partner, David Hamton.

"Christi did the drawings, taking ideas from owls, hamsters, and the like. But in the end, we purposely developed a critter like no other, a three-dimensional being with 'emotions.' A kid could invest hours in making the furry friend anything she wanted it to be."

Next, the Chungs produced a video commercial and took it to the toy companies. "We didn't go to Mattel or Hasbro, the big guys," says Caleb. "With only thirteen weeks left to Toy Fair, 1998, time was running out. Tiger Electronics, a company light on its feet, was our choice. They bought it on the condition that David, Christi, and I would work for them to see the product through, bring it to life."

And to life it has come! With 1.5 to 2 million tiny Furbies selling every month, the Chungs' brainchild is possibly the most successful toy ever made. "You hope for a big hit," says Caleb. "Then you hope for longevity. Only time will tell."

An Eclectic Group

Time is on the side of toy makers, with all those youngsters under 14 wanting—demanding—their favorite advertised playthings.

According to the Toy Manufacturers of America, Inc. (TMA), total industry sales for 1998 hit $27.2 billion. That's a 20 percent increase over 1996 if you don't include video games, a 10 percent increase if you do.

What's selling? "Stroll the aisles at your local Toys Я Us and you'll see a Barbie, a vehicle, an action figure, a plush, and a video game aisle" says Martin Caveza, toy design department chair at Otis College of Art and Design in Los Angeles. "It's classic toys to interactive entertainment, and everything in between."

Those who design these toys form a varied group. "Few of us are engineers with degrees," says Eric Ostendorff, of Mattel's Hot Wheels design group. "Most, perhaps 80 percent, have an industrial design background. Many are art school graduates."

"The best designers," David Voss, design manager for the Nerf and vehicles division of Hasbro Corporation in Cincinnati, Ohio, explains, "are those who understand three key areas: design, engineering, and marketing. Often, we get new hires who are completely focused on design. Not good. You have to ask, 'How are you going to market the toy, how are you going to make the darn thing?'"

Caleb knows how important the latter skill can be. "You must be able to draw, to build, to make the prototype," he says. "You won't know something is fun until you build it. If you can't construct it yourself, you'll have to talk someone into doing it. If they don't think it's a good idea, it never happens."

"Our job is to bridge the gap between what marketing wants to sell and what the customer wants to buy," adds Eric. "You must be a jack-of-all-trades, and not just with your hands. Do you understand costing, safety, marketability, advertisablity, and playability? As toy designers, we wear many hats."

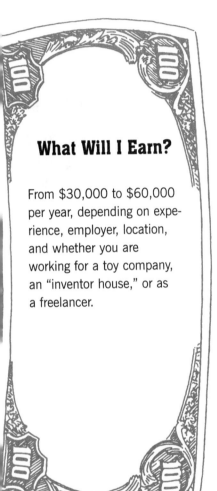

What Will I Earn?

From $30,000 to $60,000 per year, depending on experience, employer, location, and whether you are working for a toy company, an "inventor house," or as a freelancer.

Child's Play

Playability—that's kids' stuff, isn't it? "Yes," says Martin, "and it is critical. Is this something a child is going to pick up and play with? That's always the question. You have to understand how children think and act. What they want."

"I'll give you an example," Eric adds. "If I could get a toy car to levitate, that would be a major technological achievement. Yet, only an adult could appreciate the feat. Test that technology against a set where the car does a simple loop and smashes into other cars, and a kid will opt for the latter every time."

Appealing to kids and their wants is not enough, however. A product, including a toy, has to be made and then sold. Adults are involved.

Elliot Rudell, founder of Rudell Design, a new product development and invention company in Torrance, California, and one of the most respected inventors in the field, puts it this way: "A guy will come to me and say, 'I have a great idea for a toy, kids will love it.' My face does not move. In the real world, I too have to love it, the guy at the conference table has to love it, his company has to love it, and the buyer has to love it thinking it will sell to the kids, and, more important, their parents. As a toy designer, you're in a creative field. But if you are going to be commercially creative, that puts restrictions on you. Can you live with those limitations? If not, do something else."

Easy on the Technology

Though the toy business is up, competition for the entertainment dollar is, too.

Sales of video games, for example, which may or may not be considered a toy depending on who you ask, are blasting off: $6.2 billion in 1999 compared with $3.6 billion two years earlier, a 72 percent increase. Video games now outgross movies.

But can the same technology used in these electronic games help propel traditional toys to new levels of sophistication? "We are now involved in technologies that don't typically get put into toys," Steward Imai, a partner in Toy Innovations, says. "That makes them unique. However, such technology has to be transparent to the child."

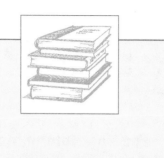

What to Read

Toys and Games
by John Williams.
Raitree/Steck Vaughn, 1998.

Elliot echoes that sentiment. "With electronics costs going down, we can now afford cool stuff. About 60 percent of the new toys unveiled by Mattel's Fisher-Price unit in 1999 came with a computer chip. That's up from less than 10 percent only three years ago. Yet, we must sober up to the intoxication of technology. At day's end will the kid play with it?"

Eric agrees. "I last worked on these cyber-racers with a computer inside. Not a great hit. Though they spewed out information, kids still went for the 99-cent cars. Being a good designer is realizing when something is good enough, then moving on to the next thing."

Toy College

On the fifth floor of the toy design department at the Otis College of Art and Design, Gabriel Delatorre is carving a four-inch piece of wood into a VW bug. "I'll vacuum-form it with styrene later, then paint and detail the mold," the 19-year-old junior explains. "I'm learning to execute a prototype model."

Gabriel is a full-time student at one of only two "toy colleges" in the United States, the other being the Fashion Institute of Technology in New York City.

When Gabriel completes his studies, he'll have earned a bachelor of fine arts in toy design. Otis, which has a distinguished reputation in the fine arts field, began offering toy studies in 1997. They graduated their first class in June 2000. "Our program trains students in developing soft and hard toys," says Martin. "Of course, we also cover safety issues, game theory, child psychology, and business practices."

The curriculum is demanding and diverse, as Gabriel will attest. "I'm taking courses in technical illustration [CAD], model making, toy design, blue sky concepting, childhood and society, art history, and children's literature. I love it all."

Why did Gabriel choose this career path of toy design? "Heck, where else can you get a job assignment to design a really cool toy?" he responds.

Gabriel knows toy design won't be all fun and games. "I interned at Mattel last summer," he says. "I discovered it's not just drawing up your latest fantasy. A toy has to make sense. You have to know how it would be made, how it is to be marketed."

Dig Deeper

Indeed, it is not all play. "You have paperwork, bureaucracy, as in any company," says Steward. "Sure, if you could do the movie *Big* every day that would be great."

"Considering the time frame and amount of product generated every year, on any given day your odds of coming up with a licensable, potentially successful toy is close to zero," Elliot states.

Even the big boys, the star companies, have their good and bad days—or years. In 2000, Mattel Inc., the world's largest toy maker, was forced to sell off its troubled Learning Co. operations for an estimated $200 million, a mere 5 percent of its purchase price of $3.6 billion. Yet later in the year, Mattel snagged a contract from Time Warner, Inc., to make toys and other products based on the books and films of the popular children's character Harry Potter.

Then there's that question everyone asks: "You're a what—a toy designer?"

"In the design world," says Dave, "other jobs are looked on as a bit more prestigious than ours. Car design for example. But then you could be drawing taillights for two years."

True, and Dave wouldn't trade his career for any other in the design field. "I get no greater thrill than knowing that what I sketch today some kid could be tossing around in the playground a year from now."

So, how to get started? Caleb gives clear, important advice: "Your goal as a toy inventor, working freelance or for a design and innovation firm [known as an 'inventor house'], is to place a product with a large toy company and get royalties. First, go to toy college, whether it's a place like Otis or on-the-job-training at Mattel.

"Next, buy a ticket, hop on a plane, and get to Toy Fair in New York every February. Then, haunt your local Toys Я Us. You must know everything that's in the store and why it's changing. Make the place your research facility.

"Finally, throw away your first five ideas. They've already been thought of. Dig deeper. Always dig deeper."

Cool Web Sites to Visit

Design a Toy
www.algilbert.org/design/kidsinvent.html

LEGO Mindstorms
www.legomindstorms.com

Toy Tips-About Toy Tips
www.toytips.com/toystuff/contest.htm

Hot Concepts!

Workable Wardrobe

"Dress for success" is a phrase that has entered the mainstream. Yet, though there are jobs where impressing by dressing is a factor, for most jobs, dressing appropriately is all you really need to do.

What you wear on the job, however, is different from what you should wear to your job interview. On the job, you dress to be included, as others dress who do the same work. For an interview, it is always acceptable to dress upward, a little more formally than you would once on the job. At the interview, "Play it safe," says Gordon Thomas, of Menswear Solutions. "Wear something that you don't have to worry about—no wrinkle-prone fabrics. It's fine to be overdressed at the interview, but you're in serious trouble if you are too casual."

Some guidelines:

- In traditional fields—business, law, medicine, insurance, banking—tailored conservative outfits are best.
- In creative fields—journalism, publishing, multimedia, advertising, graphics, art galleries—your own style is more important.
- With service-oriented jobs—retail, restaurants—it is all about looking presentable.

The bottom line—dress appropriately. Once you find out what everyone else is wearing, do pretty much the same. Looking good is looking right!

TRAVEL AGENT

*It used to be that being part of a fun and glam-
orous industry, with its so-called familiarization trips
made up for entry-level pay below the poverty line.
That's not the way it works anymore.*

T he trip commences in a week, and Susan, excited, is making
sure all travel documents are correct and accounted for. With
a Brendan Tours tote bag at her side, she sifts through the
paperwork on her desk (tickets, reservations, insurance forms),
checking it against a printed itinerary. "OK," Susan mutters, "arrive
in Amsterdam on the 20th, stay at the Novotel Amsterdam; take a
train to Brussels on the 21st, Jolly Hotel Du Grand Sablon; return to
Amsterdam on the 22nd, pick up Brendan Tour and proceed to
Rome. . . ." All is in order. As she leans back, a satisfied smile
crosses Susan's face. "It's going to be a great two-week vacation,"
she says, "too bad I won't be going."

Though a seasoned traveler herself—England almost every year
for the past 20 years, among other destinations—Susan's career is
not traveling, but arranging travel for others. "A time existed when
travel agents received free travel and we went everywhere. Those
days are gone," she says. "While we all love to travel, travel per se
is not what it's about. For agents, it isn't liking to travel, it's liking
to *sell* travel. Remember, this is a business."

Out and About

Travel agents, about 250,000 nationwide, according to the International
Airline Travel Agent Network (IATAN), give advice on destinations,
make arrangements for transportation, hotel accommodations, car
rentals, tours, and recreation or plan the right vacation package or
business trip. Constantly changing air fares and schedules, a proliferation of vacation packages, and business/pleasure trip combinations

can make travel planning frustrating and time-consuming. Travel agents are there to help. The demand for such travel advisers is soaring.

"The good news for travel agents," Tim Simmons (CTC), editor-in-chief of *TravelAge* magazine, says, "is that business is expanding, with a lot of retail growth. More front-line travel agents are needed, though the number of travel agencies [33,000] is declining."

Annette Alden, director of relationship management at the Institute of Certified Travel Agents (ICTA), agrees. "Leisure travel is no longer considered a luxury but a necessity, at least for those seeking a well-rounded education. As a result, travel agents are more in demand. However, their role is changing. We used to dispense information, issue tickets. Now we're more an interpreter of information. We are travel consultants."

Taking Off

Susan, a certified travel counselor with 20 years in the business, has experienced the transformation. "Before, I worked for a pediatrician in the front office. But dealing with people who didn't want to be there began to wear on me. I needed to be with people who were excited about going somewhere, doing something fun." A travel agency course at Learning Tree University (LTU) in Los Angeles gave Susan the chance to switch. She's never looked back.

Though Susan has worked both sides of the industry, retail and supplier, she now sells leisure travel to an upscale clientele at Town & Country Travel in Thousand Oaks, California. "I specialize in northern Europe," Susan explains. "Dublin to Moscow."

Yet, upscale types, with plenty of discretionary income to spend, have many choices, travel being but one. According to Roger Block, executive vice president for Minneapolis-based Carlson Wagonlit Travel, "We are competing against a vacation home versus a new TV, versus a fur coat, versus a new car. Someone has to convince the consumer that spending $5,000 on a week-long trip will create more satisfaction than a big-screen TV."

The travel industry has seen good times and bad. "Ten years ago, we took a real hit," Susan volunteers. "In 1986 three tragedies,

What Will I Earn?

The U.S. Department of Labor reports the median annual earnings for travel agents was $27,880 in 1999.

all in Europe, practically did us in. Chernobyl, a TWA hijacking in Greece, and the Achille-Lauro cruise ship seizure in the Mediterranean were a disaster for the travel business. It was a year of refunds."

But that was then. Today business is up, though the work is more demanding than ever.

"The most difficult aspect is figuring out what will be perfect for your client," Susan says. "But when you do, they come back. And repeat customers are key to our success."

Sande Davidson, owner of Davidson Travel in Phoenix, Arizona, and a 26-year veteran, knows what it takes to please. "I like putting the puzzle together," she declares. "I concentrate on FIT—foreign independent travel. It's for those who want to avoid the standard tour thing. More work, but it's worth it."

"Travel Agents Do It Free"

"Worth it" in the travel business used to mean free or discounted travel, even if salaries were low. "Accessorizing the travel agent lifestyle," Sande calls it. "Being part of a fun and glamorous industry, along with so-called familiarization trips was supposed to make up for entry-level pay below the poverty line."

"Traditionally it's been a second job," Susan says. "And over-whelmingly female. The wife would make a little money, get the trips, while the husband earned the real income." Tim agrees. "For many, it was like a hobby. But hobbyists don't run supermarkets, banks, or sell real estate. Something had to change."

Indeed. Until recently, the commission structure from suppliers (airlines, cruise lines, tour companies, etc.) along with familiariza-tion travel allowed a bumper sticker of the time to declare: "Travel Agents Do It Free." At least that's how it looked from the client's perspective. From the supplier's, too, in a way. "Many suppliers viewed the travel agent as a free distribution system where they didn't have to pay salaries," Tim explains. "Hence, any business was great. Suppliers didn't need to check on performance."

INFORMATION

For More Information

American Society of
Travel Agents
1101 King Street
Alexandria, VA 22314
(703) 739-2782

The Institute of Certified
Travel Agents
148 Linden Street
P.O. Box 812059
Wellesley, MA 02181-0012
(800) 542-4282

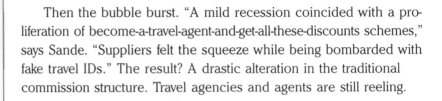

Then the bubble burst. "A mild recession coincided with a pro-liferation of become-a-travel-agent-and-get-all-these-discounts schemes," says Sande. "Suppliers felt the squeeze while being bombarded with fake travel IDs." The result? A drastic alteration in the traditional commission structure. Travel agencies and agents are still reeling.

Fees for Service

"In 1997, the airlines capped our commissions," Susan says. "Then a year later they cut them again—twice. Many mom-and-pop agencies have folded. Anyone in the business simply to play got out."

"The industry is tougher and more competitive," says Tim. "Suppliers still pay commissions but more on a pay-for-performance basis. An agent must meet specific sales goals."

"Leisure agents have been forced to a fee-based system," says Tim. "But there's an upside. Now agents are less dependent on suppliers. We can make independent recommendations."

"Travel agents, more than ever, work for their customers," James Locks, manager of communications for the American Society of Travel Agents (ASTA), says. "The minute you start charging for services, you must show you're worth it. Value-added service, that's is what it's about."

Nonetheless, things could turn ugly, at least for some. Writing in *Travel Agent* magazine, Sally O'Dowd asks, "What if commissions are reduced further—or worse, eliminated?" She quotes ASTA president Mike Spinelli as saying, "Up to ten thousand small agencies could close. Yet, it's charge fees or go out of business."

E-Travel Has Arrived

Though commission reductions and the growth of fees (about two-thirds of ASTA agencies responding to a survey said they charge fees) have altered travel agency operation in discernable ways, the impact of "electronic travel,"—bookings on the Internet, for example—is less clear. "It has its pluses," concedes Susan. "I can e-mail around the world and have a response faster than by fax."

Sally adds, "Online travel bookings are expected to increase dramatically, and the effect on the retail community is still unknown." Online sales of air, hotel, car rental, cruise and vacation travel, as well as site-generated advertising is expected to explode from a mere $276 million in 1996 to an incredible $8.9 billion in 2003, according to a report prepared by Jupiter Communications for the Travel Industry Association of America (TIAA).

In 1999, TIAA found that more than 52 million travelers, 50 percent more than in the previous year, used the Internet to plan a trip. Of those, nearly 17 million took the additional step of booking their own arrangements, an increase of 146 percent over 1998.

Are people now becoming their own travel agent, via the Web? "Some are," Susan says. "But they're the same travelers who use the airline 800 number. For the majority, travel is too complex. They need a travel agent to guide them. It's the old story—'We're drowning in information while starving for knowledge.'"

"No one's quite sure what it all means," advises Tim. "The biggest impact seems to be in corporate travel. Two years ago agents were terrified suppliers were going to do an 'agent bypass,' and go around them. That fear has subsided, however."

"Many agents thought the sky would fall when e-travel took off," says James. "It hasn't. Think about your banking. For many transactions you use the automatic teller. But the minute there's a problem, something substantial to do, you go inside."

Professional Credentials

As the travel business transforms itself, the part-time, in-it-for-the-travel travel agent is disappearing. In her place a cadre of hardworking, technically savvy, well-trained professional specialists is emerging. While on-the-job experience is essential to their success, professional education and certification play a critical role. "Suppliers are looking for a way to identify the guy who printed up business cards and goes to his Rotary meeting claiming to be a travel agent," says

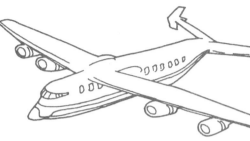

Cool Web Sites to Visit

ASTANET
www.astanet.com/ind

Travel Agent Job Profile
www.jobprofiles.com/
alltravelagent.htm

Travel Career Opportunities
www.bcdirect.net/~sstravel/
page1.html

Annette. "They need to separate him from the one who sits at a desk forty hours a week servicing customers. Certification separates the two."

Since travel agents are not licensed, certification is important in establishing professional competency. The Institute of Certified Travel Agents offers three levels of professional development. You begin by taking the 120-question Travel Agent Proficiency (TAP) test that measures basic entry-level knowledge of travel agent professionals. With 18 months' experience, completion of the 12 courses offered by ICTA, and the passing of another examination, you're eligible for a certified travel associate (CTA) certification. With five years' experience, plus additional course work and exam requirements, the most coveted designation in the field, certified travel counselor (CTC) can be yours. As Annette explains, "A CTC after your name is the hallmark of industry professionalism."

What sort of course work are we taking about?, Everything from developing communication and technology skills to business planning, cultural diversity, and employee training and development. The ICTA offers it all.

So, how to get started? "Numerous private and public institutions offer short- and long-term training in preparation for entry-level work," Susan says. "Half those taking such classes will give up. That's OK, they probably weren't in it for the long haul. But if you care about people, want them to get the best travel they can, are a good listener, and detail oriented, you have a future in an exciting field. After all, what other profession deals with people who come in happy, go out happier, and return the happiest of all?"

VOICE ACTOR

Up to two years of study, training, and application may be required for success. You wouldn't expect to produce a record after a half-dozen singing lessons, would you?

You've heard her voice:

"If you think miracle cures are only dollars away, think again. Wasted hopes, wasted lives, today at five, only on Channel 4."

"There is a way to make a women fall in love with you. All it takes are the words, and the passion, of a poet."

"Walt Disney presents Pinocchio *to keep, to share with your children."*

Of course, just reading the promo excerpts that you'd hear on Kit Paraventi's demo tape doesn't allow us to capture her slightly husky quality, her flair for the dramatic—or her compassion. "My feelings come through in my voice," this versatile, experienced voice actor of 16 years says, "be it in promos, commercials, or animation."

Or, in celebrity voices you think you hear—but don't. "I've been the voice of Katharine Hepburn, Roseanne [Barr], Madonna, Liza Minelli, and Joan Collins," Kit says. "Then there's the voice of Trash, Garbage, and assorted leftover foods in the National Network Glad Bag spots with Tom Bosley, the voice of Norman Bates's *Psycho* mother in the Bud Light Halloween TV spots, and the voice of Juiceberries for Cap'n Crunch. Whoever's hot and not available at the time, I'll be there."

Speaking Up

Voice actors, or voice-over artists, do the offscreen voices you hear in commercials, trailers, narratives, and animations (which is a voice-over field of its own). But broadcasted voices are just part of the picture. "Voice actors are heard on CD-ROMs, voices for toys, audio manuals and training guides, books on tape, audio Web sites, and infomercials," says Yvonne Viner, casting director for Kalmenson & Kalmenson, a voice casting agency in Burbank, California. "Also, don't forget translations and voice-on-hold telephone messages. Anywhere a voice is needed, a voice actor is ready to talk."

And everyone, it seems, is eager to speak up. Kalmenson & Kalmenson has over 8,200 voice-over talents in its database. "Some are big name actors, too," Kit says. "Tom Hanks was Woody in *Toy Story*, Robin Williams, the genie in *Aladdin*. For film stars, voice roles are relatively undemanding."

Though competition is keen—this is the entertainment industry, after all—opportunity abounds. "So much more programming is going on," Kit says. "Every cable station needs promos. As they struggle to forge an identity, a signature voice can achieve that goal."

Getting Personal

Into the second hour of a three-hour introductory voice-over seminar Kit is conducting at the Learning Tree University in Los Angeles, 11 participants are reading "Strip Scripts," short, one- to three-sentence snippets of commercial dialogue.

"You want to know the hardest thing about maintaining an exercise program? Getting started," recites Candace Adams, a self-admitted class clown in her school days.

"It isn't easy being man's best friend. It isn't even easy being woman's best friend. Your dog deserves Nature's Recipe," reads Bob Francis, a cruise ship entertainer.

"Look, it's a computer, not a car bomb. You don't have to be afraid to touch it," is Jim's line. He states it flatly.

"Try, Jim, to create a scenario in which it will be natural to conduct a conversation," Kit advises. "It's a conversation that needs to take place between you and someone else. The more vivid and specific you can make your scenario, the more truthful and natural your delivery of the message will be."

Jim gets the point. A good "performance" is not the idea. Conversation, talking on a personal level, one-on-one, that's what it's about. As Julie Williams, of Spectacular Voice-Over in San Antonio, Texas, says, "Think! Is this how I would have sounded if I were talking to my best friend? Make everything sound like you're talking to someone. It's not announcing; it's a dialogue with another person."

Burton Richardson knows the difference, he's been doing both announcing and voice-over for 20 years. The booth announcer voice for *The Arsenio Hall Show*—"*Now can you stand it, it's Arseniooooooooo Hall*"—he defines the difference this way: "On the air, you're being yourself, in voice-over, you are a voice actor. The worst thing you can say to an on-air personality is, 'I heard your show the other day and it didn't sound like you.' Yet, that's the best thing you can say to a voice actor."

"Some folks get their training though radio," says Julie. "I have to untrain them. Announcing isn't what it is all about. But such people have a good base, they have trained themselves to control their voice. It does help."

Speakers of the Truth

Controlling your voice is needed if you're playing a character. But while a voice-over artist is an actor, he or she must be true to who they are. Kit explains, "Of the four factors needed to succeed in this career—skill, signature, a promotional package, and a knowledge of advertising trends—signature is critical. It is your elemental identity, displayed in every creative thing you do. It is how you can be recognized."

Here from Kit is a typical signature description for a voice-over actor:

"Clever, blue-collar, know-it-all, savvy wit, homespun philosopher, East Coast, wise guy, earthy, quirky, likeable, thirties-forties, loveable

What Will I Earn?

It depends on experience, how often you work, and if you're in a union. Don La Fontaine, acknowledged as the "King of Promos and Trailers," is reported to have earned $6 million in 1998. The average annual salary, however, is closer to $27,000.

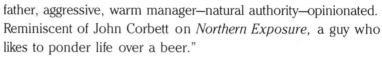

INFORMATION

For More Information

National Association
of Broadcasters
1771 N Street N.W.
Washington, DC 20036

father, aggressive, warm manager—natural authority—opinionated. Reminiscent of John Corbett on *Northern Exposure,* a guy who likes to ponder life over a beer."

"To understand signature," Kit advises, "look at stand-up comics. They don't become successful telling great jokes. They succeed with strong identifying signatures. They are speakers of the truth—their truth."

Session Pay

To determine just what voice actors can earn, pick up a copy of the *Voice-Over Resource Guide*, the industry standard, published by Dave & Dave Incorporated. The following is taken from the guide and lists some sample category sessions and fees for June 1998.

- RADIO Session Fee: $200.00
  This Session Fee is paid for each spot you record. A like amount is paid each 13-week *renewal* Cycle while in use.
- TELEVISION Session Fee: $359.95
  This Session Fee is paid for each spot recorded. A like amount is paid each 13-week *renewal* Cycle for use or HOLD (Holding Fee).
- CABLE TV Session Fee: $359.95
  13-week "Commercial" Rate
  Minimum RATE for UNLIMITED airings in a 13-week Cycle. A like amount is paid each 13-week *renewal* Cycle while in USE or on HOLD (Holding Fee). A higher RATE could be paid based on a combined total Cable Subscription where aired.
- DUBBING ADR WALLA LOOPING Session Fee: $559.00
  This Session Fee is paid for recognizable voicing of five lines or more in Theatrical Film, MOW, TV Series, or Pilot. Residuals are paid based on each airing either Network, syndication, Cable or Foreign and Video or Multimedia release. These residuals are activated using the same formula as *in-front-of-camera* performers. The voice performer is placed on the production's CAST LIST.
- ANIMATION Session Fee: $559.00

This Session Fee is paid for a single program or segments of programs over ten minutes in length. Up to *three Voices* may be performed per program. If more than Three Voices you shall be paid an additional Session Fee. Also, an additional ten percent is paid for the *Third Voice* in each group of *Three Voices* performed. Residuals are based on Producer-optioned payment schedules.

- MULTIMEDIA/INTERACTIVE I.E., CD-ROM, CDI, 3DO
  Session Fee: $522.00
  This Off-Camera Session Fee is paid for any single Interactive Platform performance of up to Three Voices during a Four Hour Day. For the Fourth and Fifth Voice, add an additional FEE of $168 each. For the Sixth, Seventh, and Eighth Voice, the FEE would be $1,008 and an Eight Hour Day. There is also a One/Hour/One Voice Session Fee of $261. Voices used on any ON-LINE or NETWORK Platform or used as a "LIFT" to another program, add an additional 100% of the original Session Fee in each case.

Nice work, if you can get it.

Wanted: Voice of a Pot

In the offices of Kalmenson & Kalmenson, Cathy Kalmenson, a savvy, high-energy casting director, is busy at work. "We supply the sponsor with voice choices," she says. "I discover talent from voice-over agents, theater, comedy clubs, showcases, and from our classes."

With a flick of her computer mouse, Cathy calls up signature notes on voices. "I'm looking for the voice of a pot, and the voice of a pan," she says—seriously. "It's for an SOS commercial. From my database, I'll select fifteen actors to audition. The directed, recorded voices will be sent to the ad agency producing the SOS commercial. They'll then choose the two they want for the pot and pan."

How were the actors' signatures derived in the first place? "From a demo tape each has produced," Cathy says. "Usually a

What to Read

The Art of Voice-Acting: The Craft and Business of Performing for Voice-Over by James R. Alburger. Buttersworth-Heinemann, 1998.

Voice-Overs: Putting Your Mouth Where the Money Is by Chris Douthitt. Grey Heron Books, 1997.

minute and a half long, the tape should be professionally made, costing the actor anywhere from $500 to $1,000, or more. Yet, the demo tape is your calling card—it must be done right."

But what if you have no broadcast commercials to include on the tape? "It's not a resume," Julie says. "Nor is it a sample of what you've done. It's a sample of what you *can* do."

Kit is sometimes asked, "Will I emerge from your three-hour introductory seminar ready to produce a demo tape?" "No, not at all," she replies.

"Up to two years of study, training, and application are necessary," Cathy says, "before you might succeed. You wouldn't expect to produce a record after a half-dozen singing lessons, would you? The same is true with voice-over."

"My guess is that 99 percent of the population has a good enough voice to do commercials," Julie says. "If you're counting on that 'edge' to get you there easily, don't quit your day job! With that knowledge in mind, you'll need training, a good, professionally produced demo, and, in L.A., an agent. Is it something you really want to do? Or are you just responding to encouragement by people who know nothing about the business? If it's the former, great! If not, thank your acquaintances for the compliment and go on with your life."

But if you are prepared to make the investment, do so. Contrary to a popular belief, this is not a closed field. You can break in. "Comfortableness with self, awareness of your personal signature, ability to translate your truth to commercial copy, choosing an attitude, sense of humor, personal permission to ad-lib and improvise, flexibility, luck, timing, and commitment, these are the elements of a winning formula," Cathy concludes. "They will allow you to impose your personality on the world."

Cool Web Sites to Visit

Radio and Production:
The Magazine for Radio's
Production Personnel
www.rapmag.com

Springfield Zone
www.student.qulufi/~keskiaho

Star Wars Cast
*www.phantomenace.com/
cast/oz*

WEB MAGAZINE EDITOR

An online magazine provides the random search of a newspaper with the immediacy of on-air broadcasting. When you pick up a newspaper, you can go immediately to the sports page, the funnies, the business section. The Internet, with its many branching paths, works the same way. You have the freedom to choose.

H aving a great name, *Herald Tribune Online*, is a definite asset in a world of over five million Web sites and more than a billion Web pages. Still, making the transition from a traditional ink-splattered community newspaper, serving the "Inland Empire" east of Los Angeles, to an all-online cyber "rag," hasn't been easy for this San Gabriel Valley publication.

"I remember the month we reached forty thousand hits," says Victoria Erickson, the *Tribune's* managing editor. "The office went ballistic. Then we crossed the magic one hundred thousand mark. We couldn't believe it. Yet, it didn't stop there. In June 2000, the paper was receiving an astonishing six hundred fifty-six thousand online visits a month. Every time those advertising banners rotate, it's considered a hit. Exactly what those hits mean, however, is anyone's guess."

Indeed it is! Publishing an online magazine or newspaper is still an iffy proposition. For every "e-zine" that launches, more than a few fade from cyberspace. And though there are clear economic advantages to publishing online—no printing and distribution costs, to mention the most obvious—attracting advertisers to these often ephemeral enterprises is tough. While advertising on the Web is expected to climb from $4.7 billion in 2000 to an astonishing $33 billion by 2004, Victoria is a bit skeptical: "I wish someone would throw a couple hundred thousand ad dollars my way. Even though our prices are lower than in the print media, and the ads go up immediately, grabbing those advertising dollars, the key to any magazine's success, online or off, is a constant stretch."

Part of the Routine

No one knows how many Web magazines exist, not only because the number changes daily, but because the definition of just what they are is open to debate. From the "in-your-face" zines (pronounced *zeens*, as in magazines), often self-published Internet "flyers," to the almost staid exemplars such as *Salon* and *Slate*, you can find Web magazines catering to every subject and passion. According to Anthony Tedesco, author of *Online Markets for Writers: How to Make Money by Selling Your Writing on the Internet*, as of mid-2000 there were probably fifteen hundred online magazines worthy of the name. "While not all, by any means, are making money," he says, "quite a few are dishing it out—to writers in the form of $1, even $2, a word. Web publishing is definitely for real: for publishers, editors, and writers."

What about for readers? Is the online reading experience being taken seriously? Anthony gives some stats:

- The average Internet user is 32 years old.
- Sixty-four percent have at least a college degree.
- Forty-two percent are female.
- Users have a median household income of $59,000.

OK. But just where, and how, are these savvy connected folks partaking of their read? They can't be sitting back, downing a cappuccino while flipping pages. "We are seeing a new ritual," says Greg Tally, associate editor at *Boardwatch* magazine, and managing editor for *ISP World*, trade journals covering Internet service providers. "At the beginning of their day, folks are logging on to check stock quotes and look at information they deem important. It's included as part of the routine, not at the kitchen table, but at the office desk."

Does this mean the print magazine is dead, destined to no longer leave a paper trail? Hardly. In a given month, nearly 180 million magazines are received by subscribers or purchased at newsstands. Yet, just 4.6 million adults read online magazines in the same period. Though the online group is growing by 24 percent a year, and though print magazine readership is actually declining slightly, 3 percent from 1998 to 1999, the Web magazine is unlikely to eclipse its progenitor any time soon.

What Will I Earn?

Zero to $100,000 or more per year, depending on success and profitability of the magazine.

The Daily Post

Web magazines are a different read than their print counterparts, however, and online editors must provide a reading and viewing experience that works for the Internet surfer.

"Keep in mind, content is on the *screen*, not on the page," says Geoff Keston, of Faulkner Information Services. "As a result, formatting is different, the fonts are varied, and paragraphs must be shorter. A modular approach is required."

Anthony agrees: "Writing online is not the same. It should be done in small chunks. You must break up text. No reader wants to scroll through page after page of material."

Yet, Chris Colin, associate editor at *Salon* magazine, isn't so sure length is a factor. "We have run long stories that have been every bit as compelling and readable as the short ones," he says. "There's no hard and fast rule on length. The ability to tell a good story is still key."

Getting out an online magazine is unlike anything in the print world. "The Internet is daily," says Rick Anthony, editor and publisher of *L.A.F.M., Los Angeles Film and Music.* "And coming out daily, putting up new content all the time, requires maintenance. It's no different than having a swimming pool. You must keep the Web site functioning all the time."

"Your schedule is driven more by industry events than by predetermined operational procedures, as in the print world," comments Geoff. "Sometimes you simply don't know what you'll be writing about when you arrive in the morning. You just can't plan in the same way."

"An online magazine provides the random search of a newspaper with the immediacy of on-air-broadcasting," adds Greg. "When you pick up a newspaper, you can go immediately to the sports page, the funnies, the business section. The Internet, with its many branching paths, works the same way. You have the freedom to choose."

All this immediacy, with its need to get content up quickly, does have its perils. "Sometimes we're too quick to post," cautions Victoria. "Do we check our sources as well as we should? As online editors we must work even harder to make sure it's right."

INFORMATION

For More Information

American Society of
Magazine Editors
919 Third Avenue
New York, NY 10022
(212) 752-0055

Electronic Publishing Special
Interest Group
P.O. Box 25707
Alexandria, VA 22313-5707

Magazine Publishers of America
919 Third Avenue
New York, NY 10022
(212) 407-5700

Ads Tell The Story

It is no secret that magazines make money by selling advertising space. Some, such as job search magazines, rely entirely on such income, having no subscription rate or, with a few exceptions, a newsstand price. Journals, on the other hand, rarely take advertising, relying almost exclusively on subscriptions for an income stream. As a result, most, even the better-known ones, are highly subsidized by private donors, corporate sponsors, or government agencies.

The same is true for Web magazines. Those in the business of earning a profit must, like their print counterparts, attract and hold advertisers. While online ad revenue is currently growing at a much higher rate than other forms of advertising, the effectiveness of such advertising is questionable. "Only about one percent who see those infamous banner ads actually click on them," says Anthony. "Most view such ads as an intrusion. Even when they do click on the ad, less than two percent continue on if they realize it is a promotional site, not a content site. No doubt about it, online advertising has a problem. And a problem with online advertising is a problem for online publishing."

"If you already have a print magazine, you can often correlate advertising there for the Net," says Rick. "If not, you are going to have a hard time. Advertisers will argue with you about the number of hits and the difference between hits and visits. Still, we're lucky. We have advertisers who believe in us, what we are doing. Hopefully, they will stick with us."

No Hobbyist Adventure

Crisp magazine was lucky, too, at least initially. Created by Anthony Tedesco and a few friends back in 1995 when Mosaic, the first graphics-based Web browser appeared, it sought to provide assistance for young artists, activists, and entrepreneurs. "We included some fiction, women's pieces, and a technology section," says Anthony. "There were six of us, slaving away for equity only."

As of this writing, *Crisp* is on hold, though it's projected to launch again soon under a revised business plan. "We had advertisers, the likes of BMW and CityBank," says Anthony. "We were recognized as

one of the top seven online magazines. And we reached three hundred thousand unique visitors a month. Still, we simply weren't making enough money. It was just physically impossible to continue without the necessary funding. We will relaunch under a different, we hope more successful business model soon."

John Lee has been publishing his "baby," *Inline First*, as an online labor of love for some time now. A programmer by profession, he has placed over three thousand movie descriptions into the magazine's database. "In another six months, I'll have it completed," he says. "Right now it's just for fun. My overhead is practically zero. As long as I keep it as a hobby, I can stay ahead of other dot.com companies struggling to make a buck. Yet, if it ever gets the attention it should, there's the potential to make money on the back end with e-commerce. I could do my own advertising or seek it out on a profit-sharing basis."

No hobbyist adventure, *Salon*, established in 1995, is considered one of the more successful online magazines to date. Based in San Francisco, every day *Salon* publishes stories about books, arts, entertainment, politics, and society. Featuring original reviews, interviews, and commentary on topics ranging from parenting and sex to technology and travel, the widely admired *Salon* receives approximately three hundred thousand visits a month.

Chris, at 25, is probably one of *Salon*'s youngest editors. Unlike most of his compatriots in the online editing profession, Chris does not come from a print background. "Actually, I'm too young to have come from much of anywhere," he confesses. "I started by sending the magazine a fiction piece..They ran that story and, soon after, others. Then, all of a sudden they made me an offer to come on as associate editor. I write an article or two every month, edit daily features, read blind submissions, and assign stories, just like associate editors everywhere."

So Hip

Though Web magazine editors come from varied backgrounds, most began their professional careers in print, Chris aside. "It is quite helpful to have had traditional journalism experience," says Rick. "You know how to dot your *I*s, cross your *T*s. In other words, you've done it."

What to Read

Online Markets for Writers: How to Make Money by Selling Your Writing on the Internet by Anthony Tedesco. Owl Books/Henry Holt, 2000.

Writer's Market by Kirsten C. Holm. Writer's Digest Books, published annually.

"Many of the same skills apply for both print and the Web," adds Greg. "Good reporting is good reporting. But you can't yell, "Stop the presses," when online. It's just like in broadcasting, the urgency of getting it right the first time is great."

But don't you have to be technologically savvy to work online as an editor? What about all this HTML stuff? "In the beginning, with Internet publishing, we saw nothing but tech types," says Anthony, who interviewed over 25 online editors for his new book on the subject. "The content was weak, typos were everywhere. It was techies trying to be creative. In the next wave, creatives came online, but they lacked technical understanding. Now, we are seeing the morphing of both worlds, tech-savvy creative editors who know at least a little HTML. It's a dynamite combination."

For such editors, the Web is a truly exciting place to be. "I think it gives you more variety—the Web as opposed to print," says Geoff. "Don't forget, with an online magazine you see your work published much quicker. It's that, and the ability to respond to events in a more immediate fashion, that is a high for me."

But what is the downside? "It depends on your point of view," Geoff responds. "Your day is definitely more unpredictable. You must be flexible, ready to drop what you're doing for something more immediate. Some would consider that a plus, however. I do."

"The potential is tremendous," says Anthony. "As an online editor, the barriers for entry into publishing have been lifted dramatically. Get some experience, learn what content works best on the net, and build up a Rolodex of writers. From there it's only a matter of time before you're publishing your own rag."

Despite the various struggles, there have been more pluses than minuses for Victoria. "It's been quite a ride," she exudes. "I have enjoyed it. There are so many advantages over print—the immediacy, the ability to hot-link. I'll stay with it for now. Besides, even though it is at times quite routine—after all, we do all our own production—everyone I meet thinks I'm so hip being an online editor!"

Cool Web Sites to Visit

Boardwatch
www.internet.com

Salon
www.salon.com

TidBITS
www.db.tidbits.com

WEBMASTER

Anyone can do it—poorly. But designing a Web site that people find clear, simple, and easy to understand and download is another matter. Patience and a design sense are required.

Go to *www.dodgers.com*, and though you may not be a baseball fan, you'll undoubtedly appreciate this well-designed and functional Web site.

From the home page, under Dodger News, you discover plans for stadium renovation. In the Press Box, you scroll through colorful logos that invite you to click on ticket information, Dodger merchandise, player information, and the season schedule. There are audio tips from coaches, games, contests to enter, and fan forums. Even text-based game updates, live, are available.

It's easy to see why, from its debut on April 24, 1996, this L.A. Dodgers site has conquered the charts, catching 41,000 to 50,000 discrete user sessions per day. *USA Today Baseball Weekly* gives the site a 9 for content, 9 for presentation, and 9.5 for bells and whistles—27.5 out of 30—way ahead of 29 other Major League sites scored.

For Steve Buchsbaum, president and CEO of Creative Edge Enterprises, Inc., in Calabasas, California, a stat like that qualifies as a grand slam.

"We've begun our fourth season with the Dodgers, designing, updating, and maintaining their Web site," he says. "It's been an experience. Back in the beginning, during the first season, we were thrown a few curves."

Steve remembers a unique design challenge, when he and Mark Stone, vice president and CFO, began reporting games live on the Web site. "We took a picture every couple of innings and added description," Mark explains. "But then we were bombarded with e-mail—cyber Dodger fans wanted more. So we cranked it up to a picture and description every inning. Still not enough, so we went with every batter, every play. Folks loved it. A popular feature for a year and a half, it showed us the Web's power to communicate via a new medium."

Who's Afraid of the World Wide Web?

Exactly how powerful the Web is is anyone's guess. In the first 100 days of 1999, Internet usage doubled. The creation of the World Wide Web, the graphics-based organizing system for the Internet, is what made this possible.

"As the millennium dawned, there were more than five million Web sites in the world," says Brian Benson, president of Stellar City, a Web design company. "The total number of pages—one billion. There's plenty to visit out there."

People involved with this explosive endeavor, as designers, programmers, and managers, have various titles: site designer, developer, and Webmaster, the latter rightly conjuring up a sorcerer's image.

"Opportunities are there for designers," David Taylor, author of *Creating Cool HTML for Web Pages*, says. "Those putting together sites for a company's intranet and internet communications are doing well. A clear trend is in high-speed, high-quality communications between businesses, and businesses to customer. It's simply erupting."

Charlie Hess, art director of *Buzz* magazine for its first six years, agrees. "People from the traditional media are going into Web design. For example, editors are becoming producers, overseeing site development. Los Angeles, along with New York and Silicon Valley, has a huge interactive design community. There's plenty of work out there."

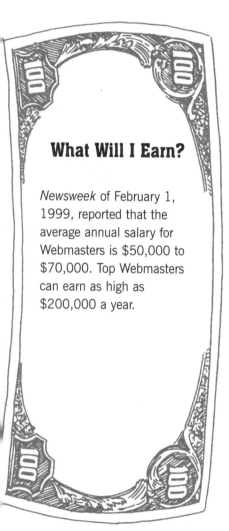

What Will I Earn?

Newsweek of February 1, 1999, reported that the average annual salary for Webmasters is $50,000 to $70,000. Top Webmasters can earn as high as $200,000 a year.

A Team Effort

Plenty of work wasn't always the case, as Steve and Mark can attest.

"Initially," Steve says, "we formed Creative Edge Enterprises, Inc., to design and promote our own sites. Our first venture, Casino Net, was a directory of Las Vegas casinos and sports books. We were going to sell advertising to make money off the sites. We didn't think about designing for others."

That changed in May 1996, when Creative Edge linked up with the L.A. Dodgers. "While it's been up and down—there's a certain feast-or-famine aspect to this business—we're doing quite well now," says Steve. "We have created over two hundred sites. Some are quite small, requiring a day or two to design, others demand weeks, even months, to bring online."

Creative Edge, like most Web design firms, takes a team approach to site development and maintenance.

Steve, with his degree in motion picture, film, radio and television from UCLA, and with over 20 years in the film and television post-production industry (*Star Trek: The Next Generation, Quantum Leap*, and *The Quest*), oversees the design effort.

Mark, a lawyer, provides legal counsel and directs corporate finance. He runs the business end.

Steven Besser is vice president of operations and marketing. His job is to bring in the business.

Thom Porter, with his strong background in programming languages such as C++ and Perl, is director of programming.

So, how does site design actually proceed? "Two types of clients come to us," Steve answers. "Some are starting an online company and have nothing, not even a logo or a name. Others will hand us their business card, brochure, and logo. We take it from there. Either way, most clients have little idea as to what they want. Sure, they've visited the Web. But now we must create the look and functionality the client needs."

"Once we have an idea," Mark continues, "we channel it through our staff. Then, after the client signs off, our programmers get started; basic layout and content generation begins. Cut and paste, computer-style, eventually leads to a final product. To date, we haven't had a dissatisfied customer."

Beyond HTML

Jerzy Gorecki, an electronics engineer, is staring at his computer screen. "I'll show you how to design a Web page," he says, as he opens Microsoft Word. "Once we create our document, I can save it in HTML [Hypertext Markup Language], a set of special codes placed in text to add formatting and linking information.

"All HTML information contains HTML *tags*. These *tags* tell an HTML browser that the document is written and marked up in standard

INFORMATION

For More Information

Careers College Association
750 First Street N.E.
Suite 900
Washington, DC 20036

What to Read

Webmaster in a Nutshell
by Stephen Spainhour
and Robert Eckstein.
O'Reilly and Associates, 1999.

HTML. Popular browsers are Microsoft's Internet Explorer and Netscape Navigator."

In the next half hour, Jerzy goes through Web page design basics: creating an introduction, establishing hyperlinks, making e-mail connections, and doing color formatting. Then, with a mouse click, the page is ready.

Evidently, creating Web pages is easy, especially with more advanced, off-the-shelf programs, such as Microsoft FrontPage, FileMaker HomePage, and Adobe Page Mill, which allow you to design without writing a single line of code—without knowing what HTML even stands for.

But like all design efforts, the tools are one thing, knowing how to use them to create a great product is another.

Lawrence J. Magid, writing in the *Los Angeles Times*, makes the point: "Saying it's easy to build a page is like saying it's easy to take a photograph. Just about anyone can take a picture, but some people are a lot better at it than others."

"The key," Brian says, "is understanding layout, usability, and user friendliness. And, above all, keeping it simple."

"My approach to design is as an art director," Charles says. "It's about communicating the site's message as simply as possible. A well-designed site is clear, simple, easy to understand, and downloads quickly."

"There are crucial elements to every site," Mark explains. "Basic information about the client, the ability to e-mail back and forth between visitor and client, and a merchandising capability, to name just three."

What skills are needed to design such sites? "Two are critical," Dave says, "patience and some sort of design sense. Can you look at the world and see what's working? Why do we have different colors for stop and go on a traffic light? Because it's a faster way to communicate than with words."

"This is where the professional comes in," Mark adds. "Letting your fourteen-year-old nephew have a go at it is fine. But when he doesn't finish, or it won't work, maybe it's time to call in a pro."

Web Sites Forever

So, where are Webmasters coming from, are they primarily designers with a graphics background, or are they computer programmer types?

"More and more," David reports, "programmers are competing with quality off-the-shelf solutions. If you have an ability for programming, great! But many more Web designers than savvy programmers exist. With large design teams, the ratio is ten to one, ten times as many content providers, graphic designers, and managers than programmers."

OK, then how do you get started? "If you're working in a company, get to know the individuals doing site design," suggests Brian. "Volunteer to work with them, let them know you are interested."

David agrees. "Go to your local church, temple, scout troop, or homeless charity and ask to design their site. Then, when you're ready for a paying job, you'll have gone beyond the classes you have taken. You'll have sites to display."

When you do go after a job as a master, expect to sell not only yourself, but what you do.

"While the situation is changing rapidly for the better, many old-line companies," Dave continues, "still don't know what it means to have a site. Management hasn't bought into it yet and executive-level people view the whole thing as a nuisance. Everything you try to do will encounter opposition. That's not a real fun work environment."

Once you're working, whether alone or on a design team, basic business decisions must be made.

John Petrovich, an attorney specializing in Web-related issues, puts it this way: "The contract is crucial. How you'll be paid, the rights of a client to terminate the agreement, and how design credit is given on the site are important issues. Credits, for example, can mean the difference between getting referrals, and staying in business, or going under."

Yet, a Webmaster's future is bright. "More than anything, you want people to come to your site not once, but over and over again," Steve says. "If they visit once and get everything they need, they won't be back. Thus, a changing site is essential. You can make more money updating and maintaining a site than you did with the initial design. Let me tell you, in this business, it's only going to get better."

Cool Web Sites to Visit

Webmaster Resources
www.webmaster-resources.com/

Webmaster's Notebook
www.cio.com/WebMaster/wm_notebook.html

ZOOKEEPER

Do you think working with animals is fun? It is.
But it's only one side of the story. It's difficult,
demanding, and dirty work. And it can also be
dangerous. Of the eighty or so elephant keepers in
the United States, one is killed every year.

When the Burbank, California, apartment manager put out a "No Pets" sign, she trusted it would keep her building dog- and cat-free. Thank goodness she never found out about the tenant in apartment 101, who was sneaking baby mountain lions up the elevator under her jacket.

"I had to," says Jami Shoemaker, a 34-year-old zookeeper at the Los Angeles Zoo. "I was training them for a show we were doing. To gain their confidence, to build a relationship, I had to spend practically twenty-four hours a day with the cubs. After all, I couldn't have them developing bad habits."

Bad habits are something Jami knows all about.

A bit obstinate as a child, she began demanding a pony at the age of four. By nine, she had actually won one in a church contest. "That's when it started for me, my fascination with animals," she says. "Oh, my poor mother. In the next few years I brought home everything from possums to wolves."

Not a particularly good student at the time, Jami dropped out of high school in the 11th grade to join the closest thing to a circus: an animal act in Las Vegas. "That was a disaster," she recalls. "I high-tailed home to finish high school."

Three years later she had done considerably more than that. With an associate of science degree from Moorpark Community College's acclaimed Exotic Animal Training and Management (EATM) program, in Simi Valley, California, Jami was ready to begin a serious relationship with animals. That relationship has led to the hard-won position she now holds: zookeeper.

Zookeepers—Keepers of the Faith

Zookeepers, of which, say the American Association of Zookeepers (AAZK), there are approximately five thousand, used to do little more than feed animals and clean up the inevitable result.

Not so anymore. Since zoos have changed from their role as a source of entertainment to the role of animal caretakers, zookeepers have become respected zoo professionals—many hold bachelor's degrees in subjects such as zoology and environmental studies.

Today, according to *Chronicle Guidance Publication #288*, "Zookeepers observe and get to understand animal temperaments, personalities, and ways of interacting with other members of the group. They become aware of the animals' daily cycles of activity and rest, what they like and do not like. Keepers report any illnesses to the veterinarian. And they often assist in the regular physicals given to the animals."

Furthermore, as Lyndia Frazier, also a zookeeper, stated in *Zoo View*, the magazine of the Los Angeles Zoo Association, "As keepers, we take care of our animals as parents should care for their children—with love, concern, protectiveness, worry, support, and hope for their happiness, health, and comfort."

Animal Trainers—Behaviorists at Work

Zookeepers are animal caretakers. While zookeepers will often perform some form of animal training (which Jami does on a regular basis), for the most part they are an entirely different breed. Animal trainers, among which dog trainers are the largest group, work to alter the behavior of animals, it is hoped in a positive, supportive setting.

Robin Kovary, executive director of the American Dog Trainers Network (ADTN), has been doing just that for more than 17 years. Voted "best dog trainer" for two years in a row by *Manhattan File* magazine, she is the cofounder of the Society of North American Dog Trainers and a charter member of ADTN. Robin has authored numerous books on dog training, including, *From Good Puppy, to Great Dog!* "It's a growing profession," she says. "Our organization

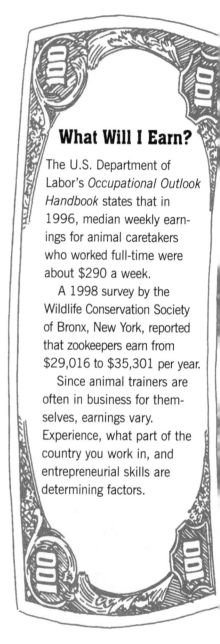

What Will I Earn?

The U.S. Department of Labor's *Occupational Outlook Handbook* states that in 1996, median weekly earnings for animal caretakers who worked full-time were about $290 a week.

A 1998 survey by the Wildlife Conservation Society of Bronx, New York, reported that zookeepers earn from $29,016 to $35,301 per year.

Since animal trainers are often in business for themselves, earnings vary. Experience, what part of the country you work in, and entrepreneurial skills are determining factors.

is deluged with inquires from those wanting to be trainers or behaviorists."

Robin has strong opinions as to just what makes a good trainer. She says a good trainer:

- Has lots of tools in his or her toolbox, and knows how to use them well
- Strives to learn as much as possible, from as many sources as possible
- Knows there's always more to learn, and keeps him- or herself up to date by attending seminars, workshops, and conferences as often as possible
- Has a strong behavioral background
- Has an open mind
- Does not behave in an arrogant manner (toward their clients or the general public)
- Has a strong sense of ethics
- Doesn't misrepresent him or her self with bogus or mis-leading titles and credentials
- Loves dogs (if a trainer doesn't love dogs, she or he has no business training them)
- Has patience, and understands that anger and abuse (of any kind) have no place in dog training
- Treats their students (both the two- and four-legged) with respect and kindness. Empathy, compassion, kinship, and encouragement towards one's students is essential when training dogs
- Has good teaching and handling skills
- Has a good sense of humor
- Is passionate about living and working with dogs

Robin knows who will make a good trainer the moment they call to inquire about the career. "If the first thing out of their mouth is 'How much will I earn, how soon can I start making money?' I get suspicious," she says. "What we want to see are those who have a true devotion to dogs and want to work with people."

Glamorous It's Not

Working with animals, as a zookeeper or a trainer, is often less than glamorous. It's *hard* work.

"Most people think working with animals is a lot of fun," said Lupita Limon Cerna, public relations specialist at the Los Angeles Zoo. "In truth, it's difficult, demanding, dirty work."

It can also be dangerous.

According to the *Elephant Managers Association*, one of the most dangerous jobs in America is elephant zookeeper. Susan Chan, managing editor of *Animal Keeper's Forum*, reports, "Of the eighty or so elephant keepers in the United States, one loses his or her life every year."

Jami knows about this type of danger—she spent time as an alligator keeper. "Yes, I jumped right in with them. At first I was intimidated. But I would go in with a stick and hook, bang on the side of the pool, and feed the giant lizards dead rats, rabbits, and trout. As long as I knew where they were at all times, I was safe. If they were ever to snap at me, it would be because I did something wrong."

In general, zookeepers do not interact directly with the animals. Why? Because zoo residents are wild animals, and the zoos want to keep them that way.

Becoming an Animal Caregiver

Zookeepers don't just work in zoos. Sometimes referred to as animal keepers, they can also be found in amusement parks, aquariums, wildlife parks, and research institutions—anywhere animals need care or training.

Regardless of where they're employed, zookeepers should be dependable people, excellent observers, and have good oral communications skills to help visitors learn about animals and the role of zoos as their caregivers. And, says Lupita, "They must be physically able to perform the hard work required in keeping the animals clean, fed, and healthy."

INFORMATION

For More Information

The American Association of Zookeepers (AAZK)
635 S.W. Gage Boulevard
Topeka, KS 66606-2066
(800) 242-4519

American Dog Trainers Network (ADTN)
161 West 4th Street
New York, NY 10014
(212) 727-7257
www.canine.org

International Marine Animal Trainers Association
1200 South Lake Shore Drive
Chicago, IL 60605
www.imata.org

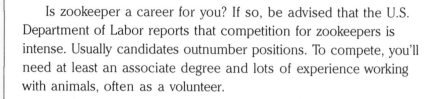

Is zookeeper a career for you? If so, be advised that the U.S. Department of Labor reports that competition for zookeepers is intense. Usually candidates outnumber positions. To compete, you'll need at least an associate degree and lots of experience working with animals, often as a volunteer.

Training the Trainer

Those interested in animal training need to be trained themselves, of course. The ADTN recommends that in learning how to train dogs, you should attend at least two dozen one- to four-day seminars and workshops on a variety of dog-related subjects. Here is a list of just a few topics that should be included in such training:

- The History and Development of the Breeds
- How to Choose and Raise a Puppy; Developmental Stages
- House Training and Crate Training
- Competition Obedience Training (all levels)
- Animal Behavior, Behavior Modification, and Problem-Solving Techniques
- Effective Handling Skills
- How to "Read" and Evaluate a Dog
- Canine Health, Nutrition, Medicine
- Handling and Training Aggressive Dogs
- Dog Sports and Activities
- Protection Training
- Bomb and Narcotics Detection
- Search and Rescue
- Trick Training
- Pet Safety

Seminars and workshops can show you how to handle and train dogs for TV, film, and advertising. Then there are full-fledged dog training schools. Many are reputable; for an approved list,

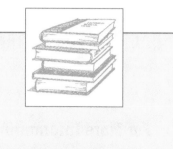

What to Read

If You Were a Zookeeper
by Virginia Schomp.
Marshall Cavendish, 1999.

check ADTN's Web site. However, some training schools will short-change you, and subsequently the animals under your care. Such programs fail because they teach and promote harsh compulsion-style training; are limited in their scope or cover topics superficially; they offer limited and/or unsound information to their students. Avoid such institutions as you would rabies.

Also, you are advised to keep away from mail-order training programs. "Yes, amazingly, there are now actually self-proclaimed 'animal behaviorists,' so-called animal behavior centers, and dog trainers that are selling people mail-order courses to become 'certified' professional dog trainers and 'certified canine behavior therapist,'" says Robin. "It can't be done, online or by mail."

Then how long will it take to be ready to train dogs? Must one have a Ph.D. in dog training and 20 years of experience to make it in the profession? No, of course not. As Robin explains, "It generally takes at least three to five years of intensive study and hands-on training and handling to become a good novice trainer. No trainers' school is going to teach you everything you need to know as a dog trainer in just a couple of months. If you have aspirations for becoming an experienced 'master dog trainer' after only a few months of study, dream on."

Nonetheless, if you have a passion for animals, if you want a career as a zookeeper or animal trainer—go for it. Like any career, there will be good and bad days. As a zookeeper, nursing a sick flamingo back to health would be an "up" time. However, sometimes the sick don't make it. As Jami, our zookeeper, said, "I have had my heart broken by animals more times than I have by people by far—*by far*."

Cool Web Sites to Visit

Canines of America Trainers Network
www.canines.com

Real Zoos in the United States
www.smcoe.k12.ca.us/msd/gh/soopg5.htm

You Want to Be a Zookeeper?
www.members.aol.com/abgie44/zoo.html

Hot Concepts!

Flex-Time

Surveys suggest that employees, particularly in the service sector, are working a lot longer than official numbers indicate. Supposedly, the average service sector workweek was 32.9 hours in 1999, down from around 38 hours in 1964. Yet, try telling that to the round-the-clock, 24-7 folks working in the new economy. As Juliet Schor points out in her insightful book. *The Overworked American*, most of us are working an extra month a year, officially or more often, unofficially, than we did three decades ago.

As a result, telecommuting, part-time work, job sharing, and compressed workweek arrangements are gaining in popularity. But how do you get beyond 9 to 5, how do you convince your boss to grant you "flex-time," a flexible schedule that will work for you and for your company?

Pat Katepoo, of WorkOptions.com, tells how to avoid the two most common mistakes when requesting flex-time arrangements. One, don't "wing it. Set an appointment with your boss to present and discuss your proposal," she says. "And, be as prepared as you would be for an important job interview or business presentation." Two, "having no proposal document deflates the seriousness of your request and the strength of your desire."

In sum, if you want a flexible work schedule, present your request in a well-thought out, professional manner.

We Have EVERYTHING!

OVER TWO MILLION EVERYTHING® BOOKS SOLD

Everything® **After College Book**
$12.95, 1-55850-847-3

Everything® **Angels Book**
$12.95, 1-58062-398-0

Everything® **Astrology Book**
$12.95, 1-58062-062-0

Everything® **Baby Names Book**
$12.95, 1-55850-655-1

Everything® **Baby Shower Book**
$12.95, 1-58062-305-0

Everything® **Baby's First Food Book**
$12.95, 1-58062-512-6

Everything® **Barbeque Cookbook**
$12.95, 1-58062-316-6

Everything® **Bartender's Book**
$9.95, 1-55850-536-9

Everything® **Bedtime Story Book**
$12.95, 1-58062-147-3

Everything® **Bicycle Book**
$12.00, 1-55850-706-X

Everything® **Build Your Own Home Page**
$12.95, 1-58062-339-5

Everything® **Business Planning Book**
$12.95, 1-58062-491-X

Everything® **Casino Gambling Book**
$12.95, 1-55850-762-0

Everything® **Cat Book**
$12.95, 1-55850-710-8

Everything® **Chocolate Cookbook**
$12.95, 1-58062-405-7

Everything® **Christmas Book**
$15.00, 1-55850-697-7

Everything® **Civil War Book**
$12.95, 1-58062-366-2

Everything® **College Survival Book**
$12.95, 1-55850-720-5

Everything® **Computer Book**
$12.95, 1-58062-401-4

Everything® **Cookbook**
$14.95, 1-58062-400-6

Everything® **Cover Letter Book**
$12.95, 1-58062-312-3

Everything® **Crossword and Puzzle Book**
$12.95, 1-55850-764-7

Everything® **Dating Book**
$12.95, 1-58062-185-6

Everything® **Dessert Book**
$12.95, 1-55850-717-5

Everything® **Dog Book**
$12.95, 1-58062-144-9

Everything® **Dreams Book**
$12.95, 1-55850-806-6

Everything® **Etiquette Book**
$12.95, 1-55850-807-4

Everything® **Family Tree Book**
$12.95, 1-55850-763-9

Everything® **Fly-Fishing Book**
$12.95, 1-58062-148-1

Everything® **Games Book**
$12.95, 1-55850-643-8

Everything® **Get-A-Job Book**
$12.95, 1-58062-223-2

Everything® **Get Published Book**
$12.95, 1-58062-315-8

Everything® **Get Ready for Baby Book**
$12.95, 1-55850-844-9

Everything® **Golf Book**
$12.95, 1-55850-814-7

Everything® **Guide to Las Vegas**
$12.95, 1-58062-438-3

Everything® **Guide to New York City**
$12.95, 1-58062-314-X

Everything® **Guide to Walt Disney Wor** Universal Studios®, and Greater Orlando, 2nd Edit
$12.95, 1-58062-404-9

Everything® **Guide to Washington D.C**
$12.95, 1-58062-313-1

Everything® **Herbal Remedies Book**
$12.95, 1-58062-331-X

Everything® **Home-Based Business Bo**
$12.95, 1-58062-364-6

Everything® **Homebuying Book**
$12.95, 1-58062-074-4

Everything® **Homeselling Book**
$12.95, 1-58062-304-2

Everything® **Home Improvement Boo**
$12.95, 1-55850-718-3

Everything® **Hot Careers Book**
$12.95, 1-58062-486-3

Everything® **Internet Book**
$12.95, 1-58062-073-6

Everything® **Investing Book**
$12.95, 1-58062-149-X

Everything® **Jewish Wedding Book**
$12.95, 1-55850-801-5

Everything® **Job Interviews Book**
$12.95, 1-58062-493-6

Everything® **Lawn Care Book**
$12.95, 1-58062-487-1

Everything® **Leadership Book**
$12.95, 1-58062-513-4

Everything® **Low-Fat High-Flavor** Cookbook
$12.95, 1-55850-802-3

Everything® **Magic Book**
$12.95, 1-58062-418-9

Everything® **Microsoft® Word 2000 Bo**
$12.95, 1-58062-306-9

For more information, or to order, call 800-872-5627
or visit everything.com
Adams Media Corporation, 260 Center Street, Holbrook, MA 02343

We Have
EVERYTHING KIDS'®!

Everything® Kids' Baseball Book
$9.95, 1-58062-489-8

Everything® Kids' Joke Book
$9.95, 1-58062-495-2

Everything® Kids' Money Book
$9.95, 1-58062-322-0

Everything® Kids' Nature Book
$9.95, 1-58062-321-2

Everything® Kids' Online Book
$9.95, 1-58062-394-8

Everything® Kids' Puzzle Book
$9.95, 1-58062-323-9

Everything® Kids' Space Book
$9.95, 1-58062-395-6

Everything® Kids' Witches and Wizards
$9.95, 1-58062-396-4

Available wherever books are sold!

For more information, or to order,
call 800-872-5627 or visit everything.com

Adams Media Corporation, 260 Center Street, Holbrook, MA 02343

Everything® is a registered trademark of Adams Media Corporation.

7569